T0149628

Mr. Lonely Again

Adventures of Philosophic Reflection
Volume I

Nino Plazola

Translations
Albert Nino
Rega Lupo

authorHOUSE®

AuthorHouse™
1663 Liberty Drive
Bloomington, IN 47403
www.authorhouse.com
Phone: 1 (800) 839-8640

Original Title
On Time with Mr. Lonely

First Edition Volume I
Winter 2016

Audio CD
Winter 2016

Certificate of Registration
Number TXU1-167-111
United States Copyright Office

2004 Author of Copyright
Nino E. Plazola

2004 Translation Copyright
Albert Nino

2017 Narrative CD
Mr. Lonely

Printed In
United States

Published by AuthorHouse 10/04/2016

ISBN: 978-1-5246-3942-6 (sc)
ISBN: 978-1-5246-3940-2 (hc)
ISBN: 978-1-5246-3941-9 (e)

Library of Congress Control Number: 2016915115

Print information available on the last page.

THANKFULNESS

My dear sons...**Albert, Rega, and Alvin**
My lovely mother..**Arminda Plazola**
My lovely aunt..**Irma Medina**
My lovely uncle...**Mario Alberti**
My best friend..**Villi Ardavin**
My lovely Lady...**Yadira Vargas**

To them I appreciate having put their talents and aid, in helping someone who is not a writer, furthermore, for giving me the valor to realize and produce a format of unique communication in two languages of writing.

To all those people, guilty or not, that have lost their freedom, to those who have lost their loved ones, to those who have lost their health and fortune, to those who have fallen to drugs, and have not been able to recuperate, to those who do not have a place to inhabit.

To critically ill, to single mothers, to lonely elderly, to the poor, to those who work cleaning the streets, and finally, to those people who day after day, fight to survive without asking or knowing what tomorrow brings. Will be agreeable, whoever have the opportunity to read this humble book, to all these marvelous people, as a show of love and respect.

"To all these people I dedicate this book"

JUST A NOTE

I just want to inform you, as to why he is intentionally give it one name in English "Mr. Lonely", and another in Spanish "Don Triste", without it being an error in translation. Thank you for your understanding. I hope this cleared up any entanglements in its literal translation.

Thought:
There is no such thing as darkness, only the absence of light. Cold does not exist; it is merely the absence of heat. Black does not exist; only the absence of color separation. Ignorance does not exist; it is merely the absence of knowledge. Intolerance does not exist; it is the absence of comprehension.

Just the same, evil does not exist; it is the absence of God. Do not blame him for the evils that ail you. Do not blame him for the crimes or the tragedies of life it is merely an absence of God that affects our lives.

Albert Einstein stated this when he was young.

Mr. Lonely grew up in a world where the absence of God was very noticeable, and accentuated. That is why he did not believe in God. He never prayed, but it was only due to absence. May it be a lesson, so that the same does not happen to you, avoid being on the side of the absence.

CONTENTS

Introduction xi

Benito Friendship Neighborhood 1

The Law 5

The Rag Picker 12

Artist or Thieve 15

Perkins the Wise 20

The Boxer 32

A light on the Eyes 36

The Search 43

The Wall and the Faith 49

The Yellow Boots 55

The Uka Puka Phenomenon 67

The Truth and Only the Truth 73

Sad Story of an Impossible Dream 97

Spanish Version 163

INTRODUCTION

Through out many years, Man has searched threw out any means: Happiness, Richness, Health, and Eternal Youth. Wars, Diseases, and Natural Disasters have contributed to slowing down the search for all these subjects but yet and against everything. Great Men and Philosophers have found these things, and revealed them to the world as discoveries, for the benefit of the Human Race.

This is the history about an ordinary man with a vision close to fantasy. With a point of view that is unique and special, that will make us remember times in our lives. That will never be spoken or heard of again, but will always remain in our hearts because he talks about Friendship, Faith, Love, and above all, hope for all People who have lost track of their only right and true path to follow, the one of Happiness.

Mr. Lonely and his magic will take us to a world of the unexpected, with dramatic situations, and in occasions fun but extraordinary, every minute with solutions, and mistakes that will make us laugh, and think in a different sort of way, because we will be traveling through the world of Mr. Lonely.

Have your passport ready to travel to through trails full of mystery, and incredible people known for their bad habits, and others for their bonds, which you will be able to identify with other people you know. However, remember, whatever likeness these characters have to real people is either pure coincidence, or pure reality.

Thought:
Travel is an opportunity to see the life with the others eyes, think and develop ideas with the others minds. Discover the world, and all the varieties with the others amazements, and knowledge. However, remember the important is, do not change, be the same to yourself and for the amazements of others.

BENITO FRIENDSHIP NEIGHBORHOOD

Where and when Mr. Lonely was born was long time ago in a place called Benito Friendship Neighborhood located next to Desperation, in the Sector of Fright, in the Country of Faith, in the Continent Dream.

Mr. Lonely is born as one more member into a family of fishermen and restaurant owners dedicated secretly to the twisted business of the Mafia. His parents traveled a lot, especially his father, who was a diplomat hired by a foreign country, one which gave him his new citizenship with a motive to transfer his residence to America. The life of Mr. Lonely was fun, healthy, and serene, all thanks to the natural wisdom of his mother who gave him the best of everything.

When he was only two years old, his father was kidnapped and assassinated by political revenge, related to its work, reason to which his mother decided to give him an education in his home country. He returned to her side only during the summers, because his mother remained in the previous country with the hope that her husband would appear and everything would just have been a minor obstacle in life. Unfortunately, this was not the way he had disappeared forever.

Mr. Lonely traveled from Europe to America, and vice versa, at the early age of six years old. His infancy was normal yet fun, but he resided with an uncle in various cities, schools, religious schools, and military academies. This is how his first ten years of life were spent, studying culture and the forced religion, developing the fear of God as a supreme punisher and avenger.

In the streets and schools, he was very popular, admired, and had a good reputation, Friends and strangers envied him because of his mental quickness and special abilities for everything including sports, culture, mischief, and more.

MR. LONELY AGAIN
BENITO FRIENDSHIP NEIGHBORHOOD

He had short hair and his slenderness gave him an aspect which was simple yet fun at the same time. The opposite sex, girls, at that time caught his attention at such a level that he participated in ceremonies and religious rituals in order to be near the most beautiful girls, that assisted such events in the church.

He stole flowers from saints and virgins, making money from selling them to the girls that were not so beautiful, giving them to the most beautiful ones. He obtained their favors and embraces, discovering the strange enchantment that the flowers brought to the girls.

In everyday life in the churches, he discovered how the priests manipulated the followers with ease, how they would lie, and cheat them supposedly, the priest was not to have intimate relations. However, in reality, they had lovers and children, whom they supposedly protected out of bondage.

The truth confused his mind. Everything in religion deals with interests and money just like politics. They were hypocrites, all in the name of God, and they always insulted, and condemned people to hell if they did not follow the rules; rules that they made, but did not respect. At the end was a dirty game that you had to learn to play or be silent Mr. Lonely played by his own rules.

He dedicated part of his time investigating the illicit activities of the priests. He studied their activities inside and outside the church, which proved they assassinated, stole, and involved themselves in politics with high priests to decide the destiny of the city, state, and country making this an activity full of atrocities and misery. After investigating and realizing everything about religion, Mr. Lonely decided to investigate, analyze governments, people, teachers, schools, institutions, politicians, etc.

His major dissolution was that history, the scholastic books, and cultures, written and approved by those who succeeded and conquered with personal interests. Mr. Lonely remained studying in Europe with his beloved uncle, during the summers in America with his mother. Occasionally, he studied in America, and returned in the summer to be with his uncle in Europe.

At the end, it was eternal traveling between the young continent, and the old continent. The relationship between nephew, and uncle became strong with much understanding and compassion, being the true joy living under the protection of his uncle Mario Alberti.

The island where they lived was into four sectors; a protector dominated each sector. The Godfather, the maximum authority of the mafia, controlled these four protectors. The Godfather shared and received unlimited power from the government authorities just like the Catholic Church, composing a trio so powerful that they controlled the entire country, involving themselves in activities legal and illegal in the entire world.

The succession of the Godfather a term used inclusively for movies was not so complicated in reality. One of the protectors would be as the successor of the Godfather, making them the reigning Godfather.

Mr. Mario Alberti, uncle to Mr. Lonely was the protector in the sector of the capital; him being the most important of the four sectors made him the most powerful candidate to be the next Godfather.

The family of Mr. Mario Alberti was grand, living in a home with two floors occupying an entire city block. It was so beautiful, and as large as having twenty-two bedrooms, ten bathrooms, six kitchens with their respective dining room, four living rooms, six studies, and a giant hall for reunions.

MR. LONELY AGAIN
BENITO FRIENDSHIP NEIGHBORHOOD

The center of the home was a huge patio with an interior parking lot. There were twenty-six automobiles of all kinds; cars, station wagons, utility vehicles, luxury cars, and limousines.

Twelve dogs and a strong group of security made up of people who were dedicated and committed to the family throughout generations, protected the house. In one of the corners of the house, you could encounter a semi luxurious restaurant, that throughout generations, was the family business for certain it was called "My Family"

It was easy to find Mr. Mario Alberti in the office of the restaurant, which was the center of operations for all his business, the members who made up the family possessed everything, and it was for everybody. For example, Mr. Lonely could use any vehicle at whatever time, but he was not to think or say that it belonged to him only, because everything belonged to everybody.

When a member of the family got married, their spouse or husband became one more member of the family coming to reside in the house, having their own bedroom being able to cook their proper meals in whichever kitchen.

They could work with Mr. Mario, receive money to start their own business, or simply work in the restaurant, and be paid a suitable salary like everyone else. They could also make use of whichever automobile was in the parking lot.

Thought:
Family can be your happiness, or your downfall. How do you know who is good for you, and who is not? Do not torment yourself with the selection, just follow your heart, and the rest is mutual. Since a true family always does everything in agreement, it is easy to identify. Respect and love are easily recognized.

THE LAW

As everyone knows, the government and its institutions form the authority which corrects, regulates, and orients the citizens, giving them all types of support and protection as well as countless other services.

However, this law has a price; it can be bought and sold by bitters with no feelings. Well that is the impression that Mr. Lonely had when he meets the law for first time in his life.

Mr. Lonely was used to walking late, not minding that he was a minor. One night, on his walk home, a gray official van supposedly dedicated to the protection of minors detained him. It would pick minors up and take them to protection centers. Where they were given clothes, meals, education, and at an appropriate moment, give them a family.

In a few words, they became subjects of adoption so they would not wander the streets alone and without protection. Mr. Lonely mentioned that he had family, as well as a home. He showed his identifications and his schoolbooks, but the representatives of the authorities did not hear a word, and put him in the van and moved him to a detention center for minors called "Protection Center for Minors"

There at the detention center, after taking his money, watch, and all the things of value, he was sent to a dormitory with who knows how many others minors. They said he was to sleep there, and the next day his situation would be clear up in the end more tired than surprised, he decided to sleep wherever he could and however he could.

It was around 6:00 am. The next day when, another minor named Benito, who told him to get up, awaked him to clean the messy room, and prepare for his shower. Mr. Lonely did as he was told at the same time as Benito, but his new friend had a great fear reflecting in his face.

MR. LONELY AGAIN
THE LAW

Into the dormitory walked six kids between sixteen and seventeen years of age. One of them seemed to be the leader. He ordered all the little ones to remove their clothes, form a line, and enter to the shower zone they all obeyed crying.

One after the other, they entered the famous bathroom, being pushed savagely into the interior of a whirlpool with ice-cold water in which it was impossible to swim. They could only grab the edges, which were slippery. To make things worse, the kids in charge proceeded by punishing them with belt whips.

Pressuring them to cross the whirlpool, the older ones helped the much smaller. After leaving the whirlpool, they entered the showers, where they continued to receive ice-cold water, and the unforgiving belt whippings.

Later, they returned to the dormitory to dress, but sometimes, their clothes would disappear, making things worst because they lacked towels. All the while, a continuing concert of belt whips, guiding them towards a patio for them to finally have breakfast.

They once again formed a long line where they received trays with bread, and meals of miniature portions, but they could pay, and receive extra food; using clothes buttons as the official coin.

Mr. Lonely understood why everyone lacked buttons in their clothes. The kids in charge had long necklaces with buttons of all colors, with which they bought items, received favors, or avoided punishment.

Mr. Lonely remembered that his sweater had buttons made of gold plated steel, which were valuable in this place, so Benito and he ate extra rations, since he traded the metallic buttons for four necklaces made of plastic buttons.

THE LAW

After that about a hundred children sat down to take in the sun, not leaving the designated area, which was about forty square meters, where they were not allowed to play or leave the sun area except to use the restroom. All days bathed in sunlight, later take lunch, and sure, the buttons trade in every moment.

Benito explained to Mr. Lonely that he did not know when they would be set free, since they had no communication with the exterior, they received no responses to their pleas to be communicated with their families if they have relatives if not, they do not have a good future. Come nightfall, they moved to the dormitories, and the next day the same cycle repeated.

Mr. Lonely and his friend Benito watched four more days pass without any certainties of their future, in order to eat well and use the restrooms whenever they pleased, Mr. Lonely used one of the necklaces made of buttons, leaving him only three remaining, which would last, at most eight more days. After that, who knows?

The situation began to turn critical since Mr. Lonely had an infection in one of his eyes, and no longer has shoes, since they were stolen, reason for which he decided to do something to escape.

He told Benito his idea and contacted with one of the kids in charge, in order to carry out the attempt of escaping. For a few buttons, they were allowed to go to the restrooms at night, suppose in search of their liberty.

Candles illuminated the place; and a boy told them that they were to sell their souls to the Devil, if they wished to escape from the place. The boy grabbed a piece of chalk and drew a circle on the floor, filled with symbols. He danced and invoked the Devil.

MR. LONELY AGAIN
THE LAW

The scene turned grotesque when the boy pulled, from within his clothes, a shard of glass which he used to cut his hand, in order to smear blood on the symbols, and on the faces of those who wished to escape, which at that moment, were a great many, Benito and Mr. Lonely fled towards the dormitory, with the intent of finding a more secure and simple way of escaping, leaving behind the ugly and unusual ceremony.

The next morning, after showering, they could not spot the kids, which participated in the soul selling ceremony for the Devil. The kids assured that the Devil had set them free, just as it had occurred times before.

Mr. Lonely faked being extremely sick and was taken to the infirmary room once there he put to use the tricks he had learned in his neighborhood forcing over doors and desks, he found the information, which told him where he was. It was a home for minors called "Protection Center Number Two", which was controlled by police authorities of the northern part the city.

In the infirmary, were the infants and kids less than four years of age, which were up for adoption? He also found information, which connected the Center with Hospitals, which carried out transplants, surgery operations, making sure that the kids were the involuntary organ donors, with no benefit for them. Later, Mr. Lonely incorporated himself with the sunbathing group, but he had papers and pens, which he stole from the infirmary he wrote his name, address, uncle's phone number and a reference where he could be found he did the same thing on another piece of paper with Benito's information.

Later, using buttons as payment, he bought more paper, and wrote hundreds of little notes, with straws tubes made of paper; he launched the notes turned into darts at paper airplanes creating a fun game that even the kids in charge joined in. The only exception, Mr. Lonely' darts flew out over the walls that guarded the place.

For three days they launched darts with notes, in search of liberty, of course, paying with buttons. A woman, neighbor to the place, found one of the notes and called Uncle Mario Alberti, who was anguished by the disappearance of his nephew. He spent various days searching for him in hospitals, and jails with no results, but when he received the call, he shed tears of joy, and immediately departed towards the center number two in the northern sector of the city.

Once there, he asked for his nephew they told him he was there, but he could not be released, since Mr. Mario Alberti was not the father nor the official caregiver besides, they had plans to move him to a different detention center, making it a more difficult and complicated task of his freedom.

Mr. Mario Alberti begged them to return his nephew, but the authorities of the sinister place denied him, why was he being held captive, it was never known be he was in a state of imprisonment, the uncle offered a thousand dollars that he had on him for the release, but they required five thousand dollars and just cash. After hearing the arbitrary decision, and not believing who he was, he left without another word.

Once home, he made some phone calls, and minutes later, he had two assault trucks with thirty armed men at his disposal, as well as two cars with people he trusted, who were ready to help. They entered the center, and savagely beating the guards, he accomplished an attack, which overcame everyone with force the head of center placed on his knees in front of Mr. Mario Alberti, who ordered the return of his nephew in exchange for their lives.

Minutes later, he was brought forth. He was dirty, thin, shoeless, bruised, had an infected eye, in other words, he was a disaster. Uncle and nephew shared a hug Mr. Mario kissed him livingly picked him up and intended to leave, but his nephew spoke to him of his friend Benito.

MR. LONELY AGAIN
THE LAW

As well as the babies in the infirmary the military force was informed of the situation, for which a commando and trucks were sent to arrest all of the center's personnel, to be detained at a military facility without any possibility of going free with impunity, after learning the terrible truth about the place, Mr. Mario Alberti gave the order to free all the kids.

The babies in the infirmary were picked up along with all the identifying paperwork they left the place setting it a blaze not much later the minors were dropped off at the nearest hospital, along with all the paperwork, so that identification was possible, as well as notification of their parents and relatives.

The next day, Mr. Mario Alberti ordered the City Mayor, and the Chief Police to dismantle the remaining three detention centers. If it was not done, he threatened to destroy all the families of those involved in the corrupt business. All they did was sell babies disguised as adoptions, so they could sacrifice the rest in order to sell their vital organs. All this was carried out easily since the babies were too young to recognize their families. The older ones were sacrificed with the advantage that they had no families, or after some prudent time, left missing. They were treated just as the Jewish were during the Second World War.

Those missing kids, who took part in those strange soul-selling ceremonies for the Devil never knew it, but in the lapse of two weeks, everything ended and the detention centers were officially shut down, the bruises on Mr. Lonely healed quickly, but he found out that his uncle was an active member of the mafia, in a high position, with limitless powers. He was guilty of many crimes, but because of his enormous love for his family and friends, everyone loved him. Only his competition envied him.

This is how he realized that his uncle loved him very much, and remembered how he would help those in need. He was a guardian angel for the neighborhood, as well as the city.

The relationship between nephew and uncle became stronger, full of understanding, and mutual comprehension, making it a place to live, under the protection of his beloved uncle Mr. Mario Alberti.

Thought:
What does it mean to be good? What does it mean be bad? They are difficult questions to answer in a correct way, and more difficult to understand. The good ones almost killed him. They deprived him of his freedom with no reason. The bad ones liberated him without any condition sending him back to his normal life filling him with love, and at the same time filling him with confusion.

THE RAG PICKER

Mr. Lonely met one of them, a man of the streets, dedicated to picking from the trash, all types of paper, rags, glass, and all types of bottles, in order to sell them by the pound. It was said that these men kidnapped minors and infants to sell, or enslave them as their workers, but this he never proved.

The rag picker had his own territory, which he traversed day after day with his inseparable friends, twelve dogs as dirty and flea bitten as he always at the end of the day, the rag picker crossed the neighborhood as he headed to his dormitory, outside of an abandoned theater. He formed a fabulous bed of paper, rags, and dogs, upon which they dined on waste, leftovers, and occasionally, pieces of bread.

The rag picker was the unconditional protector of his twelve apostles (the dogs), to whom he spoke to and treated with great respect and friendship, as if really dealing with the twelve apostles; seeing as how he named them after each one of them; Peter, Pablo, etc.

This provoked a definite curiosity in Mr. Lonely, who knew and treated with a different, yet special person who lacked a name, or never had one. In the afternoons, Mr. Lonely awaited him with food for him and his twelve apostles, which he appreciated by telling him stories as strange as fantasies, and marvelous adventures of all types, assuring him they were true.

After approximately three hundred afternoons, it occurred that Mr. Lonely inappropriately used some money, since it meant to be used to buy a mathematics kit, which was needed for classes with deadlines. To not have it was to run the risk of losing the class and the semester, reasons for why his sorrow was great, at his saddest and most desperate state, the rag picker and his twelve apostles appeared, just like every other afternoon. He offered his help, but Mr. Lonely answered that in being poor, it was not likely that he could be of any help.

ADVENTURES OF PHILOSOPHIC REFLECTION
THE RAG PICKER

Because of the rag pickers insistence, he told him about his problem after attentively listening to Mr. Lonely, the rag picker revealed from within his papers and rags, a wonderful mathematics kit of great quality and high price, arguing that in the trash, you find things as useful and beautiful as the kit, which was so necessary at that very moment.

The rag picker hugged him, and told him that life is much like a giant trash can, and that in it, you will find wonderful things, if you search with faith and without getting grossed out. But you would have to search with your heart, and be happy with your finds.

That marvelous afternoon, the rag picker kissed and blessed Mr. Lonely, wishing a good night as always, but with the difference, that we never saw him again, nor did anyone ever know anything about him or his twelve apostles.

He disappeared forever from the neighborhood, and from the life of Mr. Lonely, but the mathematics kit remained by his side as proof of the rag pickers existence and giving; a marvelous philosopher with characteristics of a historic character.

The greatest gift was not the mathematics kit but the valuable things like the stories he told Mr. Lonely, which he kept in his heart and mind because they came from a just and wise man known only as, the rag picker.

For days and nights, Mr. Lonely kept asking himself, where did the rag picker come from, where did he and his apostles go, and what kind of special being was he? Why doesn't one encounter that kind of person every day?

Answers, he never received, but he kept believing that the world was a giant trash can in which, with faith, he would find the rag picker, or perhaps another just as valuable, and as intelligent as the first.

MR. LONELY AGAIN
THE RAG PICKER

Wherever he and his twelve apostles may be, may god care, and conserve them, because Mr. Lonely was fortunate in meeting them. I hope that others can meet the rag picker and be as fortunate as he.

Thought:
The University of Life, the school of the streets with the most surprising people as its teachers People who graduated from the known faculty of street philosophy, homeless individuals, those who live in the world of the forgotten, they are not failures, not stupid. They chose to live a different way of life, renouncing themselves, living happy by simply narrating stories and living in the moment. Without fear or worries for the future. Is it them who have been mistaken in their choice? Alternatively, is it us who have been mistaken?

ARTIST OR THIEVE

It was during those fantastic times in which the modern world introduced the television, the transistor, the space race, the cold war, Marylyn Monroe, Martin Luther King, Nikita Krushov, and Mao Tsetung, John Fitzgerald Kennedy, Cassius Clay, Edson Arantes Do Nacimento "Pele", The Beatles, Bobby Vinton, James Dean, The Rolling Stones, Stanley Kubrick, Dean Martin, Frank Cinatra, and many others.

Mr. Lonely met a painter named Rupert in the time. Not quite famous, but his art was on exhibition, and sold in the best and most prestigious art galleries in the capital city. Rupert was deeply in love with the impressionistic view. Therefore, his paintings were of the purest form of impressionism, but Mr. Lonely thought it lacked quality.

Yet, art was art. Rupert enjoyed his afternoons painting, and listening to the music of Ray Connif, Petula Clark, Tony Bennet, The Beatles, etc. Motive for which Mr. Lonely did his homework alongside Rupert; simply to listen to such marvelous music, as well as contemporary narrations about the artists, politics, and sports.

Always the comments made by Rupert were accompanied by succulent dinners that he cooked himself, showing that he was a better cook than painter, or so thought Mr. Lonely, who was a real little critic. Mr. Lonely responded to that generous attention for him, by washing the dishes and cleaning Rupert's place up a bit. This was like an unmentioned deal that they both accepted, as if something part of the ritual called friendship.

They were friends every afternoon, getting together with only one goal. To enjoy each other's mutual company, share experiences, interchange ideas, opinions, and jokes until 10:30 p.m. the time that Mr. Lonely left for home to sleep, in order to be ready for the next day to attend school.

MR. LONELY AGAIN
ARTIST OR THIEVE

Mr. Lonely trusted Rupert with everything, not caring that he was a full grown man of approximately forty-five years of age. He, as well, trusted in Mr. Lonely even though he was a mere child of school age with extravagant ideas.

There were many nights of conversation, and music without any extraordinary changes until one day; Mr. Lonely confessed to Rupert that he would not buy his paintings, because they lacked quality, Just the same, they lacked profoundness in every one of the intended themes, but he respected his friendship, and the honesty with which he showed in every aspect of his life.

Rupert was left silent for a few long and seemingly unending minutes when he later said that his paintings were not great because he was not a painter, and much less, an honest man with his only ability being to steal. The painting was only a cover up, to hide his true profession; he was a thief.

It was very difficult, for Mr. Lonely, to comprehend what he had just heard from the lips of his greatest friend, but his analytic abilities told him it was true, and that Rupert was indeed a thief the supposed painter told his sad story, because every thief has his story to tell. Rupert had a happy family in a distant city. He stole, protecting himself with the lie that he was, in appearance, a professional photographer. He sold his photographs in very prestigious art galleries and museums.

One certain occasion, his family discovered his truth, and asked, why? He answered that it was the only thing he knew how to do and he did it well. He provided them with all types of commodities, adequate of the times. They lived a good life without any economic pressures. Due to religious convictions that were as intense as they were unchangeable, they did not want to know anything more about him, and he was cast out on the streets, with the threat of being reported to the authorities, and without any hope of repair between them.

ARTIST OR THIEVE

Rupert begged, but they did not bother to listen to him. They only said to be ashamed of him, and his dirty profession giving him only the option of voluntarily leaving their lives and being forgotten, after many failed attempts to be accepted back into his home; he grew tired, hungry and was without money in his pockets.

He decided to steal in order to send money to his family who accepted it without any remorse as long as he never returned much time after and so many robberies, problems, cities embarrassments risks, and fictitious jobs he took like destiny to the neighborhood where Mr. Lonely lived, it was there where they met, and became great friends. That was all his sad life. After that, he kept silent, anxiously awaiting a response from his little friend.

Mr. lonely only asserted to hug him, and tell that he understood and cared for him. He also proposed to learn to be a thief by soliciting his teachings. School's good, but it has many lies. So, why not learn something interesting. Furthermore, the next day, initiated his new class with the best of teachers, he learned that stealing is the finest and most wonderful art, worthy of the Nobel Prize. You should always share the wealth with those who need it. Do good things with the wrongfully earned money.

Rupert unconditionally aided his neighbors. He loaned them money that in all reality, they did not pay back, but he was happy because for the moment, he solved their problems. He paid the fees for students, in order to give them futures. The sending of money to his family continued, he donated money to the Red Cross, homes for the elderly, orphans, etc. He was totally an angel, protector of the less fortunate. In the eyes of Mr. Lonely, he was a hero. The classes included physical education of high quality. He needed to be as strong, fast, and agile as an Olympic champion; he needed to see, and walk in the pitch-black of darkness, as well as the technology involved in alarm systems, electricity, electronics, etc.

MR. LONELY AGAIN
ARTIST OR THIEVE

He learned to control his emotions, and the emotions of others, how to use his instincts, develop his common sense, deduction, and deductive analysis, which was in the end, an education far superior in every aspect, with time, came the practical anxiety, much like the final exam.

In the early mornings, they would walk the streets, and with great ability, they would penetrate businesses by scaling walls, dodging dogs, security systems, and accomplishing clean robberies, leaving not the slightest trace.

Mr. Lonely greatly enjoyed his new hidden job, concealing it with scholastic activities, and helping those in need. Rupert entrusted Mr. Lonely with a system of sending people to the galleries to buy his paintings, and that way justify his earnings.

Gaining more fame as a good artist, certainly, there did not lack any ingenious people who, influenced by false buyers, bought his paintings. Others were expert art critics, or so they claimed to be, but the outcome was a positive one for the good Rupert.

This fun and rare friendship lasted for at least twelve months. Until one day, Rupert had to change cities for security reasons, as well as retire from his job, and invest his money in a less dangerous, and more tranquil, business he carried out the convenient preparations for the move and gave his goodbye, and advice, to Mr. Lonely.

He ordered him to retire immediately. Rupert disappeared, from his life forever, leaving behind marvelous lessons, in his heart and mind.

Never steal from someone you know, never steal from your friends, nor the poor, nor honest rich people. Only steal from those who steal, and the dishonest. This way, you will still be a thief, but at least one with a code of honor.

Therefore, be an honorary thief, and be honest with yourself. Certainly, Mr. Lonely remembered Rupert as a friend and artist, more than he remembered a thief honor and glory, to the giving painter of miracles, with magic in his acts of true partnership and friendship teacher of Excellencies only known as Rupert, with Mr. Lonely's heart, being his greatest steal.

Thought:
Being noble and good, allows others to take advantage of you. Being sweet and tender allows others to humiliate you. Do not allow it, but do not change. Continue being noble, good, sweet, tender, and comprehensive, so that eventually, they can understand that they are mistaken. However, the true reason is simply so that you can be happy with you, and yourself besides, in the end, it is the only thing that matters.

PERKINS THE WISE

During the marvelous era of college, Mr. Lonely studied at the vocational of physical sciences and mathematics. His colleges were considered one of the wise people and lunatics Mr. Lonely was one of the lunatics, all though he considered himself a genius. Outside of college was a library surrounded by an immense park. This park served as a recreation area, which held sports encounters and uncountable ferocious boxing matches between students, as well as a reunion center for lovers. In general, it was a classic, scholastic conjunction, and recreation area of a big city college.

What made the park special was the presence of a stranger of impressive personality. No one knew where he came from but he quickly became the center of attention in the park, school, students, and the very cathedratic professors. In the mentioned great college of mathematical sciences, and lunatic inhabitants that student or professor who demonstrated recognition and knowledge was respectably known as, Perkins, but the character from the park was so special and surprising that he was called, as well as for respect, admiration, and kindness, "Perkins the wise."

As if he were an employee from Monday to Friday, Perkins the wise accustomed himself to arriving punctually at the park at noon. He installed himself in the same bench, situated various pencils, and a pencil sharpener. Dogs that would occasionally accompany and surrounded him.

Sometimes two, other times six. Simply put, not all of them followed him daily. The majority of the time his clients waited for him, there were many anxious students who solicited his services for mathematics in exchange a drink for him and some food for the dogs.

There were students from the college who required his help to resolve calculus problems which were assigned daily by professors as homework.

PERKINS THE WISE

These were so complicated that on occasion, a student could take as long as forty-five minutes on each one to accomplish solving them, this of course with all the resources, including a scientific calculator. Perkins the wise used only a pencil and paper. He spent something like fifteen minutes per problem. On the more complicated ones, between twenty and twenty-five minutes, and, I affirm that he did not use any scientific calculator. He did not make mistakes and his responses; it was a complete cathedratic he was asked for an explanation as the way to solve a problem.

Perkins the wise took within his dirty hands the sheet, or sheets, that contained the questions. He analyzed them for about thirty seconds and emanated his response, which went something like this, well, these problems will cost you a quarter liter bottle of beverage, and a pound of meat and bones for the dogs, in those times, it was the equivalent of half American dollar.

This way they agreed on the price to resolve the problem, or problems. Then the student walked about two streets length, until he reached a liquor store and bought what wise man Perkins solicited, after that, he would walk back to the park. Usually when he arrived, before minutes, Wise Man Perkins finished his homework. Throughout the day, until 4:00 in the afternoon, it was coming and going to the park and to the liquor store that resembled a parade. The dogs ate until the dragged themselves.

Some disappeared, to return the next day in search of food. Others would leave with Perkins the wise, thankful for his kindness at four in the afternoon, he carried his beverage bottles and abandoned the park with unknown direction, returning the next day to realize his joyful task of helping the students.

As time passed, Mr. Lonely' curiosity took him to observe Perkins the wise, proving that the nickname.

MR. LONELY AGAIN
PERKINS THE WISE

Wise fit him small he was an extremely able and intelligent man it could, be said that such intelligence could only be compared only to that of a wise man, yet his appearance was that of a beggar, or a simple rag picker full of curiosity as well as respect, he neared Perkins the wise with the idea of conversing, discovering that it was not his joy to talk.

He only solved problems and gave cathedra's just like mini conferences about the mathematical sciences there was no friendship, nor talk of personal matters. Daily, Mr. Lonely observed him. Inclusively, he tried to investigate about the special character in all reality, no one knew more than he did, that is, nothing. He tried various times to establish conversation with him. Evading conversation a thousand times, he refused to give him his name, responding that he was Perkins, and nothing more.

Perkins the wise drank just like any alcoholic. During the four daily hours that he worked, he would not taste food what so ever. Suppose he ate because if not he would have died a long time ago, that is how Mr. Lonely came to ask himself what it was that Perkins the wise ate, and what he liked to eat. That moment on, he gave food to Perkins the wise as well as the dogs. He would put the food in his clothes, or share it with the dogs. He always gave thanks for the food, but he continued without establishing any conversation with Mr. Lonely.

This is how various days passed and Mr. Lonely could not make friendship with Perkins the wise. Later, Mr. Lonely prepared the best sandwiches you can imagine, using various types of cold meats and cheeses at the same time using the best of his culinary ability.

He accomplished some very delicious sandwiches. Well, he took them to Perkins the wise, and he was thankful, as usual. Mr. Lonely mentioned that he had prepared them especially for him.

ADVENTURES OF PHILOSOPHIC REFLECTION
PERKINS THE WISE

It so happened that Mr. Lonely got sick. The illness was not that serious, but it required him to rest in bed. Because of this, he did not attend classes for a week, which seemed to be an eternity for Mr. Lonely his friends frequently visited him at his house during his rest. His college friends said that everyone missed him. Even Perkins the wise had asked for him. That was the best news he had heard all day, and only waited for the next school day, to go in searches of Perkins the wise.

At the end of the noon class, Mr. Lonely ran towards the bench in the park. He was in search of Perkins the wise, but found only students that also awaited him everyone was confused because, in reality, Perkins the wise was always punctual. Later, Mr. Lonely returned to class. The school day finally ended and at 2:00 in the afternoon and Mr. Lonely, once again, ran towards the park, but on the bench, there were only three dogs, sad because they did not eat that day.

Mr. Lonely ran to the Liquor store and bought meat and bones for the dogs. He returned to the park and distributed the food amongst the dogs just as Perkins the wise would have. He remained at the park, playing ball with his friends every day, but he was always watching Perkins the wise bench, which remained empty. It was already 4:00 in the afternoon and his friends decided to leave, each to their own home.

Mr. Lonely seemed troubled, what if Perkins was ill. Nobody could help him. After all, he had no idea where he could search for him. He headed home, stopping at the liquor store as a last resource, he entered the store and asked the attendants if they had seen Perkins the wise. They said they had heard of him, but they have never seen him in person. Mr. Lonely said goodbye, thanking them for the information provided, and continuing his way home, feeling very hungry.

He was hurrying his step when he felt a hand on his shoulder, as he heard a familiar voice saying;

MR. LONELY AGAIN
PERKINS THE WISE

I see you have gotten better. It pleases me. When he turned, he found himself before Perkins the wise showing a friendly smile never before seen on his face, Mr. Lonely reacted by asking if by any chance he was sick because he had not attended the park. The dogs, as well as the students, seemed sad. Perkins the wise showed satisfaction from Mr. Lonely's words, but only said that he also needed vacations, just like any worker, and that this day was his day off.

They said goodbye almost instantly, merely mutually saying; good afternoon, see you tomorrow at the park, as usual. Without more, they headed in opposite directions, but deep inside with the thought and sentiment of the new friendship. The next day was no different, and Mr. Lonely waited for noon in order to reunite with which he considered his friend. Once in front of Perkins the wise, he asked Mr. Lonely to help him quote what he considered his work.

Mr. Lonely mentioned that he was not wise, but Perkins the wise showed the same smile from the previous day and said; the secret to knowing how to charge for a job is: first, knowing how to do it right, so that it seems easy to you. Second, observe the client, and do not charge more than what he can pay. This way, he will feel thankful to you, and you will be happy with your work. Although it did not seem difficult, Mr. Lonely preferred to observe in order to learn, and with times help, both smiling, they agreed that is how it would be.

Perkins the wise continued solving problems, but out loud, for Mr. Lonely to learn. By the way, you have never been a client of mine, why? Perkins the wise asked are you smart? Mr. Lonely only smiled, answering that he was not bad at his studies, besides, he had his tricks, and he did not like to go shopping at the liquor store. Mr. Lonely spent his time with Perkins the wise doing his homework. When they both finished with their respective obligations, they occupied by conversing, and the innumerable daily adventures with Mr. Lonely.

Of course, Perkins laughed at his occurrences because they were entertaining. Perkins the wise showed facility and ability to solve problems the two would play with riddles, and sometimes, in that department Mr. Lonely defeated Perkins the wise. They had lots of fun but punctually, at 4:00 in the afternoon; they said their goodbyes without asking each other anything, only promising to see each other the next day. This is how three school semesters during which their friendship grew. Perkins the wise kept drinking daily, but together they shared sandwiches.

On occasions Mr. Lonely brought sandwiches for lunch from home, and on others, Perkins had someone buy them, from either the school cafeteria or a place nearby that Mr. Lonely recommended. In the end, they were great friends, and both were completely satisfied with their friendship. It implied no compromise for either of them, since they never spoke of personal matters that could injure the good relationship between the two.

Mr. Lonely was curious as to why a man so intelligent was drunk, dirty and did not worry about anything, but because of the fear of lost their friendship, he only concentrated on enjoying the moment. Truthfully, it was surprising to watch Perkins the wise enjoy watching Mr. Lonely play soccer. He was a very good player. He played with such enjoyment, only comparable to his ability.

He was the best player at the school and at the park, he was an idol, but his biggest fan was Perkins, and he let him know by telling him that just as easily as he solved the mathematical problems, Mr. Lonely easily solved the games.

To Mr. Lonely, being able to count on his friendship with Perkins the wise was something special.

MR. LONELY AGAIN
PERKINS THE WISE

He appreciated the luck of being the only student that sat at his side just to talk. He did not go for mathematical help, and he did not have to make the trips, back and forth, to the liquor store. Unfortunately, not everything that goes well last eternally. Therefore, the distancing between the two friends began its process. Someone said that when you have a good friend, you enslave a part of him within you. It is very true because it hurts you when something affects them, and whatever injures them, injures you as well.

Perkins the wise, one day asked Mr. Lonely what was his nationality. Why did he act different, in fact, his sandwiches have a European style? Mr. Lonely grew pale, and said that perhaps he was different because he traveled a lot as a child to different schools in Europe, and that an uncle taught him how to make that kind of sandwich.

Perkins, the wise looking at him, mentioned that the first occasion when Mr. Lonely prepared sandwiches for him, pleasant memories from his family life came to mind. He remembered having eaten that type of sandwich in Italy during his honeymoon. The taste of the mustard, and the cheeses moved him to wonderful times of his life. He intended to ask Mr. Lonely, why that very simple act of the sandwiches, but he could not do it because Mr. Lonely remained absent for a week due to sickness.

The next day, Perkins the wise preferred to wait far from the park. He waited at the gates of an abandoned building near the liquor store, and observed how Mr. Lonely bought food for the dogs, and later came back to ask about Perkins the wise. It was then; he decided to be friends with the young lunatic that had a certain charm, creator of sandwiches with the taste of pleasing memories. This is how Perkins the wise opened the doors of his heart to Mr. Lonely.

PERKINS THE WISE

With time, he came to like and admire him for his able playing. After a silence with a melancholic flavor, Perkins the wise asked Mr. Lonely; well, when did you decide to be my friend? Mr. Lonely, smiling, answered that in another country, in another time, he had a marvelous friend that he called, the rag picker. He was homeless, alcoholic, philosopher and with dogs. He appeared and disappeared without any warning.

Mr. Lonely knows there are more characters like that. The first time he saw Perkins the wise, his curiosity was reborn, as to whether or not he was a special character, like the rag picker He discovered that he was special and full of Wisdom, but what was his secret, or disgrace, that makes him live a life so full of shame and solitude? Perkins the wise, with a clear voice, told his sad story; which turned him into Perkins the wise. He said he was a student poorly sustained and supported by his mother's love, which proportioned him the means to have a university education. He never knew any father, but even so, he graduated the best in his class. Very young, he accomplished became one of the most brilliant mathematicians in the nation. He met a marvelous woman, which he married and had two daughters with, creating along with his beloved mother, a happy family.

He gave conferences around the world, becoming cathedratic at various universities. In this manner, he earned enough money to provide his family with a life very different to the one he had during his infancy. In the end, happiness was his friend, and accompanied him daily When the media interviewed him, he said that his secret to success was the four women he had for a family. They had a lovely home in which together, they shared the majority of their time that was possible.

MR. LONELY AGAIN
PERKINS THE WISE

Since his time was occupied with work giving all sorts of cathedra's and conferences around the world So huge was his success, that NASA became interested in obtaining the services of Perkins the wise, offering him work at the space center located in the city of Houston, Texas in the United States This had been one of his dreams for years, without wasting any time he bought airplane tickets for his entire family. His intention was to sign the contract while his family had fun, and searched for a house to live in the city of Houston, or perhaps its surrounding areas.

With two days left for the trip, a cathedratic friend became ill, and could not replace Perkins to give the conference as it had been agreed, so he would have to travel one day after the date that had been agreed on. The simplest thing to do was not to cancel all the airplane tickets for his family and him to travel to Houston on the day after the conference. This way, they only cancelled one ticket.

They boarded the plane, as decided. The family traveled towards Houston, while Perkins the wise participated in the conference that he could not cancel. After the conference, he would go home and the next day, travel in order to reunite with his family. After participating in the long conference, he went home. Upon arriving, he expected to find some sort of message from his family, but there was nothing.

Later, tired of waiting for a phone call, he decided to call the hotel where his family was staying, but his family never arrived. He called the airline to ask, if the flight had been delayed but it had not been so. The flight had suffered an accident. He went to the airport and received confirmation that passengers and crew died in the accident, with no hope of finding survivors.

ADVENTURES OF PHILOSOPHIC REFLECTION
PERKINS THE WISE

After crying for hours and days, not knowing how many miles he walked with no set direction. He ate no food, only a bit of water, which he casually found in bottles and public water fountains. He was homeless with no direction for days, drinking only alcoholic beverages, trying to drown the shame.

Then, the money he had, finished, but he did not return home. Who kept his home, cars, and his fortune? He did not know, nor did he care. He decided to live forgotten. With his ability for mathematics, he installed himself outside of what one-day was his college, and decided to solve mathematical problems in exchange for drink, and a bit of food for the dogs that surrounded him, being his occasional friends. He would sleep where he could drink alcohol and eat, so long as not to die.

He discovered, that he easily made enough to drink, so he would leave early to get drunk, forgetting his shame. He does not know how many years passed like this, maybe three, or four. He did not remember, nor did he want to he said that during his infancy, the only thing of value was his mother. Later on his wife to complete his world with two lovely daughters, total four women who completed his world of happiness. Perkins the wise blamed nobody. He did not bother anyone. The only thing he did was mind his own physical resistance, so that one day, not too far away, he could die in some alley and this way reunites with his family. During this whole time, he never asked for help, condemning himself to live, or half die, in this manner, but was his choice. Mr. Lonely attentively listen without interrupting at any moment, Perkin's heart-rendering story.

Lonely only managed to clean his tears, and suddenly hug him; telling him that he could always count on him since they were friends. Perkins the wise said that he did not want to involve himself with anyone else.

MR. LONELY AGAIN
PERKINS THE WISE

Since it was time to disappear and leave the bench for some other character that arrives at the park They said good bye and walked in opposite directions. Mr. Lonely was crying because he knew that he would never again see Perkins the wise. He knew it was goodbye. He suddenly ran towards Perkins the wise and told him that he was doing bad in mathematics, and needed his help.

He said that he could not abandon him in such a difficult moment. Perkins the wise smiled just like the first time, telling him that he already knew Mr. Lonely tricks to passing mathematics, and other school subjects a soccer player of his category is passed in his subjects with no importance to whether or not they studied, in order to play with the college team and try to win as many championships as possible for the establishment Just as the recognition of having the best soccer team in the nation is the dream of every coach in every school district, you do not need me, but thanks for the attempt.

Without saying any more, they both took their paths, but Mr. Lonely continued crying without end until he reached his home. He later grabbed a mathematics book and began studying; in honor of Perkins the wise. He knew that Perkins the wise would not return. Just as it had happened with the rag picker, but he also knew that he was very fortunate to have met people like them, and to be able to tell it.

Maybe someday, he would write his experiences that made him feel better about losing Perkins the wise. Mr. Lonely never imagined that another person would write, and tell his stories. The important thing is; that they were not forgotten from the next day on, he was never seen, nor was anything known about Perkins the wise. Everyone missed him. Everyone liked him. For some time, they searched for him in alleys near the school, and in various liquor stores. With time, the students returned to their daily activities in the park. Even the dogs stopped going in search of Perkins.

PERKINS THE WISE

Mr. Lonely never looked for Perkins the wise, nor did he again play soccer at the park. He simply limited himself to study mathematics, so as not to do the soccer trick, in honor of his friend. Mr. Lonely finished college and did not return. The park lost forever, the wise man and the soccer player, both being its greatest attraction. Today, perhaps no one remembers, but I do.

Thought:
When you have a good friend, you enslave a part of him within you Gibran Jalil Gibran said. It is true, but it is also true that when a friend gives you his time, his compassion, and when you need him he is there for you. But as much friendship exists, there is always the person that prefers to heal his pain in the most complete solitude.

It is hard to respect that solitude because it sounds like abandonment, or because of fear of becoming absence Love, friendship, and loyalty are only a question of decision, not of sentiment. You like someone, or someone likes you, because that is what was decided, it is only a proud choice of respect. Friends are forever and ever.

THE BOXER

Mr. Lonely and his cousins worked in the restaurant only on the weekends, making school their primary activity. On a certain evening, a foreign client insulted a waiter without reason Mr. Lonely had to intervene, but the client threw punches, and he received an answer from Mr. Lonely, a lesson in boxing so unforgettable that he did not know he started his new profession, which brought him glory, satisfaction, and a lot of bitterness.

The client, laid flat on the ground bathed in his own blood as if he had been run over by a truck. Mr. Lonely had not a single scratch on him Mr. Mario Alberti had observed from beginning to end without intervening, and then called his nephew and directed him to the interior of his office. He asked his nephew how what just happened had been possible. Mr. Lonely wanted to explain his innocence but his uncle again, asked how it was possible, referring to his ability in boxing; which he classified as very fine, elegant, and effective.

That same night, uncle and nephew went out together to watch professional boxers fighting illegally, for enormous amounts of money. Mr. Lonely, for the first time found himself at the center of illegal fights. He felt scared, but the respect that everyone showed towards his uncle brought back his confidence the place was a big underground parking lot, where you find people of all social and economic levels. Police officers, priests, politicians, artists, businesspersons, and mafias, escorted by beautiful women, but everyone obsessed with betting their money on their preferred boxer.

The rules were professional with a referee controlling the actions. When the fight passed around number three, time was no longer stopped, nor did rests exist. The fight continued without stop until one of the boxers won or lost in a few words, after the third round, the fight became a mortal fight without space for a draw, with some exceptions. For security reasons, the fights took place in different places.

Which were confirmed by phone the day of the fight. With a discrete dignity of the system created by the organization called or known as, the mafia, which controlled the event, from beginning to end the good boxers won up two thousand dollars per fight, but the money was split between the sponsor, the trainer, the physical trainer, a doctor and two fighters that completed the team that prepared the boxer before and after each fight.

Mr. Mario made a proposition to Mr. Lonely to become a professional fighter, to which he did not like the idea, but accepted due to obedience later, a gym was set up in one of the house's living room. They hired a trainer, two physical trainers, a doctor, and two sparring partners a week later, began the hard trainings for Mr. Lonely, which continued studying since the deal was that he would not abandon school.

Three months later was his grand debut. Easily winning these fights obtaining in a few months' fame, and the title of being presently undefeated. His fine and elegant boxing impressed because of its effectiveness the admiration he felt for Cassius Clay motivated him to fight, imitating him to the perfection, exactly the same style, only with different weight and size. He counted on a great speed of hands that just scratched the limit of incredible; these being his best weapon just like his unbeatable defense.

Mr. Lonely did not receive money directly for his fights, but he had all the luxuries at his disposal, since Mario Alberti spoiled him and did not charge him for expenses, just to please him anyway, his likes were, regularly traveling and getting to know places far away, to forget his career as a fighter, and turn himself completely into a traveler. It was about twenty-six months of fighting; Mr. Lonely was considered one of the best. His record was; one hundred five fights, one hundred wins, two draws, and three losses.

MR. LONELY AGAIN
THE BOXER

Seventy of his victories where the result of his enormous luck which accompanied him to every one of his fights the characteristic thing about his fights was that he always lost the first round, since he never could hate his rival, dedicating himself only to defending without attacking his corner crew passed desperate moments; they never understood his nature, being his reaction after receiving hits, changing his tactics, and utilizing his quick offensive.

He would finish always winning with certain ease. Other fights, he won with miracles, since at the end he was taken to illegal hospitals to recover from the terrible punishment he received during the match Mr. Mario and the corner crew won a lot of money, and always thought of how to make more, while Mr. Lonely only thought of how to retire, since some of those fights became savage and brutal, as if they were criminal fights.

In reality, he never liked the idea of fighting, after all that time, he continued his studies, sports, and adventures, just like any student. There were never any changes in his behavior, since he maintained his life as a fighter separate from the one as a student. He did as long as he could his terrible activity of professional street fighting he did not like the idea of fighting any longer always thinking of how to retire on time, before ending up completely beat up he himself did not know how to stop, until the unexpected reached his life. The result was in a form of a drastic change in his life, which made him the Mr. Lonely as in this story.

Thought:
It has been said that fighting is an art it is aside from being quite complicated the greatest joy of this art is the fine ability to defend you. It can maintain your physical and mental integrity, saving you from aggressions, without having to be aggressive or offensive.

However, the only possible defense in a fight is reason. To win you must always be reasonable about what you are doing, or do not do it at all. The lesson is clear. Reason drives to not fight, only to defend you.

A LIGHT ON THE EYES

On a certain occasion, a young woman named Inia arrived at the neighborhood. She was scared, beaten, and asked for protection Mr. Lonely, asked why and from whom? Inia told him about when her mother died, only two days ago. Her stepfather sexually attacked her sister, and intended to do the same with her, beating her first, but Inia was excellent in fighting and defended herself by attacking him with a liquor bottle.

The consequences were not made to wait since he threatened her with death. He was under protection by the "Protector"; a protection he enjoyed because he was a distributor of drugs, with great dividends for the "protector" of the sector they lived in the situation became critical for Inia, due to armed individuals looking for her with strict orders to kill her, which is why it was best for her to flee to another sector, and request protection.

She knew that Mr. Lonely was a fighter, since she had been present at some of his fights as a spectator, and that he was nephew to Mr. Mario Alberti. The situation was critical yet simple at the same time, since he did not help her, no one else would do so, because of the fear of the vengeance of the "Protector"

Mr. Lonely explained the situation to his uncle, asking for his help Mr. Mario Alberti spoke to the "protector" of that sector, and everything was solved, with the condition that she would not set foot ever again in the other sector. Inia, although beautiful, had a dirty past but kept good feelings.

Since she learned to rob, and dirty tricks from an early age, as a necessity, using them to survive in a dirty world which she was assigned just for being born with drugs and robbers in addition, assassins as company, in the end, she was not to blame for being how she was. She was born into the worst and fought fiercely to be good and sweet.

Inia asked Mr. Lonely to no longer fight since every fight turned into a pain for her. It was difficult to withstand his famous first round, which he always lost besides, he would no longer have to train, leaving more time to enjoy their mutual company Just a few days ago, they had fallen in love, and what they looked for was more time to be together Inia inhabited a hotel room, and Mr. Lonely stayed with her, but secretly, since Mr. Mario did not really like Inia.

Partially due to her past and partially for being the cause of retirement for Mr. Lonely; from the savage activity of street fighter Mr. Mario did not rejoice the relationship between the couple, since he considered the dirty and lost relationship between them so he reduced to a minimum the allowances of his nephew so that he would not have means of going with Inia, but the opposite happened, since they were always seen together at all hours enjoying their love to their greatest heights.

Inia and Mr. Lonely went to other sectors, assaulted drunks outside of bars and cantinas. Once they had enough money, they would go have dinner and then sleep at the hotel. Very early, he would return home, entering secretly, pretending he had been asleep in his room he ate breakfast and went to school while Inia ate breakfast and lunch at a restaurant. She looked for something to entertain herself with until the afternoon arrived, to go and search for her love, since she only lived for him.

No matter how much they tried, they could not be separated, since their relationship turned into something special. They never spoke of formalities, since their relationship was solid and permanent. With or without money, they enjoyed simply being together, sharing it all.

This way is how they spent seven months with adventures and romance. The nocturnal assaults began to get increasingly dangerous, and they gained fame as thieves and much more.

MR. LONELY AGAIN
A LIGHT ON THE EYES

One night Inia gave Mr. Lonely a pistol, which he refused, arguing that for nothing in the world would he use or carry a weapon he returned the weapon to Inia, telling her it would be best if she kept it for her protection, since some nights she remained alone while he studied for his scholastic exams.

One night, Inia told a story so strange and incredible, that Mr. Lonely did not know what to say. Inia and Mr. Lonely had a light in their eyes so intense, it was special. There were occasions in which at a distance they recognized each other, and in the dark, manifested like a shine of great splendor, which only seen by them she would say that her mother, before dying, told her that the light in the eyes was the symbol of a different generation with special abilities. They could tell each other apart by the light in the eyes, and the common person could not perceive such shine, only those which possessed it.

The people with the shine have the quality to do good or bad, but in great proportions. When you find someone with the shine, this person could be your happiness, or your disgrace Mr. Lonely and Inia were happy in these moments, just as said by Inia's mother. He did not know what to say, but understood that they were happy, and liked to look in each other's eyes, since the shine motivated them to continue loving each other as they did at that moment.

Inia said that the shine was the symbol predestined them for something great and unique, but understanding it, and finding the path to follow was difficult, since it required knowledge and mental ability, as well as time to understand it. Finally, it was an extraordinary yet interesting, but nothing more. At least, that is what Mr. Lonely thought.

She said she loved Mr. Lonely like she never thought she could ever love somebody, promising that if she were to perish, she would return to him and help him, because they were inseparable.

A LIGHT ON THE EYES

Mr. Lonely said he did not believe the dead could return, but Inia said she believed it to the extent of promising, with tears in her brilliant eyes, that she would return to him after death. Mr. Lonely said his goodbye and went home to study for his exams leaving Inia in the same hotel as always, but with the gun for her protection. The next morning, his best friend suddenly awoke Mr. Lonely, Villi, which seemed sad and alarmed, asking Mr. Lonely if he had spent the night with Inia. He answered with a no, saying that he left her at the hotel around 10:00 pm. before coming home to study.

Villi said that at the hotel, they had found Inia dead supposedly assassinated with three bullet wounds. Mr. Lonely left without words. He could not believe what he had heard, but the sadness in Villi's face confirmed what he had said they quickly left to the hotel, where the police detained and arrested Mr. Lonely as a suspect in Inia's death, considering the possibility that the case was a passionate assassination it was three horrible days, during which Mr. Lonely remained detained in prison for the investigations of the case.

He was released on lack of evidenced they could not find his fingerprints on the homicide weapon, as well as Mr. Mario's testimony, stating that his nephew remained at home studying that night during this time Inia buried in a dignified manner, Mr. Mario took charge of all the funeral expenses, and even allowed for the burial in the family cemetery, showing repentance for having misjudged Inia, whom resulted to be a good person.

During the past three days, Villi told Mr. Mario how Inia purely loved Mr. Lonely, and that her dirty past was circumstantial, since she did not chose that way of life or that neighborhood. It was cruel destiny that gave it to her Mr. Lonely locked himself in his room, devastated, for he'll never see Inia for his last goodbye. Now, he only has a tomb as the reminder of that wonderful woman which he loved, whom loved him.

MR. LONELY AGAIN
A LIGHT ON THE EYES

From that moment on he became known as Mr. Lonely, just as he is known in this story, remembering Inia's promise to return to be with him. Day after day, he searched in the eyes of people, that marvelous shine which was once happiness, but now was his downfall. The police did not solve the crime; archive it as another unimportant case. Villi on the other hand had come to his conclusions, as well as being at the crime scene. He found a triangular Fender pick, the ones used to play guitar, which no one noted as an important clue in the assassination.

Villi and Mr. Lonely went to the sector where Inia had lived and grown, in search of any clues to solve the crime. For days, they found nothing, but one night, while they dined at a musical café they spotted a poster of Francis, a guitarist who was very popular for, phenomenal interpretations for the songs of The Beatles. Aside from being a gigolo, drugs addict, gangster, and criminal. They found out that Francis had been in jail for choking his lover with a guitar string in a hotel room without consideration or remorse.

In addition, he played guitar using triangular Fender picks, saying it was his preferred. The same kind found at the crime scene. Villi and Mr. Lonely located the music store where Francis got strings and picks for his guitar they found out that the triangle Fender picks came in three sizes, thin, medium, thick, and that Francis used the thin for them, this signaled the first clue to solving the crime, since the pick that Villi found was thin, so they had one suspect.

Now, it would not be enough to find him and prove that he committed the crime, something not quite that easy, but they would try anything.

They began their search for Francis, but he had moved to another tourist city, where it was easy for him to find work as a musician, he was the best musician in the area when it came to interpreting The Beatles.

Looking for the motives of the crime, they returned for the sector where Inia once lived frequently. Bribing friends of Francis, they found out that he loved Inia like crazy, but was shot down. He insisted but never accomplished anything, so he motivated her stepfather to give her a hard time, which would cause her to flee home and take refuge in his arms, but this never happened Francis and Inia's stepfather constantly being drugged and went crazy trying to get sexual favors from Inia, which aside from being beautiful, she was sly and always escaped their pretensions.

She finally fled to the sector where Mr. Lonely lived, and received the protection of Mr. Mario Alberti, thus leaving no possibilities for Francis. Therefore, he stopped bothering her, but it only appeared that way later they learned that the weapon that Inia had, was the same one with which she was assassinated. It was a gift from Francis for her protection and as an apology for all that had previously occurred between them.

Mr. Lonely did not have the means to go after Francis, since the expenses would be great. Just the same, he did not know how many days, weeks, or even months, this desperate search would take. Villi, his inseparable friend, suggested he could live off music; why not learn to play the instrument well? This would pay the expenses while is on the search for Francis, later, Mr. Lonely and Villi stole a guitar, beginning secretly, the difficult task of learning to play guitar.

Mr. Lonely tied the strings with a handkerchief so as not to make noise, and practiced for hours every night. Carrying out exercises with his fingers and listening to music day after day, his life became full of music in that time, the entire world went crazy for the music of The Beatles. Mr. Lonely liked them, but they did not drive him crazy. He had a universal taste, but tried to interpret them as best he could to their original discs, trying to imitate their guitar sound 100%

MR. LONELY AGAIN
A LIGHT ON THE EYES

Four months later, he could acceptably interpret the Liverpool Quartet, and was considered a good guitarist. He intensified his practices day and night, accomplishing performances two months later.

Thought:
Never fear happiness. Do not avoid it; fearing it may not be real, or definite. Only fight to maintain it by your side. No matter what happens, never give up nor let it pass you by, because with time, you will know you've made a mistake, but it will be too late. Happiness is the answer to all the questions and riddles created by sorrow.

THE SEARCH

He gathered some money and embarked on the ferry, not in search of fame, but in search of Francis. Villi, showing his enormous and valuable friendship, said his goodbye, reminding him of how dangerous the subject was, as well as the disadvantages of being alone at all times, far from home, without his protective uncle, and with few allowances after the trip on board the ferry, he boarded a train, which moved him rapidly to the most important city, on a tourist level, searching in bars, musical cafés, and every place with any relationship of rock music. It was said that Francis performed in many places, but left for another city.

Mr. Lonely performed in various musical cafés, gathered some money, and traveled in search of Francis, but this story went on for many months, and many cities so much practice had transformed him into a famous guitarist with very personal styles of play. When playing, he used a thin Fender pick, and kept the one, which Villi found in the hotel room, where Inia died by mail, and occasionally by phone, Mr. Lonely kept in touch with his mother, his uncle, and Villi, who continued relating valuable information and providing unconditional support, proper from the best friend in the world.

In one of the many cafés he visited, after listening to his music, the owner commented that he had another guitarist who interpreted Beatles that it would not be a bad idea for both of them to perform together. He mentioned that the name of the other guitarist was Francis, which provoked a sense of triumph in Mr. Lonely.

He had finally found him. Mr. Lonely asked the owner for the address, stating that they both came from the same area of the island, and that they were friends from infancy the owner recommended Mr. Lonely to take caution in the ugly, difficult, and dangerous neighborhood to cross by locals and strangers.

MR. LONELY AGAIN
THE SEARCH

In fact, the place was bad, extremely dirty, and you could smell the danger. But it was not that different from the ones Mr. Lonely knew, so he was not that worried he stood in front of the building in which Francis rented a room, located in the ruined sector of the neighborhood. Francis opened the door, and courteously asked Mr. Lonely to enter, as well as offering him a seat on an old smelly sofa.

Francis took the first word, stating that he was aware of his search, and before any revenge, they had things in common which they both needed to solve, finally. Francis asked him if he knew the story of the light in the eyes after thinking for a little, he responded that he heard something about it, but why did that have anything to do with this moment. Francis answered that it was important than he could imagine, because it was a great story that was as fascinating, as it was real.

The shine in the eyes was something more than just that. Those who have the shine can change the destinies of people. They could provoke tranquility, happiness, and even make miracles happen. Not that great, but miracles none the less, on the condition that it was in the benefit of others, and not that of their own. How to know who was in this group was easy. They identified themselves by the shine in their eyes, since the common person could not see nor feel anything special, in regards to this rare yet simple shine. Mr. Lonely looked, for the first time, into Francis's eyes, and saw the same shine as that in Inia's eyes.

When Francis met Inia, he discovered the shine in her eyes, and fell hopelessly in love with her, realizing that if he did not conquer her, he would be unhappy forever. He tried every way, to no avail, causing his pain to be greater and greater with each passing day later, he realized that if he did not conquer her love, he would be unhappy for life. This was his motive for killing her; at the same time not allow their happiness, for he knew that they both had the shine in their eyes.

Therefore, that was the one, and only reason that lead him to commit the crime, something that was nothing new to him. Now, absurd the only thing he desired was to kill Mr. Lonely because according to the story of the light in the eyes it was said that if there were only one person with the light in their eyes, in the entire world, sure this person would have unimaginable powers. Therefore, he wanted to be the only one.

He left the pick intentionally, knowing that it would serve as a clue for Mr. Lonely, to then kill him far from his neighborhood, without any protection from Mr. Mario Alberti Mr. Lonely could not believe this story, since it sounded more like a fantasy than it did a reality. Absolutely absurd, but Francis assured him it was the one true reason for all his existence.

He told him that there have been many men and women with the same abilities, and that they had used them for good, just as for bad great heroes and people in worldwide history all had in common the shine in their eyes, but they were not his heroes. In the end, they sacrificed their lives for the benefit of others, but he did not intend to do the same.

He mentioned people such as Hitler the dictator, President Kennedy's assassin, Jack the Reaper, and many other criminals which he admired, because they killed without compassion, and tried to stay alive in order to be the only ones in the world with the shine in their eyes Francis pulled from within his clothes, a pistol, preparing himself to kill Mr. Lonely, a very intense light, with the silhouette of a woman illuminated the room and blinded Francis.

In that moment Mr. Lonely utilized to throw himself upon him, which caused them both to fall out of a window. For an instant, Mr. Lonely did not know anything. Nor did he realize they had fallen two floors. He threw his gaze in the direction of the window, but to his surprise, there was no window, only solid walls, for which he felt confused and fortunate.

MR. LONELY AGAIN
THE SEARCH

Then, he felt pain in his right hand. Upon looking at it, he realized that one of his fingers was impaled with a thin metal bar he withdrew his finger, which was left bleeding uncontrollably. At the same time, he realized how fortunate he was, since he had fallen on Francis's body, which protected him from the other four bars that completely impaled the body, killing him instantly.

Mr. Lonely remembered all of his great friends. Marvelous people he knew and assured himself that they also had the shine in their eyes. He now understood, and knew the reason for his strange and extraordinary attitude the story was true, and presented him with the wonderful opportunity to be good and useful to the world and its subjects understanding that it would never be in his own personal benefit, but still, a mission so wonderful that he would have to keep following as if it were his destiny.

Besides, the gorgeous Inia would return, as part of this wonderful story, just as she promised. Mr. Lonely understood, and accepted his new destiny. Later, after bandaging his finger, he began his return home. He was in search of protection he traveled by many trains, and took the ferry back to the island. He remembered the errors he committed during his search for Francis.

He gave his name and information on the hotel where he was staying. The owner of the café could inform how to locate and arrest Mr. Lonely, so he was once again suspect number one after narrating his entire story to Villi and his uncle, he confessed his fear of being arrested. His uncle used his contacts and discovered the police had circulated a warrant for the arrest of his nephew. In dealing with Mr. Mario Alberti, they gave him ten hours' time, which was plenty for him to put his nephew far away and safe from arrest after providing him with money and contacts, Mr. Mario and Villi said goodbye, and watched as he boarded a fishing boat in route to Barcelona, Spain.

THE SEARCH

The police watched over the ferries in route to Italy, so this was the safe protected path the goodbye was sad, as expected, but Mr. Lonely left happily, having realized that his uncle loved him more than what he had imagined. With Villi, he realized he had a friend for life, thus being precious gifts to him with the money provided by his uncle, Mr. Lonely left his home and headed to America, but not before traveling parts of Europe, as the getaway planed.

Various months after arriving in America, he decided to play rock and roll music with a group that traveled throughout the entire border of the neighboring country. He learned the accent, and culture like a shell, in order for his identity to not be discovered he did not need to learn the language, only the accent, the underground language, and the customs, and the culture that, in these moments, allowed him to breathe as a free man.

Still, he awaited the return of his beloved Inia, searching in every woman for that wonderful shine in the eyes. He believed in the promise Inia had made him, of one day returning to him. It is believed that this is how he became Mr. Lonely, as he is known in this story. From now on, his life and his character would be so special and incredible, that the only thing that can be said, is that the story of the light in the eyes is true, since his life proved this for its own his stories and adventures were as fascinating as a book of imaginary adventures, but as real as his spirit, and faith that never broke, nor changed his way of life, just like, he never stopped searching for his beloved Inia.

Thought:
Revenge has two sides. Some see it as justice, while others see it as a negative sentiment that only brings more unending disgrace and problems to those who carry it out. Someone once said that revenge is like a jungle in which you can get lost. Someone else said it was a very sweet pleasure. Mr. Lonely never sought revenge.

MR. LONELY AGAIN
THE SEARCH

He only searched for the truth. When he found himself face to face with the truth, he did not get any vengeance, and saw himself entangled in unending problems. So to say, under no circumstance, is revenge correct. It will only do you harm.

THE WALL AND THE FAITH

During 1975, Mr. Lonely was heading to work, in a beautiful city bordering the sea, in which the federal government constructed a thermoelectric plant to generate more electricity, and give a better service to industry just as the citizens. The project was so gigantic that it occupied 15,000 workers distributed into three shifts. On his first day of work, he was assigned to the import warehouse because of his knowledge of the English language.

To finish the workday, he dedicated himself to finding a home, and renting it, since he was expecting to live at the port for at least twelve long months. He found a comfortable and economical home in a beautiful neighborhood near the beach, where he often enjoyed his afternoons, dedicating himself to running for long hours along the shoreline that displayed its beauty to which he felt part of.

On a precise day, he woke up dreaming that he swam in the blue of the ocean, but to his surprise, he was almost swimming, since the house was flooded due to the heavy rain that was falling through out whole night. He called his work telling them that he would not work that day, since he had problems to solve. The neighbors cleaned, and took out the water with a nature way, that provoked his curiosity asking them, how often these kind of floods occurred. Responding, they said that in times of rain, they happened every day, and that neighborhood was located in a giant ditch.

Immediately he took a taxi asking to the driver to take him to the neighborhood at the highest elevation of the sea level, with the intention of renting a house far away from the floods.

To his good luck, he found in the high parts of a hill, a house that dominated the entire city enjoying a marvelous view. Well at least it was a place where he would not have to worry, about getting flooded again after finding a moving van, and long hours of sweat, he finally got some sleep on his new and sparkling safe location.

MR. LONELY AGAIN
THE WALL AND THE FAITH

Next day he had to walk more than three stone blocks, to get to the main avenue to catch the bus to work. This route was free of charge to workers going to, and from work. A huge wall as big as one full city block caught his attention, to say the truth there were four huge walls. Puzzled he asked what was inside, and found out it was a cell-unit to seize detainees, it was a prison.

A feeling of disgust made him grab a stone between his hands, and throw it against the wall, wishing to end what seemed to be a division of two worlds, fine and dreadful people on both sides of the wall but condemned only the ones inside. For him that was no justice so he reached for another stone, and again threw it against the wall. After that he, continued his way for work. Once the workday was over, he took the bus home. Walking the same route, he soon reached the wall. Not even thinking twice he grabbed a stone, and threw it as hard as he could with the intention of destroying the wall.

Later he went on with his usual walk to the beach throwing stones to the wall every time he passed by it. This started without knowing a daily routine, which as symbolized a protest for the innocent people wrongfully locked up. The daily walk to work, the walks along the ocean, and other sporadic night outs, caused him to walk past the wall four to six times a day. This was the same number of times that he hit the wall by throwing the rocks at the wall every time he walked past it.

Later Mr. Lonely meets Gabriel, a lunatic communist, and ex political prisoner from the capital city, who worked at the same department where he was assigned. They immediately initiated a friendship that lasted for a long time, something more than they had imagined. Since they shared their house, adventures, and friends, they were popular and fun, just the same as work as in the city. Every day they walked to and from work, but the habit of the rock seemed absurd to Gabriel, and on certain occasions, his friend would get mad, and think he was crazy.

On a sunny morning, they were walking late on their way to catch the bus, and Mr. Lonely returned like always to throw his rock towards the wall, but Gabriel looked at him with anger since it was late and the bus just passing by leaving them behind. Gabriel looked at him, and pointed to a nearby restaurant inviting him to go inside, but he knew they should be on their way to work. Gabriel did not really care and literally dragged him inside.

Sitting down in front of each other, they ordered something to drink while they kept arguing about the stupid incident, and the daily annoying habit towards the wall. Gabriel argued about being late for work every day, for having to wait for the thrown stone so he demanded to Mr. Lonely an explanation after a few sips of the refreshing orange juice, Mr. Lonely explained a long story about the infamous wall, and what it means to him. He tried to explain, that even a tiny but continuous drop of water will break a rock, and he was hoping that one-day something similar would happen with the wall.

Gabriel told him it was the most ridiculous story he had ever heard, assuring him that they will die someday, and the wall would always be there. Gabriel told him that he was never going to be late for work again, from that day on, his friend never waited for him to throw the rock at the wall. Inclusively, when they had visitors, he would tell them about his fantasies, and they would ridicule Mr. Lonely, and laugh this did not anger Mr. Lonely nor did he give up his mission, and he continued to throw the rocks toward the wall.

Many months passed, in which their friendship grew, despite the ridicule, and the throwing of the rocks. Gabriel went off to solve his problems with his wife, and he finally encouraged her to come to live with him. She was a woman with an angel's character who forgave everything, and understood with smiles full of tenderness.

MR. LONELY AGAIN
THE WALL AND THE FAITH

Their relationship was that of siblings to Mr. Lonely. They watched over him, and he knew that he was alone in this place, and was responsible only in answering to them. Further, more they continued thinking that he was crazy, for throwing the rocks towards the wall every day. Finally, the day came when Mr. Lonely decided to return to the capital city to continue his studies. Other circumstances contributed to this event, but details of that marvelous story we will speak of later.

He packed his belongings, said goodbye to the entire city, and returned home to be with his mother. She received him happy, and proud of him as she always did before. Many weeks later, the media reported from the harbor, where he used to live with alarming news. They spoke of a hurricane accompanied by many tornadoes that had destroyed the port, and left it with no communication for many days.

Mr. Lonely grew crazy because he had not heard from Gabriel and his wife. The home where they lived was safe from floods, but a hurricane would surely destroy it. The house was located on a hill, at the highest in all the port. You can imagine his anguish during all this time that he knew nothing of them, during the twelve days that followed. The days went by without hearing anything from Gabriel and his wife.

Finally, it occurred to him to go to the central offices of the federal government, to ask for communication with the thermoelectric plant through their communication radio. After many hours, they informed that both were rejoicing in their health, with no problems it was a great relief to know they were fine. In addition, they mentioned that they had mailed him a letter with newspaper clippings, describing all that had occurred due to the hurricane. Later he received the letter, and read: Dear friend, we were lucky that our home resisted the strength of the storm.

THE WALL AND THE FAITH

Some of the glass windows were broken therefore all furniture were damaged by the water these were the only damages that we received. My wife and I are fine, but the wall has fallen the wall, I am referring to is the one you used to throw rocks at every time you passed by it. Only the other three walls that you never threw rocks at left standing.

We have cried tremendously, because we cannot forgive the error that we always made by not understanding the faith of you, and your Great Spirit. We write you this letter with tears longing to hug you, and ask you to forgive our stupid ridicule we want to tell you that we love you with all our soul, and that you have our eternal respect for the great faith that you have shown disbelievers like us. with love from your brothers.

P.S.
They started to rebuild the wall, and now my wife and I throw the rocks daily in your honor. On the weekends, old friends who used to ridicule you visit us, and they too throw rocks at the wall. It hurts to know that only you can make it fall, and we need you to bring down many more. Immediately, he took a newspaper clipping, and he read the following: The hurricane destroyed one of the walls from the prison, in which ten prisoners took advantage of the chaos and confusion of this natural phenomenon and escaped.

Another clipping mentioned that six of the prisoners had been captured, and that the authorities for resisting arrest had assaulted the other three. The authorities stated that there was no other way but to have a confrontation one of the prisoners never found, and the people believe that he left far from this place, into another country where it would be difficult to capture him.

He must have read the letter and all the newspaper clippings about thirty times, after that. He could not imagine how his faith had benefit to someone else.

MR. LONELY AGAIN
THE WALL AND THE FAITH

I hope that the free prisoner was innocent so that he could justify all the faith he had to destroy the famous wall of the prison, because if this were not so, then all had been done in vain.

As time went by, Mr. Lonely and Gabriel reunited in the capital city. They spoke poetically about the event, and they continued to remember it as a poem dedicated to the daily routine of throwing rocks at the giant wall. This was, just a small boy full of faith, and armed with rocks, which were never hard to find. I hope someday he can destroy the walls, of the misunderstanding which separates the just men from the not so just, the rich from the poor, the wise from the not so wise, and overall the philosophers from the politicians, so that we may live in a world without walls.

In time, he came to know about how the Berlin Wall, which separated a nation of brothers, was brought down. I would like to tell you that Mr. Lonely was out there throwing rocks as well, but this would not be true although I am sure he would like to have thrown a rock, at the famous Berlin Wall.

Thought:
Liberty is the most precious gift to all living beings. When you lose your liberty, you stop living, and only dream of it. It is better to have it, and dream of what you could do with it. Remember, it is yours, do not risk it, only live it, day after day.

THE YELLOW BOOTS

During the time when Mr. Lonely worked in construction in the thermoelectric plant, in that pleasant port where he remained for ten months or so, occurred a day in which he was reviewing the various requisition orders of lading for pairs of workers boots for peons and noted an error in one of the order.

Two hundred pairs of boots destined for the department of lowly peons had been directed to various engineers from other departments; these boots which belonged to the peons. Mr. Lonely reviewed the requisition numbers, compared them to the detailed schedule of shipments, and verified that this was due to some kind of mistake.

He immediately presented himself before Mr. Palacios, the head of warehouse departments' chief, and revealed the requisition and delivery orders explained that the pairs of boots had been sent to the wrong department and that the engineers' shipment will not arrive for at least another 60 days.

Mr. Palacios was reviewing the information he had been given while Mr. Lonely grinned with satisfaction at his foresight and attention to detail; but to his surprise, the chief explained that it was in fact he who ordered the switch in deliveries and that all the information was correct. By the time the engineering department received the delivery the other delivery will be arriving for the peons, by in by it wasn't something he should be concerning himself with; surely these peons could wait.

After leaving the office, Mr. Lonely immediately visited all of the warehouse departments to review all orders for the last ten months. The results were as follows: the requisition orders for pairs of boots were for the peons of the plant, due to this particular department being the largest, depending on approximately 3000 employees of whom 2800 are given minimum wage, they were in dire need of these boots.

MR. LONELY AGAIN
THE YELLOW BOOTS

During the last 10 months they have only received 200 pairs of boots, the rest of the orders had been redirected, to other departments, the lowly peons, and others had to wait until the other departments' orders had arrived. That instant, Mr. Lonely traversed the plant-taking inventory of who had pairs of boots and who had not, he found that the total number of peons had no pair of boots at all. The 200 pairs of boots that were turned over to the other departments were for the personal technician for the plant office. Not one of the minimum-wage-paid peons had a single pair of boots.

The peons used old and tattered shoes, torn tennis shoes and the majority used sandals. They were subject to various reprimands for lacking protective footwear from lacking boots; an indignant and embarrassing event to suffer on top of being denied that very footwear. The next day Mr. Lonely continued to review the orders and inventory of boots and discovered that the departments whom received the various shipments of boots included: engineering, accounting, administration, transport and welding. In short, those workers who earned lower wages and all of the peons who earned minimum wage could not take part of the benefit of free boots.

The conclusion was simple and easily understood. This was all a kind of abuse done my Mr. Palacios, chief of warehouse departments. He blatantly gave favor to his own department and other departments he wished to have a good standing with at the expense of everyone else which he left nearly barefoot. Mr. Lonely confronted Mr. Palacios, asking him directly why he indulged favoritism.

Why leave simple peons bootless and barefoot in one's own plant? Mr. Palacios argued that being chief of warehouse departments the boots where his to do with as he pleased. Mr. Lonely glanced at the chief's shoes and noticed that he donned a lavish pair of company boots. During the next three days, Mr. Lonely spoke with the purchasing department.

ADVENTURES OF PHILOSOPHIC REFLECTION
THE YELLOW BOOTS

He explained the situation to them and asked them to request the manufacturers make and deliver 4000 pairs of boots within no more than three weeks. The manufacturer explicated how difficult it would be to comply with the request in such short amount of time. Mr. Lonely's reaction was to inform the purchasing department to search for pairs of boots wherever they could, even if they had to look in another city. The manufactory owner reconsidered his initial reaction and prepared his team to work extra hours and overtime, he expressed his desire to comply with the delivery request.

Having made a profound investigation in all the departments, asking peons and officials, Mr. Lonely realized that the situation of abuse was far more common than he originally anticipated. This had been going on for several years, which no one had done anything to change. Everyone's conformity and negligence resulted in the detriment of everyone with a low salary. The pairs of boots, due to their economic value, required for delivery the signature of recipient on a form as proof of delivery or when it would be returned. These forms are to be signed by the department head or assistant to the department.

During the 3 weeks of production for the 4000 pairs of boots, Mr. Lonely prepared forms under the names of each of the peons being roughly 3950. He also informed them to be present at the time of delivery. They were all in eager anticipation for the upcoming delivery of those much-desired boots; that were constantly, illegally denied them by the negligence of the company and even more specifically by Mr. Palacios, chief of the warehouse departments. The days went by and some rumors began to manifest: some speculated that just as it had occurred during the last three years the delivery would be redirected to a different department, others maintained their confidence in Mr. Lonely saying he would not permit any such injustice from happening any longer and that furthermore the pairs of boots would be delivered as promised, some remained silent not offering any opinion.

MR. LONELY AGAIN
THE YELLOW BOOTS

Either way but retained their hope that Mr. Lonely would not sway under any coming adversity during this entire time, Mr. Lonely continued throughout his days unencumbered by struggles; he continued to stone the wall of the prison on his walks between work and home. His inseparable friend, Gabriel and his wife supported his endeavor to aid the peons of the plant by assuring they received their just-deserved boots. Gabriel, being a communist, praised to Mr. Lonely's idea and said that these pairs of boots belonged to the town and for the town and the right of any poor laborer who contributed to the country through hard work. Surely a communist government would allot someone to defend their workers, especially those with a seemingly little voice.

To conclude, Gabriel made a number of eloquent discourses over the issue. He spoke so much about it that any would assume he himself had begun what Mr. Lonely had started; a credit he unknowingly gave himself and did not deserve. This did not worry or concern Mr. Lonely however; he had resolved himself to complete his task with or without help. The fact is that the purchasing department opted to help Mr. Lonely because they collectively despised Mr. Palacios but more than that because Mr. Lonely was closely acquainted and had good relations with most in the company.

He treated everyone with respect be they peons or directors; incidentally, he would alternate his lunch to eat with every department he could. This allowed him to increase work relations, which exceedingly helped him, communicate between departments and workers. This level of dedication earned him the title of coordinating director and it helped that he was tireless in his focus and work care.

Everything has a reason for happening, even that which; seemingly, has no reason at all; this just so happened to be the case with the yellow boots that are mentioned in this chapter.

THE YELLOW BOOTS

The outcome was something of an unexpected occurrence unpredictable by anyone except Mr. Lonely whom knew well what events were unfolding. He did not care not did he desire to change his decision or his behavior because to do so would be to change the person that he is. A simple a thing as being gifted with inner light based on the value of justice and to always be disposed to self-sacrifice for the good of others who require such reprieve.

All necessary installments were met and finally the boots are delivered to the plant by the purchasing department, of course, it was all done with a hermit's diligence and almost secretively. Mr. Lonely had asked the peons to file in at the department furthest away from the chief of warehouse department's office; Mr. Palacios' office, to buy them the most amount of time if he were to become aware and try to impede on the plan.

Now the first pair of boots was delivered the first department head and his assistant refused to sign the delivery form. Mr. Lonely had anticipated this and was unfazed; he knew that signing one's own name on the form was equivocal to signing a termination of employment form. As you may imagine, someone at the caliber of coordinating director of the warehouse departments signing the form was more than enough to accept responsibility and get the delivery through to the peons.

The delivery began at approximately 7:30 am and prolonged until almost 4:00pm. Mr. Lonely, in an effort to not waste time, had not eaten in that phase. Delivering the masses of boots involved receiving the proper measurements, signing the recipient and receiver (Mr. Lonely); even organizing the forms in alphabetical order was a time-consuming chore.

Mr. Lonely took on the responsibility of organizing yet signing each document alone caused his fingers and hands to ache with pain; but the grateful smiles of every single peon.

MR. LONELY AGAIN
THE YELLOW BOOTS

Was recompense enough to excuse his fatigue and conclude his extensive assignment as the day of deliveries ended, Mr. Lonely said simply divine justice, realized by a virtue of wanting to serve others. Those employees who happened to be present throughout the event of delivered boots gazed at Mr. Lonely with respect and admiration. They knew he dared to do the just thing which none of them would have dared.

Fortunately, Mr. Palacios never became aware of the salubrious affair that day. During the next day, the accounting department required 100 pairs of boots and not a single available pair was seen. They harassed Mr. Palacios because they were aware that the day before, 4000 pairs of boots were delivered to the plant Mr. Palacios asked what had happened the all the pairs of boots and learnt of the marathon events of the day before. Perceptibly, his next move was to summon Mr. Lonely and reprimand him for doing wrong in delivering the pairs of boots without speaking with the chief of departments first.

Mr. Lonely only responded with "I did the right thing." There was no reason to concern the chief of warehouse departments with one particular order when in a single day and amount of important shipments were processed and accepted by many of the departments which did not require his authorization; they only required his intervention when they were replacements, which was not the case in this circumstance. Any way you look at it the delivery did not warrant the involvement of Mr. Palacios.

He exploded with fury and told Mr. Lonely that he was fired; he was to go to the accounting department and pick up his final check; meanwhile, Mr. Palacios overstated on a lengthy report the improper actions of Mr. Lonely and the reason for his termination of employment. Mr. Lonely decided to speak to the secretary general of the union about the situation.

Mr. Fong, chief of the union, asked if he was aware that he had committed a grave fault in the incorrect delivery of the pairs of boots without authorization from his chief. Mr. Lonely replied that the order of boots was correct and that furthermore he had not committed any wrong.

Meanwhile Mr. Palacios was turning in his report to the accounting department, stating all the wrong doings of Mr. Lonely, expressing his anger and citing the destitution caused by Mr. Lonely. All of the employees supported Mr. Lonely, spoke out on his behalf throughout the thermoelectric plant about the situation, and offered their help and voice in an effort to discharge Mr. Lonely.

The minutes that followed came as a grand surprise to Mr. Palacios and the chief of the accounting department. To see 4500 personnel, peons and others (that is almost the entire plant) gathered just outside the office was am astonishment to say the least; all where there in proclamation of Mr. Lonely's justified and well-to-do actions. They exclaimed for Mr. Lonely to remain employed at the plant, they would not budge until they were assured of his continued employment as coordinating director of the warehouse departments.

Mr. Palacios fled to the union chief, informing him of the critical situation at the plant. Both Mr. Fong and Mr. Lonely presented themselves at the plant and the scene before them all Mr. Fong asked Mr. Lonely to request the workers return to their posts, he acquiesced and bid the employees return to their stations, he thanked them for their support and assured he would be all right. Every one of the employees, after listening to Mr. Lonely, began to remove their boots as a buffer to alleviate the blame Mr. Lonely has incurred.

Just as they began to remove their boots, Mr. Lonely spoke with great authority to halt their actions or everything he worked for would have been in vain; besides, he had two documents.

MR. LONELY AGAIN
THE YELLOW BOOTS

To prove his innocence. Mr. Lonely stated that everything would be ok and that he would be seeing them in a few hours as coordinating director. He said it would be best if they simply returned to their stations. One by one, they reluctantly returned to their designated workplaces. It was now that chief of accounting, the infuriated Mr. Palacios, Mr. Toledo (chief of purchases), Engineer Fabre, general director of the plant, Mr. Fong and Mr. Lonely assembled.

At the meeting, Mr. Lonely presented the requisition orders for the pairs of boots for the departments as well as the delivery orders and contract forms, all in all they were every bit of paperwork required to allot the marathon delivery which Mr. Lonely executed. This was enough to absolve him of any technical fault and served to illustrate that he did not undermine Mr. Palacios.

Mr. Toledo, purchasing manager, had copies of the requisition orders and purchase forms that were exactly like the ones Mr. Lonely presented, meaning the delivery of the pairs of boots had been correct and the accusation against Mr. Lonely, not. Mr. Fong commanded Mr. Palacios return Mr. Lonely's position to him as coordinating director of the warehouse departments immediately.

The chief accounting director and the general director awaited Mr. Palacios' restitution for his mistake. Mr. Palacios apologized to Mr. Lonely and dually restored his position at the plant. He could not hide his disgust and stormed out of the office. The accounting director destroyed the report made against Mr. Lonely along with the plant general director.

The chief of purchasing department gave Mr. Lonely a big hug and congratulated him on his ample triumph doing the right thing as accomplices without falsifying any documents. They can be regarded as accomplices because the purchasing department chief disliked Mr. Palacios.

THE YELLOW BOOTS

For his abuse of the peons who were by far the noblest of workers. Mr. Fong, who himself had been the one to suggest that Mr. Lonely work at the thermoelectric plant, extended his hand to Mr. Lonely as proud thanks saying that he certainly did no wrong, thanking him and reiterating his optimal decision in recommending him work at the plant. He told Mr. Lonely not to worry about Mr. Palacios; he would speak with him later.

Mr. Lonely expressed his gratitude and commented that he had the intention to leave for some time, this event gave him more incentive to do just that: return home to see his mother and finish grad school which was now his objective. With that, they bid each other farewells and Mr. Lonely asked that Mr. Fong take care of the loose ends regarding his departure, for the sooner he would get his final check the sooner he would march on home.

Smiling, Mr. Fong bid Mr. Lonely return in the afternoon of the next day and everything would be ready; incidentally, he also stated that if he so wished Mr. Fong could transfer to another building altogether by then Mr. Lonely smiled and retreated, moments later after leaving the thermoelectric plant all of the employee's in mass demonstrated their appreciation to him, hugging him, shaking his hand, giving him pats on the back, an endless array of gratitude. He then boarded the bus home like any other day right by Gabriel and they rode home.

Mr. Lonely recanted the story to his friend but omitted his intent to leave the city. The descended the bus and after tossing their stones at the mural wall of the prison, Mr. Lonely explained to Gabriel and his wife his plans for tomorrow; to pick up his check, say farewell to everyone at the plant, give himself a few days of rest and finally part ways to the capital to enroll in the university and stay with his mother. The following day he did just as he said. He went by to pick up his check, greeted and bid farewell to everyone stating he was returning to study.

MR. LONELY AGAIN
THE YELLOW BOOTS

Three days passed by with rest, site seeing and occasionally visiting the dance halls. In those three days he happened to meet a charming woman, no one knew where he met her or what happened but it is certain that Mr. Lonely deservingly had a great time off after his exuberant effort to have all of the employees receive their yellow boots.

Gabriel spoke at the thermoelectric plant, letting them all know the day Mr. Lonely would depart and that he would do it from the bus station named Oriente so he would sleep and travel by night to arrive at his destination in the morning. The day finally came to be on his way, Gabriel, his wife and several of Mr. Lonely's friends were there to see him off.

After receiving his ticket to board the bus he was surprised to see some peons with yellow boots all around and others still arriving. All of them donned their yellow boots and fifteen minutes later, the station was filled with yellow-boot-fitted peons. There were people all over, in and out of the station. It was a small station everyone had someone with them too, family, friends, kids, approximately 9000 people gathered with thousands of yellow boots carrying chickens, turkeys, baskets of fruits and vegetables, flowers, young lamb and young pig.

The employees of the station and the security, like police on a call, presented themselves thinking this was some kind of distinguished politician, a famous artist or someone of the like. They had never seen so many people at the station. They were grateful peons who decided to give Mr. Lonely a hero's farewell because that is how they saw him and that is how they would remember him: "the hero of the yellow boots"

As he was fixing to board the bus Gabriel and his wife gave him a hug wishing him the best. The peons began to say their own goodbyes trying to gift him the young pigs, flowers, fruits and vegetables, etc. Mr. Lonely held that they being poor could not possibly accept their gracious gifts.

But above that, he just could not fit all of them into the bus. He would neither accept one gift of a peon above anyone else's either but extended his had to each and every one of the peon's present you can imagine that extending your hand out to so many people who cried and smiled as if seeing off your best friend or a close relative took more than one hour. It was still not close to being over when the driver and security asked Mr. Lonely to board the bus because of being late due directly to him. They could not have known what was happening much less who Mr. Lonely was.

So it was that without another delay he boarded the bus and bid final farewells out the window. He was able to see the great line of yellow boots jumping towards the bus on its departure; he saw hands rising to wish him the best. It was all an unimaginable experience, more than special finally, the bus departed the station and Mr. Lonely cried as the sights of all those yellow boots faded in the distance, which flooded the station in his honor. How long he had cried was not a memory he retained for a deep sleep engulfed him soon after which lasted until arriving at the great city only to awake with a great smile which marked the end of his adventures in that beautiful port.

Thought:
Across universal history and religion, we find chapters where tales of hero's acts are recounted and other miraculous stories that are remembered as singularly special. Why are heroic acts and miracles not occurring daily?

There are mothers without family, without husband or without anyone to support them. They sustain their children day after day, giving them love and protection, suffering all kinds of calamities but happy to be taking on the role of mother what is to be said of those fathers who give everything to their family throughout all their lives without expecting anything in return, making all kinds of sacrifices to grant education.

MR. LONELY AGAIN
THE YELLOW BOOTS

Sustenance, happiness and a world of benefits? To me those are miracles and those are heroes who fight every day I remember that story of the yellow boots, in which one simple individual aided near 4000 people, doing what is just without fear of losing his status.

It was far more satisfactory to help the humble people; he has given a lesson in justice to those who have power. Mr. Lonely used his power in benefit of others. Today, few remember it, others do not recall but what matters is that it happened. Fortunately, I was a witness and to this day remember it like "the miracle of the yellow boots"

THE UKA PUKA PHENOMENON

The Uka Puka phenomenon is just as antique as it is modern, because it is actually still useful and extremely developed across the nations, the so-called economic societies. In 1,650,000 B.C., Humanity found itself in what is called the age of cave men. All individuals where born free, and were proprietors of all that surrounded them, it was enough to take to have it.

The cavemen were owners of everything imaginable: rivers, trees, animals, insects, etc. When they liked a certain area, of course, with water, it hunts, and it fishes, it became the appropriate place to live. They would settle until circumstances changed. On occasion the curiosity of what is beyond the horizon taught them to journey for a safer place with hunts and fish that guaranteed security and good being.

These antique societies were converted, into groups, tribes, villages, and towns, the initiation of actual societies, and communities. Some reigned as matriarchs and others as patriarchs, but the result was the same; they were small communities guided by their own rules. They contained members in charge of security of the tribe something like an army. They contained members in charge of hunting and fishing to feed the tribe, these where hunters, fishers and gatherers who were not only respected, but admired for their ability and knowledge of discovering new ways to fish and hunt.

The women in general cared for the children, and took charge of the feasting process that consisted of the skinning of animals to then cut them into small pieces that were distributed among the members of the tribe, giving double portions to the hunters, fishers, and of course, to the patriarch(s) they were communities in which frequently they were reorganized because of its discoveries, they had enormous difficulties expressing their ideas, because they do not have language. Instead, used signs, gestures, and guttural screams, that was the beginning of what is to be called voice, and later language.

MR. LONELY AGAIN
THE UKA PUKA PHENOMENON

It was so difficult to communicate that sometimes, it ended in a fight; so cruel and bloody that they killed each other, over a simple misunderstanding, much how it occurs now in our times by cause of language. In the year 1,521,327 B.C., at noon central time Mr. Ag made one of the greatest discoveries in history. His discovery consisted of planting seeds to obtain something similar to actual Soya, only with more protein, and without the problems created by modern artificial fertilizers. Mr. Ag planted as many seeds as he could, and every time it harvested more herbs than Soya, reason for which little by little he was occupying more terrain to plant the Soya.

After various months around something like a Saturday afternoon he discovered the effect of water on the farmland, and so he decided to settle in this area, creating the watering system so as not to travel further for food this discovery was beneficial for humanity; this allowed the opportunity to feed when there were no hunts or fish, not all discoveries come accompanied by benefits, they also brought collateral negative effects. It was the year 1,521,326 B.C. at 6:30 a.m. central time.

Mr. Ag began to situate stones all of similar size around what could be considered a farmland. It took him various hours and days, because the area was something like a square consisting of two acres. After finishing his work, he acquired a club of similar size to a baseball bat, but Mr. Ag did not pretend to play baseball, what he wanted was to protect the surrounded acres by the stones he had placed during the days.

Later at 5:00 p.m., a neighbor entered into the acres crossing through the stones; he had not walked very far when Mr. Ag came upon him with the club until he made him leave the farmland. Once outside, Mr. Ag signaled to the rocks, and with guttural louder scream "Uka Puka" giving him the understanding that the farmland belonged only to him, and no individual could enter without his permission.

The neighbor ran to find other members of the tribe, with which went to the farmland of Mr. Ag only to receive a club, and the guttural louder scream "Uka Puka". Later, several days passed, and the tribes-people became accustomed to not passing through the farmland of Mr. Ag and to avoid the multiple hits by the club. Later on, at the passing of time, other cavemen followed his example.

Others chose more acres. They surrounded it by stones, and with a club yelled "Uka Puka" as a symbol of property; that was how the idea of private property was born. Some yet more ambitious chose properties so big that they never finished surrounding it with stones. Later, it was entire families that, with big clubs, protected their property yelling "Uka Puka" and beating any individual who would near their property the damage caused by this discovery of private property continues to be the motive of disputes and wars to obtain properties on behalf of riches.

The Uka Puka stabilized like something normal with the idea of protecting private property, but provoked the loss of what, in reality, belongs to all human beings. All that surrounds us belongs to us all equally, but men with no measurement ambitions have taken natural community properties, turning all them in to his or her individual properties, commercializing what in reality, belongs to us all.

We know of people with fortune, and owns hundred and thousands of acres, buildings, and commercial properties. With others, it is the opposite; they are owners of not even a small terrain to build a house. Families that can only rent an apartment, single to enrich the proprietors. The families will never buy or build a house, because all the money that one wins uses it in paying rent it is unjust, but they call it business. So if you are able you will have to pay and fight to be proprietor of a terrain. Being able to be rich off purchases of land properties with the idea to rent it; that is actual business being legally valid.

MR. LONELY AGAIN
THE UKA PUKA PHENOMENON

And protected by law guaranteeing private property. Exclusive recognition by a title of property the error is accepting this situation because like human beings, everything belongs to us equally. Unfortunately, it is not like this. There are those who are owners of the water, others are owners of the trees. All these things are property of human beings without distinction to race. Today they are just seduction dreams, because today, property is bought and sold under rules of commercialization, with disregard for the humans who lack a place to habituate all thanks to the famous discovery of private property or so named in its initiation; Uka Puka.

When Mr. Ag discovered Uka Puka, or private property, he was lucky enough to not have been killed by the members of the tribe. He was lucky enough to have others as ambitious as him to follow his example. That is the reason why private property exists; this is an idea in which all human beings have fallen at some point. Inclusively, Christ himself committed the same error of considering himself proprietor of what really belongs to all of us; if you do not believe, I will explain his error in the matter with private property or the Uka Puka Phenomenon.

Christ walked through Jerusalem and found a temple dedicated to the adoration of God father; the temple was converted into a commercial market with people making all kinds of transactions: chicken, camels, food, essences, pottery, all that you would find in a market of that era Christs anger as much, and began to offend the people, saying that his father's temple was solely for oration, and not commercial purposes.

He committed the grave error to strike the retailers with a whip, and expressing its anger to drive them away of the temple. Perhaps this was one of the motives, for which the Jewish people did not want Christ, and later condemned him to die, crucified.

The people felt offended because the temple was not Christ property, he did not help during its construction, he did not even pay for the materials used. The entire town had contributed with all kinds of sacrifices because they were poor. The retailers were hard working people, and what they did was work to gain the daily bread, how God intended.

Christ mistook himself as owner of the temple, or his father's; in truth, the temple was property of Jewish people. He made the same mistake as Mr. Ag, acting as proprietor of what did not belong to him. The "Uka Puka" converted into a legal aspect with thousands of modifications, affecting the normal course of life, all possess the whole without debit to nobody. But private property fell into the hands of a few, for misery of many.

This is how the fight to own more than others initiated, with complete disregard for what belongs to us all. Do not pretend to own something that is not yours, because in reality nothing you possess is guaranteed that it is honestly yours think of how many human beings do not even have somewhere to drop dead, because the Uka Puka Phenomenon commercializes even cemeteries. We are nothing, and we have nothing, the proof is when we die we take nothing with us.

Christ committed the same error as Mr. Ag that he hit his contemporaries, all in the name of property that belonged to everyone. The error of both was big because in the process Mr. Ag discovered private property Christ discovered that the temples are God's property, with disregard that they are constructed with the money, and effort of the poorest in this world, those who wish for a better world, and life after death as a prize for their sacrifice.

Thought:
Equal share, as equals, without distinction, it had been the best discovery of the world, its existence and actuality.

MR. LONELY AGAIN
THE UKA PUKA PHENOMENON

It had guaranteed the true equality among humans, without importance to race, color, or religion; something similar to a world without borders. The lunar surface to this being commercialized, Uka Puka surpasses the planetary border, like an infinite error.

THE TRUTH AND ONLY THE TRUTH

I confess the way in which I became involved in this story, about everything related to Mr. Lonely and his marvelous world. I had the fortune of living and coexisting near him, from his infancy to his retirement. I traveled near him, but just at margin. I was his shadow, anonymous protector, and occasionally, I was almost his guardian angel. I met his marvelous friend Villi, but it was impressive to meet Inia, who was not only gorgeous he was a being with many human values you could fall in love with her the instant you saw her. It happened to me, but it never affected me, not being the one who would enjoy her love. I confess, I would have liked to, even though the pain of losing her would have turned me into Mr. Lonely, like him.

I was one more of the many kids, which after being rescued from those detention centers falsely called orphanages, found a world with opportunities to be what you desired, or simply whatever you could. After Mr. Mario Alberti rescued us, we were turned to the nearest hospital, along with the archives, for identification. Some were returned to their parents, some with uncles, grandparents, and older brothers. In the end, those who had families were relocated.

Those of us who had no family were sent to boarding schools, where we had education, shelter, and food; but with the liberty of going out on weekends. Everything was because of the intervention of Mr. Mario Alberti, with the authorities, which were responsible for us until we were of age (18 years).

In the hospital, where Mr. Mario Alberti turned us in to, we were not abandoned to our luck, because by the next day, people would be arriving, sent by Mr. Mario Alberti, that were responsible for our security. At a week's passing, Mr. Mario Alberti began his visits at the hospital, showing signs of compassion towards all that were left without families.

MR. LONELY AGAIN
THE TRUTH AND ONLY THE TRUTH

He was very kind in his visits. He took us candies, chocolates, simple toys like yo-yos, marbles, board games, and of course, all types of balls. He asked how we were, if they treated us well. We knew he worried about us. He talked with all of us, especially with me, because I told him about all the vicissitudes of his nephew, because I felt a special affection for Mr. Lonely.

This was because I watched him share his buttons with Benito and the rest of us that were near him. I explained to Mr. Mario Alberti how Mr. Lonely involved everyone in the famous game of darts, which carried messages of hope for our freedom, and he said our freedom, because he thought of every one of us that was imprison there. I confessed that I noticed the trick of the messages, but tried to cover it up because I knew he wanted good for all of us. When we were rescue, we knew that he never abandoned us, because the rescue was for him alone, but he convinced his uncle to save us all.

Mr. Mario Alberti never took him to visit us because he did not want him to remember that sad adventure, but his uncle would tell us stories of his adored nephew, as he would call him Mr. Mario Alberti said that if I behaved in school, he would give me work in his restaurant on the weekends, on the condition that I did not say that I was at the orphanage. I would only mention my new school, and never say that I met Mr. Lonely, much less at that terrible orphanage. The first Saturday which I presented myself at the restaurant was something like four months after my rescue.

My job that weekend was cleaning plates and utensils, as a form of training. At night, I was sheltered in one of the many bedrooms of that great house. The next day I returned to the same job of wash boy, staying to sleep in the same bedroom.

Very early, the next Monday morning, Mr. Mario Alberti took me to one of the house's dining rooms where we had breakfast giving me money as payment for my work, while inviting me to return every weekend I desired, as long as I continued studying. Around three or four months passed without any change, until, one Saturday afternoon Mr. Lonely walked into the kitchen and after courteously greeting me asked who I was, to which I answered, I'm the dish washer and cooks' apprentice.

He smiled giving me welcome, not knowing I had various months working. He did not know of my existence, because when he worked in the restaurant with his cousin Plinio, they did so at the cash register, or at the reception desk, welcoming clients, taking coats and jackets to place in the wardrobe because of this, both rarely entered the kitchen. Other times, they were shopping at the market to supply the restaurant usage and that of the house. Various years passed like that. In school, I received high grades, because of which, I received the benefit of going out of school on the afternoons, and coming back at ten in the afternoon without fail and with no excuses.

I always went to because I had friends, and they knew I worked with Mr. Mario Alberti in his restaurant. So, I indulged in the respect and I could be close to Mr. Lonely my friends were not big friends with Mr. Lonely's, but that situation was beneficial to me because I was close to Mr. Lonely, but at the same, I was far and unnoticed. Like this I felt good because I was, and was not, something like a phantom, but with joy and daily amusement, because that neighborhood was special, just like all its characters.

MR. LONELY AGAIN
THE TRUTH AND ONLY THE TRUTH

There, you found writers, artists, boxers, mechanics, athletes, musicians, professors, prostitutes, thieves, doctors, politicians, tailors, priests, students, etc., etc. A world of people with an infinite variety of activities and beliefs that turned the neighborhood into a unique cosmopolitan. In the neighborhood occurred all types of adventures that only occurred in movies or books, but there, you saw them live in color every day. The soccer games were something like the great final of the world cup. They played with a great passion. The worst of the participating players could have been professional in any first class team.

The best ones were so special that they had received offers to turn into professionals, but did not accept, in order to dedicate themselves to study and one day be professionals. The boxing encounters were also something fantastic, like from a movie the neighborhood was composed of friends that would group themselves in certain sectors of the neighborhood. Each group being almost enemies with the others, but at the same time, they were like one big group against some aggressor from a neighboring area. They competed amongst themselves to be the best in the neighborhood in every aspect, including the romantic. Some considering themselves "the small faces"

In the end, you had fun in participating in whichever group accepted you, or simply being neutral, but the emotions and fun were guaranteed. The groups were named by how close they were to the street number where they gathered or lived.

The ones called 28, the 25, the 21, and the 12 and there were other groups without numbers that were mentioned only by the name of their leader as a describing adjective, such as: "The Villli", "The Francis", The Bear": etc., etc. In the end they co formed the kids from Benito "Friendship Neighborhood"

When these groups played football (American) amongst themselves, they were so talented that the street turned into a playing field where they demonstrated their intelligence, clearing the very streets' obstacles, as well as the opponent. They played so beautiful that commuters stood there, becoming spectators. They did it with pleasure because they enjoyed every one of the plays, offensive as well as the defensive, where they displayed infinite joy for the game.

Their games were so competitive that regularly they were deciding by the difference of one scoring, and came to last up to four hours or more, during which fresh players would come in and out. Leaving only a few that could stand the game in its entirety, demonstrating why they were leaders they demonstrated themselves as strong, always competitive, to make them noticed without having to do it through savage means, like fighting or offending others. The goal was to be the best in every one of the games, regardless of what sector you played for.

I watched them play, turning into one more of their fervent admirers, but I never participated because of a fear of not showing as much ability or because of the contrary. If I had it I would be popular and that was not for me, since I wanted to go unnoticed.

Mr. Mario Alberti only wanted that Mr. Lonely not remember his bad experience at the shelter. Maybe I misunderstood and always tried to be "nobody," in order to not be noticed. That is not what his uncle ordered and, I repeat, that I misinterpreted, but as time passed, it was the best thing I could have decided. This way it was easy to accomplish what will later become my mission.

MR. LONELY AGAIN
THE TRUTH AND ONLY THE TRUTH

I can tell you that these street games became something incredible when they faced other neighborhoods. The competition included pride and honor of beating "the other neighborhood." It was like the cold war. No weapons in between, but in the end a war. Mr. Lonely and his friends, being the medium ones, participated in the games, but the weight was carried by the bigger ones, who were the real leaders of the neighborhood.

The absolutely respected and liked leader was Allo. The best player, the best fighter, university student, and son of a man retired from the army; Gave him all his support for him to be whatever he wanted, without placing conditions. Allo was everybody's leader, especially Mr. Lonely. Everybody wanted to be a leader who is just, and taught everybody how to play better with strategies he invented himself.

Allo was an exemplary leader because even though he was a street fighter, he fought only as a last resort, and for just causes, like protecting the helpless from the abusive. There were many, but cowards that could never beat Allo.

He maintained the neighborhood tranquil, dedicating us to sports and games as a goal for all kids. With him, we talked about the NFL in its beginnings, musical groups, television programs, etc. By the way, something interesting is that every Saturday after playing, we talked with him, but at 7:00 p.m. all the young and small ones ran to see two programs; one was "The Monkeys", and the other was" Lost in Space"

For various weeks the same happened until one Saturday, out of curiosity, he joined the young and small ones to see the mentioned programs. Once the programs ended he said he did not understand them.

And that they were programs too infantile, but that he respected our bad taste. He was happy watching "The Wild Wild West" In what we all coincided, was watching the NFL games, the FIFA world cup, the World Series Baseball, and the incredible combats of Cassius Clay. I believe that boxing was the whole neighborhoods favorite sport on television.

It was a fun time where we went to school but in the afternoons, we played all kinds of sports and at night, we had talks, music with guitars, and the moments of flirting and conquest with the beautiful girls in the neighborhood and other neighborhoods.

This brought us all kinds of problems with the people from other neighborhoods because they were jealous of our luck and popularity with the girls of that time. I will return to the topic of Mr. Lonely, since the emotions of remembering those times make me nostalgic. Because it was the golden era of "" My life passed between the school, the restaurant, the neighborhood, and my phantasmal presence of not making me noticed, but being aware of everything.

Various years passed like this. We reached adolescence, nearing when we considered ourselves the bigger ones of the neighborhood; having to substitute and take absolute leadership, along with all its responsibilities.

When Allos' father died his family moved to another city in order to dedicate themselves to study and work, so that they could help economically his mother. We never saw him again. We know he did well, and that he graduated from university. But sadly, I repeat, we never saw him again replacing him became something incredibly difficult.

MR. LONELY AGAIN
THE TRUTH AND ONLY THE TRUTH

There were various candidates. Some did not deserve it, and some did. But the comparison to with him always made them seem unready for the mission among the candidates was Mr. Lonely, but he was far too busy with his almost secret work of street fighting. Besides, he recently met Inia, motive for which leadership was not in his plans, but he was aware of who would take leadership. He proposed Villi, Villi proposed Alessandro, Plinio proposed Beticus. In the end, every one proposed. They decided that the group that had remained with Allo would share leadership. Everything would be decided by vote, like a democratic group, to avoid mistakes. It was like this for a short time but Mr. Lonely was the one who took Allo's place, by everyone's.

Will I meet Inia at a soccer game where the team from "" was playing the team from the where she lived. When I saw her among the girls in the group of friends who went to support their team, her slim figure stood out, but well formed, with long silky hair, eyes the clear brown color, with incredibly fine characteristics, simply dressed to the fashion but she looked like a magazine model, better said, a dream model. I noticed the game was passing over to second time and everybody was focused on that group of beautiful girls; but everybody looked especially at Inia. She had her eyes on the game. She knew about the attraction that controlled everyone, but she did not seem to care. She was focused on the game.

Even though she was a fan of the opposing team, she was drawn to Mr. Lonely' noble and skilled playing. During half time, I went up to her and asked her name, mentioning that I saw her enjoying the game. Looking into my eyes, she said her name was Inia and that of course she enjoyed the game, mostly watching Mr. Lonely participate.

After all he was a good a player as he was a boxer. My surprise was great and I just asked, boxer? He is Mr. Mario Albertis' nephew, how could he be a boxer? Looking into my eyes she smiled and said, you did not know he is a street fighter? He does it for money I responded that I did not know, but I could not believe her. So as not to argue much she invited me to the next fight, which would be the next day, but because of security reasons, the location would not be known until only a few hours before the fights began.

If I wanted to see Mr. Lonely fight, she would call me the next day so we could go together. I let her know that I worked on the weekends with Mr. Mario Alberti. I think that is the reason why she trusted me. The next day at school, I received her phone call, telling me to be near the fisherman's wharf, so that we could go to the boxing match together. I was very thrilled. Inia was very beautiful, and I felt fortunate, knowing that I was going to be accompanying her tonight.

We met at the agreed time, and she had a red dress that fit her nicely, bringing out her beauty. We walked towards the seafood market and, at the large parking lot, introduced ourselves. That is how I met the world of betting and its uncountable participants she noticed I was nervous, and told me to control myself because it was enough to say that I worked with Mr. Mario Alberti, and everyone would respect me. I said I worked at the restaurant, and that I was not lying. She said that she would say the same thing, but she was lying because in reality, she had never spoken a word with that great man, but that did not matter.

The good thing is that everyone believed it and they respected you. She confessed that she liked the fights, but Mr. Lonely fought so differently than the others.

MR. LONELY AGAIN
THE TRUTH AND ONLY THE TRUTH

She was attracted to him in some special way, same as when he played soccer. That is, when I knew she liked Mr. Lonely, she had chosen me only as an informant, because I worked in the restaurant that belonged to Mr. Lonely' uncle. Before I continue, I must clarify that in the time I am narrating about, we called Mr. Lonely by his name, and it was not until after Inias' death when it would change and he would be known as Mr. Lonely. I am the one who write his story, choosing to preserve his name for myself, and those of us who knew him. Like a memory, we don't wish to share with anyone because it belongs only to those who knew him.

During Mr. Lonely' fight, the same thing happened. He lost the first round, evened things up in the second, and easily won in the third round. Well, that was the way it looked from afar. He looked exhausted after the great effort of coming from behind until getting the win, it was a victory that Inia celebrated with joy and economical gain, since she had bet in favor of Mr. Lonely. We left the parking lot. I felt depressed because I noticed in her all the interest in the world, in Mr. Lonely. That condemned me to obtain only her friendship. Being so beautiful, that would not be enough, so I prepared to be only her confidant.

Naturally, she asked how I met Mr. Mario Alberti and his nephew, and without a doubt I told her the story, but when I got to the interesting part, I had to say goodbye because it was getting to be time I had to go back to the boarding school. We promised to meet the next day at the fisherman's' wharf I left practically flying so as not to be late to the boarding school. I was lucky and arrived with perfect timing. I went to the kitchen for dinner and then to bed, to dream of Inia, who would be mine only in my dreams.

The next day after my classes, I ran towards the wharf to meet Inia, who was waiting for me. She dressed well, with a touch of class, comparable only to her beauty. After saying hello, we went to a nearby cafe, where she asked me to continue the story about the orphanatorium after multiple cups of coffee with milk, the way she drank it, the story reached its end, narrating up to the point when I met her. She took my hands and said that I lacked brightness in my eyes, because of which she could not want me, but that she liked me very much, and that we would be friends forever. She confessed that she felt love for Mr. Lonely, and that he had a shine in his eyes, which indicated that he was her destiny.

The weekend was marvelous because during the day, I worked with Mr. Mario Alberti, and in the afternoon, I went out to talk with Inia. Like always, she asked me about Mr. Lonely and his activities. I discovered in her eyes and in her words that she really loved him, which is why I asked her, if she loved him so much, why did not she just go up to him and tell him she said her situation was nothing like Mr. Lonely' and that surely, Mr. Mario Alberti would never accept her, as his nephews love. I answered that it sounded like an ancient love story, and that Mr. Mario Alberti was no one to accept or reject her. We changed the subject and she let me know how cruel her stepfather was with her mother, her sister, and with her. She said she could not change the circumstances, but she could live above them. That is what she did, not only to survive, but to feel better as well.

Remember some time ago, that occasion where Inia fled from her pursues and found refuge in Mr. Lonely's arms that was her love, almost in secret, accomplishing his falling in love with her the instant he saw her. Their romance was something from a movie. They really loved each other, without room for any doubts. While Mr. Lonely was in school during the afternoons, I would meet with Inia, becoming her confidant and her friend, and becoming witness to the love that united them.

MR. LONELY AGAIN
THE TRUTH AND ONLY THE TRUTH

She was very simple and the same time, so much class that you could never imagine that she came from a neighborhood so dirty, with people so bad, and that it had nothing to do with her marvelous way of being when they loved each other the most, Inias' tragic death happened, which wrapped all life in a mantle of sadness. Locals and strangers were affected by the occurrence Mr. Mario Alberti comprehended his error through his talks with Villi. He knew he had made a mistake in misjudging Inia, and that she was as beautiful as her heart was noble. I was hit with the sadness, since she was the only friend with whom I shared secrets. After her death, I would be a very lonely person, I think, almost as much as Mr. Lonely.

Afterwards, Villi and Mr. Lonely began the investigation of the crime in order to find the culprit. I knew about Francis' visits to the neighborhood to greet Inia, and I knew about the gift of the gun, so I informed Villi about everything, that way they had clues, to continue the search for the criminal. When they finished their investigations, they discovered that Francis was Inias' murderer. Mr. Lonely thought only of looking for him and making him pay for his crime. Francis was an enemy much bigger than Mr. Lonely, with many tricks and criminal friends. In the end, it looked like a mission that would be difficult to accomplish. With the idea of learning how to play guitar in order to sustain his trip in search of Francis, everything became music in Mr. Lonely' life, with The Beatles as his greatest allies. Every day he practiced, with the idea of being able to leave on the search for the criminal, as soon as possible.

As you know from previous chapters, he found him, and by luck or whatever you want to call it, Francis found his end, paying for his crime.

ADVENTURES OF PHILOSOPHIC REFLECTION
THE TRUTH AND ONLY THE TRUTH

Once Mr. Lonely returned home, he had to leave on a merchant boat towards Spain, which would be his base for traveling through Europe, and sometime later move to America, which had always been his dream, just not in that manner when Mr. Lonely left for Spain as a fugitive, Mr. Mario Albertis' worries had no limit, and he felt powerless to help his nephew, so he had a thought. He could send someone to help and aid Mr. Lonely with whatever could happen. His first option was to ask Villi to follow Mr. Lonely by land and sea, to ensure that he was well.

Villi could not accept the offer due to scholastic reasons, and even more because he needed to be with his mother, who needed him because it had been only a year since his father died, which is why he could not accept Mr. Mario Albertis' offer. Little time later, he made me the offer, and it was very tempting. He offered me a monthly salary that was comfortable enough for me to establish myself in America, to be Mr. Lonely' shadow, but without his knowing it, so as not to make him feel bad, or in case he did not agree without much thought I accepted, and stayed in contact with Villi and Mr. Mario Alberti. I began my pursuit of Mr. Lonely. Mr. Mario Alberti acquired for me legal papers needed for Europe as well as America. My first stop was Barcelona. Mr. Lonely was living in lodging for African students, that way he went unnoticed and not recognized as Sicilian. When I arrived at the lodging, he had departed to France, Paris in particular. At the lodging, he left the majority of his of his luggage, and a months' worth of rent paid. I only had to wait for his return. Meanwhile, I dedicated myself to knowing and enjoying the gorgeous and modern city.

A month after, Mr. Lonely returned to the lodging, he was only there a few days because he was preparing a trip to Hamburg, Germany. In the meantime, I made friends with the lodge owner, and even though I paid my rent, I helped with the minor chores of the lodge, and as a kind of gesture she gave me tips so that Mr. Lonely would not know about me.

MR. LONELY AGAIN
THE TRUTH AND ONLY THE TRUTH

From the day I arrived I walked with a limp, saying that I got polio as a kid, and my leg stayed short because of the disease also, that month I made friends with the shopkeepers of a magic and trick store. That helped me disguise my nose, curl my hair, and get a different skin tone than mine. You can imagine, when I presented myself before Mr. Lonely and told him I was at his service as a delivery boy, he did not recognize me. I gained his confidence, though my bad Spanish and his good Spanish. He would correct me and help me, while I delivered letters to and from the post office, to a P.O. Box under a school counselor's name, because he did not want to give his.

I had the luxury of reading the letters and then changing the envelope, and sending them, as well as other letters to Villi and Mr. Mario Alberti. Later, Mr. Lonely went to Hamburg, just as he planned. But he would return a month later, so I was again left to wait for his return at the lodging, while I learned magic tricks, and Spanish Mr. Lonely was preparing his trip to America. Months later, he decided to go to New York, being the normal entrance into America. He left on boat, while I traveled on an airplane in order to prepare for Mr. Lovely's arrival.

I established myself in a hotel to wait for him. Since I knew the boat and date in which he departed, I easily acquired the itinerary, as well as the date he would arrive. As the arrival of Mr. Lonely neared in New York, I took advantage of the time and wrote a letter to Mr. Mario Alberti, relating to him, his nephew's vicissitudes in Europe. I had to tell him everything, without concealing details, because that was my job. The months in Spain, he utilized to unite with secret groups in resistance of the government, like the ETA who was known for their terrorist like dangerousness. His trips were only to conceal his real identity. I do not know how he came to be involved with them, but he spent days in secret camps, to which I did not have access. I knew his approximate location, since my new ability to disguise and conceal myself was almost marvelous, and above all, useful because it facilitated me following Mr. Lonely.

As far as I could. Sometimes we would cross paths, but he would not recognize me. I was the old rag picker, the street sweeper, the doctor, the barber, the postman, basically, a series of characters. He was in training the whole time. I do not know what his exact training was, but I never saw him involved in any terrorist activities. As time passed, I discovered that his learning's were musical. He learned how to play protest music, revolutionary music, music that the oppressed manifested as a peaceful display of protest, but with a profound impression that was difficult to erase, even as time passed that is what Mr. Lonely liked about that terrorist group, which began as a peaceful protest movement, but later ended up a terrible terrorist group.

Once in New York, Mr. Lonely established himself in a neighborhood near The Bronx, because he enjoyed the baseball games of his beloved Yankees I confess that after following him to all the games, I became a Yankee fanatic myself. Besides, I could disguise myself as anything I wanted without being discovered by Mr. Lonely. I remember one time, I went as a giant hot dog, and sat right next to Mr. Lonely the whole game and he never knew that it was me, his loyal guardian. Several months passed in New York, with trips to its surroundings during the weekends, including two train trips to Canada. We visited all the cafes with live music in New York City, in which he participated as an aficionado, playing music from The Beatles. Music that would always accompany him as his internal refuge in order to support the loss of his beloved Inia.

I saw him play with a melancholy that hurt and was liked at the same time, but it would make me shed tears, because I also missed Inia, and shared Mr. Lonely's pain. Finally, we traveled to the southern U.S. border. Established ourselves in San Diego, California, where we perfected our Spanish and learned Mexicans customs, some bad, some not so bad we would cross to Tijuana, Mexico, where we listened to rock and roll music of great quality, played by bands of Mexicans and Americans.

MR. LONELY AGAIN
THE TRUTH AND ONLY THE TRUTH

That together sounded like the records, and on occasions would sound superior to the original versions, by famous musicians. I must clarify that when I say that we traveled and visited Tijuana, Mexico, Mr. Lonely and I did so as friends, but you can imagine. I was born in America, son of a Guatemalan father and a Spanish mother, so my idiots' accent was justified my disguise as a crazy existentialist with long hair, stabbed perfection in a world of musicians, rock and rollers, poets, writers, vagabonds, addicts, and hippies that would all confuse each other among themselves, and formed that eras youth.

For various months, I finally enjoyed Mr. Lonely' friendship, without him suspecting that I had a salary, for protecting him and reporting his every step to Mr. Mario Alberti. I provided details of his daily activities. On occasions, I felt I had the best job in the world, and that I was very fortunate. I thought, if this were to end this very moment, what would become of me. Because of this, I came to comprehend that I was tied to Mr. Lonely's luck. Perhaps, this would be life. During this era, out friendship became firm, and with confidence, he told me stories that left me thinking forever. He said that he had friendships with some members of the ETA in Spain, but their relation was not as terrorists. The members of the ETA, in its beginnings, were members of a secret sect, so ancient, it originated from the Templar. Those horsemen, which from the years 1200 to 1400 were the most able, rich and mystical warriors in the history of human kind they were alchemists, invented the bank system, and built the great gothic cathedrals in Europe, but their greatest success and secret was that they guarded the Cradle of Life, which they brought from Solomon temple.

They also kept in secret and under their protection, the descendants of Christ, of which to this day there are two left.

A woman, and her brother. He would say that Christ was an incredibly intelligent man, but the genius behind the completely Christian structure, in the beginning and after the false death of Christ, was Judas. He planned and executed all the miracles and acts of Christ, he also replaced Christ the very moment before his arrest. The one who died on the cross was a double. Later, he hung and sacrificed one of his brothers, whom everyone confused with the real Judas, and history took charge of saying that he committed suicide, regretting his betrayal. Afterwards, both of them presented themselves before great people of the Roman government, who believed their resurrection and handed over goods and power to the resurrected.

Motive for which Christianity politically fortified itself to the point where Jesus was proclaimed the Son of God, officiated itself as the only religion, establishing Rome as its headquarters It happened 300 years after the supposed death of Christ, but it was all planned by Judas, who in reality was the genius that created the religion that is still strong to our days. Historians say that Mary Magdalene escaped towards south of France, where she rooted herself and died, but it was not like that since Christ and Judas caught up to her several years after the supposed crucifying of Christ, and with a great fortune, they established themselves in Spain. By the way, Judas remarried in France and had another woman in Spain, but that is another story. Mr. Lonely told these stories with details, dates, and names.

I do not remember it all at a hundred percent, but that was the general story. He even mentioned one of the many organizations created by the guardians of Christ's descendants. The Templar was guardians of Christ, and Judas's, descendants, assuring that to our days, they protect two women and one man. They are kept far from the teachings of Christ. Mr. Lonely admired Christ as a man, but not as the Son of God. His stories were basic on experiences he had on his trips to France, Germany, and Spain.

MR. LONELY AGAIN
THE TRUTH AND ONLY THE TRUTH

He had contact with people who participated in the secret sects, who move in an almost invisible world, only open to members and special people like Mr. Lonely. He never told me how he became involved with these people, but I know that it was true because in difficult times, someone would always appear. Someone with influences that made things easier for Mr. Lonely, sometime with no explanation whatsoever; remaining as one of the many tricks and secrets that accompanied him throughout his entire life something surprising was the fact that Judas was more intelligent than Christ and that he was secretly the true creator of Christianity, but only as an instrument to end the Roman Empire.

The Romans were the biggest and most powerful army of those times. They had the most extensive government on the planet, and of course, the wealthiest. Judas knew that the oppressed by the empire would be easy to convert into followers, by offering something that the great empire could not it was an intelligent offer that is still on the table to this day. He offered them life after death. An eternal life of happiness that was easy to attain, by simply following their rules and commands, converting them into fervent and tributary followers of their churches, thus creating the biggest empire of all time, which also established in Rome.

The Vatican is an empire distributed though out the whole planet, receiving contribution from all parts of the world, called alms. When someone would oppose its commandments, it would assassinate them with the lie of "in the name of God"

For example, remember the sacred inquisition that eliminated millions of innocent people, especially scientists, but all "in the name of God"

The incredible thing is that women are fervent followers, even though the catholic church discriminated women, attacking and destroying them, like in the time of the which burnings, and like the Peter the apostles' hatred toward Mary Magdalene. Like the ecclesiastical laws that women cannot be priests, bishops, cardinals, and much less a pope. However, they blindly keep surrendering themselves to that religion, which repudiates and discriminates them, but utilizes them Mr. Lonely said that the birth of Jesus in Belen was a lie invented by Judas, who was born in Belen, and knew the importance of his false history. Since they wanted to make Jesus divine, they started with the story of Belen, in order to relate him to King David, who was also born in Belen. This way, Jesus would be respected and adored by the Jews, who followed the teachings of King David.

On the other hand, the real identity of his birth exists in the very name, Jesus of Nazareth. Obviously, he was born in Nazareth. That story of his youth when nobody knew where he was being also false. Those years were used by Judas to train him, and write the basis of the new philosophy, which would later become miracles. It was in Belen where they stayed to make plans, and chose the ones who would later become apostles every encounter and every miracle was a chain of events planned by Judas. The only thing that he did not plan was the hate and envy that Peter had towards Mary Magdalene. The original plan was to place her as the founder of the church, since she was Jesus' messenger after the resurrection. Peters' hate, and the usurpation of Jesus' apostle successor, was what condemned the plan to a 300-year delay. To Jesus Christ they gave divinity, and the immediate officiating of the church, before a congress realized by orders from the Roman Empire. This act was delayed for so long due to Peters' wishes and ambition. Judas moved his contacts and secretly executed Peters' sacrifice. It was to elevate him to the highest levels, which he would never have reached in life, because he was ambitious, but unintelligent, more or less honest.

MR. LONELY AGAIN
THE TRUTH AND ONLY THE TRUTH

And not a follower of Christ's principals. History was written differently. Magdalene ended up a prostitute and the church founded the traitor, Peter. The religion grew under the refuge and protection of the church, through crimes and trickery the church has established the most extensive and longest lasting empire in ancient and modern history. Those who have attacked it with no reason, or to know its secrets, or because of knowledge, have had to live in secrecy. It is a subterranean world where they protect the sacred chalice.

It is not an object because the blood of Christ is nothing more than the descendants of Christ and Magdalene, as well as Judas'

Some groups claim to have the proof that makes the sacred church tremble, but it only trembles to later fortify itself, with no knowledge of when it will end. This is one of the many stories that Mr. Lonely says. He did so with details, dates, and even names of active guardians; distributed throughout the whole planet earth secrets sects that protect the conservation of proof, of these secrets that day after day are no longer secrets, or at least some of them. Like the truth that Magdalene was never a prostitute. She came from a noble family with money, and together with other women, financed the pilgrimages of Christ. She was his woman, not his lover.

She was the true apostle, and founder of the church of Christ, and had a philosophy that was very different than those of the papal church of course, the church is managed by successful economists, which strive to make their power grow by provoking and prolonging the misery and ignorance of their loyal followers, and criminally attacking those that are not followers Mr. Lonely spoke among other things, about why the written history has tricked humanity and has lied, saying things that are not true and concealing the truths. That is something that we cannot change Mr. Lonely told things so beautiful, like the act of walking.

He would say that walking was not only an exercise, but also a complex aspect of being human. Our first steps we take with our parents and at the beginning we cannot walk in the same rhythm as them, nor can they walk at ours. As our understanding advances, we walk better alongside them Unfortunately, many of us stop doing so before we reach the fullness and pride of walking along side our parents. When you observe a mother and her children walk in the same rhythm, you know that their lives are harmonic Just the same, if they do not walk in the same rhythm, their lives do not have much communication, and much less comprehension.

The second teaching is to walk at the same rhythm as your partner you are two very different beings, but you harmonize your steps, just as you harmonize your mind and heart. It is possible for her to walk fast, and him slow, or vice versa, but together, walk at the same rhythm. That is called harmony, and it causes pleasure he proudly said that Inia would walk very, very differently than any other person, but when they walked together, they did so at only one rhythm, which caused jealousy and joy at the same time when you saw them so happy.

We all know they loved each other and showed it joyfully, infecting everyone with their love for one another. I remember how beautifully the walked together. It is true; I think that walking is an art, an abundance of harmony that we should learn and practice. Now I know why psychologists recommend walking and talking with your partner, especially when there are problems. I know that there is something good in walking, but I never saw it the way Mr. Lonely did his solitude was evident when he walked alone, since there was no rhythm, no feeling, and even less direction. Walking in rhythm with your loved ones is the greatest gift your mind and legs can reach, by simply trying it. So, do what Mr. Lonely discovered. Walk with someone you care about, but try to get that rhythm, which will later become the rhythm that your life will have with that person.

MR. LONELY AGAIN
THE TRUTH AND ONLY THE TRUTH

Walk alongside those you care about, or those who care about you. Walk with them to the rhythm of love, of understanding, friendship, and comprehension. If you do not believe it, just try it. You will walk well with your own, but you will never be able to walk in rhythm with your enemies. Walking prepares you since infancy, for when you can no longer walk, and you only observe others walk, which also has its joy. It was a delight to watch Inia and Mr. Lonely walk, with interlaced hands, smiles of adventure, and promises of love Mr. Lonely spoke of incredible things, and some were incredibly marvelous.

He was a great speaker, and would move his hands to the rhythm of his voice, while sweetening the chat with his smiles, and pleasant comments he would finish a topic to begin another. I understood why Villi and many friends from missed Mr. Lonely. They missed those nocturnal chats that extended into the early morning.

I know it was like this because during the time I coexisted with him, we would talk until daybreak, and go to bed with positive thoughts that were fed by talks full of knowledge and not just adventures after so many years, I continue to miss those nocturnal chats that would make me turn pale until I resembled a vampire, due to the lack of sleep.

Even now, I would like to be talking with Mr. Lonely, rather than narrating his stories I know I have limitations to express all the things he told me. I do not know how to say things the way he did, but at least I am trying to tell you how special Mr. Lonely was.

Sometime later, we traveled to Mexico City. He went to visit an old friend of his father. He was an ex-president of the republic, now dedicated to tourism. He was president of the National Tourist Council, and the true father of tourism in the country.

It was this character, which gave his father a new nationality, and he did it with Mr. Lonely as well, so that his real identity would not be discovered. Out of gratitude towards Mr. Lonely's father, this man proportioned him with a university education scholarship. Mr. Lonely later increased his benefits, in exchange for playing soccer, showing his ability for the sport.

Mr. Lonely dedicated himself to studying, working only during the summers for the honorable National Tourist Council with important people who would later influence his life. His benefactor was a member of a group like the Masons, but a little more realists.

He secretly participated as a member of the higher range. He would unite with people that were very able, intelligent, and prepared, to procure the good of the country, and the men of science obviously, they counted on having powerful enemies, who did not like their altruistic activities. This man was his protector, giving support and kindness, comparable to that of his uncle Mario Alberti. Mr. Lonely was secure and tranquil to shape his own destiny. Through the National Tourist Council, Mr. Lonely traveled a lot during the summers, since he worked with his protector. During one of his trips, I presented myself to the president of the council, letting him know of my mission this man was so intelligent, and with many contacts around the world, he already knew about my activities. He protected me as well, giving me the opportunity to study, just like Mr. Lonely.

He maintained the secret so that I could continue protecting Mr. Lonely, and informing Mr. Mario Alberti. Mr. Lonely gained friendship, respect, and care of this great person. From then on, he made many more friends by the way, Villi along with his entire family, caught up with Mr. Lonely to begin a new life alongside him, continuing the adventures and lack of sleep because of the talks that would take place at night and last until the morning. Like an unending pleasure of great friends.

MR. LONELY AGAIN
THE TRUTH AND ONLY THE TRUTH

Thought:
If you have friends, that together you walk with rhythm, and talk in an agreeable and amusing manner, take care of them because they really are your friends.

Friends talk to make your life pleasant, and listen to you, to feel that you share time together chats are entertaining and interesting, but always fill them with something called, understanding. Walk with your kids, chatting about the daily activities. It could become the most pleasing ritual.

Parents will remember these walks, when all their kids walk far away from them. Kids will remember their parents every time they take steps far away from home.

The day will come that you will walk alone, but filled with memories that will become your rhythm, the rhythm of memories, the rhythm of love, and the rhythm of Mr. Lonely.

SAD STORY OF AN IMPOSSIBLE DREAM

It will be difficult to narrate to story of an individual, who simultaneously subjected his life to happiness and misfortune. Calling him by his name would be unjust, condemning him to jokes at his expense or sentiments of pity, which would not be to his liking. You will know him as "the Man in the Mirror"

The city of Houston, in the Texan state, of the American Union, which found itself with temperatures of 45 degrees Fahrenheit, was displaying the wintry wonders of its streets and its inhabitants. Inhabitants who dressed in accordance with the cold and, covering themselves from the winds, walked the streets of the city. Some people portrayed wealth and good taste, elegantly combining the clothes that was stored away in closets for ten long months.

Others dressed in good taste without the opulence of the upper class, and the humbler with simple dress. All of them intermixing, forming a colorful parade of street fashion where garments, both expensive and inexpensive, rabidly competed to be the most attractive or comfortable clothes of the improvised wintry parade.

The man in the mirror, I met in 2015. Our welcome encounter was on a wintry afternoon with winds upwards of 20 miles per hour, obligating you walk the city streets as though you were individuals embarking off to wreckage. My body clamored for a hot beverage and a refuge that provided shelter. My eyes, reddened by the winds, dazzled at one of the entrances to the downtown subterranean tunnels. Moving my cold body, I introduced myself into one of stairwells leading to the interior of the tunnels, and my body immediately displayed the joy, rejoicing in the 80-degree temperature, and the perk of not having to dodge the gusts of wind howling on the surface.

MR. LONELY AGAIN
SAD STORY OF AN IMPOSSIBLE DREAM

The web of downtown city tunnels is the most extensive in the world. In it, you'll find all manner of businesses, such as coffee shops, restaurants, stationary stores, bookstores, shoe stores, even a shopping mall, and the people who walk from one place to another, properly utilizing the tunnel entrances and exits in order to avoid traffic and inclement weather, such as excessive heat in the summer and cold in the winter.

After all, the tunnels boast air conditioning, central heating, as well as an excellent cleaning and maintenance service, which provide a sense of welcoming and safety. I observed a coffee shop in which the ambient was noticeably warm, so I went in and got as comfortable as I could. Immediately, a waitress came to provide me service. I requested a cafe cappuccino and a bread roll with cheese, placed my coat on the seat back after removing my gloves, and enjoyed observing my surroundings, forgetting about the cold.

Inside the tunnels, and inside the coffee shop, the parade of winter fashion continued. Among the pedestrians there were young, mature, women that caught my attention because of their beauty and attractiveness. Some of them looked like professional models. There were also old men and women that looked comfortable and happy with their dress everything around me was beautiful.

After savoring the bread, I ordered a second cup of coffee, while observing a person who nearing my table. He dressed elegantly, with his polished shoes giving the impression that he was a gentleman. His hair was white, his face, vague, as though his mind was far from the coffee shop. His figure, upright and slender, portraying a European aspect. He seemed like a good type, and I anticipated, maybe a good conversationalist I approached asking, "Hi, how are you"? Trying to start conversation he, with a smile, replied to my greeting by offering a chair and inviting me to sit at his side. I gave him my name and he responded, smiling.

SAD STORY OF AN IMPOSSIBLE DREAM

By saying that hopefully I wasn't the dangerous type, because he was allergic to violence. I asked what his occupation was. He replied that he was retired, enjoying the free time which in his youth, was limited smiling, which seemed to be his usual, he asked about my profession, I answered, that I was a writer of short stories in English and Spanish simultaneously, that were poetry novel educational book.

They were not only entertaining, or interesting, because they offered the opportunity to learn one of the two languages. Mentioning that it sounded interesting, he asked what my fountain of inspiration was. I answered, that all of my stories were real. They were lived through by the characters, some by myself. This way, I enjoyed being able to express my feelings or the feelings of the characters, while living as flesh and blood, through every one of the stories.

Writing, for me, is more than interesting because of the time that is dedicated to every story. Such as, finding and getting to know the narrator, understanding him and gaining his trust in order to, later, write the story without losing the essence. This turns into a challenge to finally produce something that is worth reading. He said that since he was retired, old, and alone, he could narrate the saddest story ever told. The only thing, that I would have to seriously listen to him, and then decide whether or not it was worth it. Of course, I was interested and wanted to know his story, so we immediately agreed to a meeting in the same place, at the same time, on the next day. Both of us smiling, with a shaking of hands, we agreed.

That cold night, I though the man in the mirror would have an interesting story, but when He said, "The saddest story ever told" my mind began to think millions of things, and at the same time, none. The next day, my doubts would be cleared up and I would know his tale, which I knew in advance, would be more than interesting.

MR. LONELY AGAIN
SAD STORY OF AN IMPOSSIBLE DREAM

The city noises and the faint light of the new day awoke me in a good mood. After getting ready and having a light breakfast, I planned a route toward the downtown of the city. It was easier to board a public bus, which would transport me to Louisiana St. This way, I would not have to search, or pay, for the parking which was expensive and scarce. After walking to a luxurious hotel, which, in its interior, held an escalator that assessed the tunnels, I would walk a mile or more to reach the front of the coffee shop, and find myself with my new friend he was already comfortably situated at the same table from the previous day. He was sporting a white shirt with a knitted tie and red beret, which Combined perfectly with his gray oxford pants and British style coat. In short, he looked Like a classic movie character from the past, showing his grace and distinction.

Smiling, he warmly extended his hand and invited me to sit at his side. In response to his greeting, I sat comfortably at his side and let him know that I was excited to learn his story because curiosity was driving my mind. My mind, which has always been the greatest instrument for writing the stories which, after listening to them attentively, I would have to understand. This was the reason I would take notes, counting on his authorization. I ordered two cups of cafe cappuccino, and suggested he try the bread roll with cheese, then ordered two as well. I prepared myself to listen to the start of his narration. He cleared his throat and began his story, which went like this: My infancy took place in a humble middle class neighborhood. I didn't have a father and must confess, I needed so much that even in my old age, I still long for his presence.

My mother worked around 12 hours daily in order to maintain an acceptable economic state. As she does not receive child support, pension, but provided me with an economic state that was better than that of the neighborhoods average, because of this, I had access to an education, clothes, books, toys, diversions, outings, and all material things those are required in infancy and adolescence.

ADVENTURES OF PHILOSOPHIC REFLECTION
SAD STORY OF AN IMPOSSIBLE DREAM

Near the end of the 50's, it was popular to go where they showed old silent black and white movies, those were exceedingly entertaining those of Charlie Chaplin, Laurel and Hardy, The Three Stooges, and so many more that, now, I cannot quite recall them all. Various cinemas were really special such as one that, every day of the week, played the cartoons with Tom & Jerry, Might Mouse, The Fox and The Crow, without neglecting the classic Walt Disney characters, such as Donald Duck and his nephews, Mickey Mouse in addition, Pluto, Goofy, Gyro Gear loose and Little Helper, and I could go on to mention so many more. The candy vendors accompanied the cinematographic projections, Popcorn, Ice cream, sodas, and many other things, who traversed the aisles among the armchairs during the movies, announcing their product, as street salesmen would. No they bothered one, and we all tried to buy some of the products from them, thus avoiding the trip to the candy area, so that we would not miss any details of the movies.

During the intermission between movies, there was screaming and chasing kids through all aisles of the theatre. Kids who would instantaneously stop when the lights were turned off, and run to their seats, initiating the show. I enjoyed those infantile days because, at first, my mother would take me to see the movies. As soon as I aged 9 summers, I enjoyed of the liberty and trust to spend my money at the theatre and on candy, going from the matinees of 9:00 in the morning up until 2:00 in the afternoon we exited the theatre like vampires, blinded after being in shadows for so many hours, rejoicing in the cartoons or movies in black and white, and including news and short cartoons at the start of the shows. In other theaters, the matinees were three adventure movies such as Simbad the Sailor, Sherlock Holmes, The Zorro, while other times they were of terror, such as Dracula or The Werewolf those movies were too fantastic that it did not matter in the least, that they were in black and white.

MR. LONELY AGAIN
SAD STORY OF AN IMPOSSIBLE DREAM

It did not bother us that they lacked color, because that was our world, it was innocent, sweet, real, and human beings could truly call us human beings, since we respected and protected one another. Life in the neighborhoods was beautiful because we knew every one of the people who lived or wander in our vicinity. This facilitated our coexistence. Of course, there was no shortage of problems and troublemakers, but they were the minority the majority, who were the good ones, imposed they, and the neighborhoods were fun and tranquil places where it was worth living. Time in December was gorgeous, with its religion pre-Christmas parties that were celebrated from the December 16th to December 24th. At the parties, there were piñatas full of candies and fruits, which the children enjoyed until they could handle no more.

All the participants, who were holding little candles and carrying sparklers, sang the religion choruses. These lights created a cozy environment where we would try to burn boys and girl's hair. It was our only form of entertaining ourselves; all the while being careful, of course, to ensure it did not turn into a tragedy. The adults entertained themselves with their famous fruit punch, to which they would add some alcoholic beverage, thus fueling the dance. Young ladies and gorgeous women were the appealing part of the parties. Of course, we kids would compete to win over the girls our age, and create romantic adventures. If you were lucky, you would find a girlfriend at each party, but during the following days we endured the anguish of the possibility that they would all find out and you would end up ignored, but not before they would insult you and deal you a blow to the nose. That did not stop us from enjoying that marvelous time of parties, which ended on Christmas Eve. The new year lead us to making an innumerable amount of promises which, after a few weeks, faded into oblivion and were promised again the following year. That was the wonderful life of black and white that I lived and enjoyed so much, that just remembering those times, it makes my lips and heart smile.

SAD STORY OF AN IMPOSSIBLE DREAM

It was also the golden age for radio. Entire families would unite around a receiver and attentively listen, for hours on end, to the musical programs, adventures, romances, etc. all of the actors were people who were multiplied by their voices. They would voice an innumerable amount of characters, making you believe a large cast, when in reality created the programs; it was only a few actors. Many of which were improvised, due to the audiences' growing demand. The special effects were created simply, using buckets, bells, saws, glass bottles, etc. In the end, it was the age when radio would delight the ears of its listeners. Speaking of the incipient television industry, they broadcasted in black and white and only two channels existed. Channels that transmitted from 6:00 in the evening to 11:00 at night. One channel broadcasted shows for infants and juveniles, such as cartoons, comedians like Charles Chaplin, Laurel and Hardy, and even some local comedians. They were all the delight of the young ones who watched television.

The other channel broadcasted detective shows, movies, show with daily episodes, local variety programs, interviews, and news programs that the adults watched. I pleasantly remember the television industry growth, which included more channels and extended hours. The incredible thing, the fantastic thing, was the first color transmissions, which at first, many did not understand. In order to enjoy the color programs, a different type of television was needed. One that was specifically made for color.

The entertaining, old, programs in black and white disappeared, giving way to modernism. It was the end of the black and white times, advancing the age of color, which brought with it new disgraces and inevitabilities in the name of progress; wars were a big distraction used by the news programs, where they bombarded us with stupid headlines and false lies. All the while, the government was doing things that were not for the good of the country.

MR. LONELY AGAIN
SAD STORY OF AN IMPOSSIBLE DREAM

We were in the decade of the 60's, where the world was changing with every turn it took. It gave us daily surprises, good and bad. The skirts came up from the knees by 5 to 7 inches, turning into a scandal. The "hot pants" came into style. These were lovely little shorts that were tailored very short, like miniskirts. They were worn with stockings, which were another new discovery, and tall shoes or boots that went up to the knees. Women's short athletic pants were no longer used solely for sports. Men fashion also changed, such as "jeans", which we would put through a special treatment.

Today, you would not believe it even if I explained it with an abundance of details. First, you bought you navy blue jeans. In those times, it was the only color available. After removing all tags, staples, etc., we would submerge them in a bucket filled with Coca Cola, of which about two gallons were needed. We left them submerged for at least 24 hours.

We used previously washed rocks to maintain them submerged, and so that they wouldn't have stains. Afterwards, we would hang them and let them sun dry automatic dryers did not exist yet, only the roller type. Once they were dry, they were coated all over with an invisible cream that was used for shining shoes. Various coats were needed for them to be completely greased. Once more, they were submerged in the same coke from the previous day for another 24 hours' minimum.

Afterwards, they were once again hung in the sun to dry. Using a wet cloth, you would iron them inside out. After all this, they were ready to be worn, and you would did not wash them again. The best part was that they maintained their new appearance regardless of the many times you wore them. Water did not penetrate the fabrics threads, and dirt and grime were removed with a simple brushing. They were the classic north American style, just as seen the movie, "West Side Story"

We wore them with a touch of distinction, combining them with polo shirts or dress shirts. It was obligatory that the shirts and socks were of matching color. We looked special, at least according to that times tastes. That was our style for various years, until the fashion changed to the bell bottom pants, which entered in the second half of the 60's decade. The neighborhoods had friendly, musical competitions. Rock music was in its cusp, and every neighborhood had one or two music groups. There were good ones, not so good ones, and horrible ones, but being a member of one elevated you to a status of popularity that we couldn't imagine, even in our wildest dreams. We dedicated ourselves to listening to rock and roll music, watching movies, playing sports, and of course, having flirting's as a pastime.

Semi professional sports turned into the hopes of many. First, to become national league players, then international league, and eventually as a reward for our consistency and caliber, to become professional players. We also dedicated ourselves to accomplishing a university career, economically aspiring for a life that was better that the ones we had. I must say, our lives were not bad, but it was normal to have economic aspirations and goals to accomplish in life. That times brought us many interesting things. I'll tell you of one that grabbed my attention. Radio, normally, ended its daily broadcasts around 11:00 or 12:00 at night, leaving the radios dead, with no broadcasts to receive. It was the era of the giant tube radios. The discovery of the battery powered transistor radios, all of them made in Hong Kong and Germany, gave us portability. Therefore, after 12:00 at night, I searched for radio stations that broadcasted from other countries. I remember well that I used to tune in the BBC of London. The fun thing, is that I caught the best rock radio broadcaster in the world, knows as Radio Rock.

MR. LONELY AGAIN
SAD STORY OF AN IMPOSSIBLE DREAM

They broadcasted 24 continuous hours a day, from a ship anchored in international waters, near the coast of the United Kingdom. That radio station was considered illegal, just like the other 150 ships that were Pirate Radio Stations. They broadcasted in English, but rock had its own language, which all youngsters on the planet understood, without needing any translation whatsoever. They could be heard in the early hours of the day, enjoying the music of The Beatles, The Kinks, The Rolling Stones, The Animals, The Moody Blues, Caravan, The Who, Herman's Hermits, The Zombies, Cream, Procol Harum, The Turtles, The Loving' Spoonful. In my city, those groups and their songs were heard with a 6 Months delay, more or less.

I was too young. Because of this, no one could have believed that I was up to date with the music, more so than young people who were older than me. Of course, I kept my secret because I would listen during the early hours. I would cover both my head and the little radio with the pillow so that my mother would not hear. If she found out, she would take away my radio because in that era, the adults did not understand rock music. They said it was noisy, the devil music, etc. The church tasked itself with Satan evil rock, so the Sunday sermons were filled with prohibitions of rock, which our parents obeyed without think. In those times, parents ruled with or without reason. Their authority was not argued, and the rules of home were respected. During the early hours, those rules did not matter to me. I would listen to my rock music while jumping and dancing euphorically until I fell asleep, enjoying what I later found out was not satanic. Yet, nobody apologized to the youth, and they continued to blame rock for all the wrongs that afflicted society. They covered for one another because all the wrongs, wars, corruption, deprivations, religious exaggerations, assassinations, hundreds of political errors with consequences for the people. They were, and continue to be, errors committed by adults, with every bad intention to make themselves richer, or obtain more power than other adults.

SAD STORY OF AN IMPOSSIBLE DREAM

The Beatles, with their music, long hair, and tight clothes influenced and provoked the start of the youth rebellion. We only sought the liberty to choose what it was we liked, and to have religious liberty. This did not imply that we would stop studying or going to church. We continued to respect our parents, and other adults. We only asked that they also respected us. Some adults understood. They allowed us a bit more freedom, loosened the harnesses they had us subdued in. Other adults did not understand. In fact, they jammed up all of our modern activities. Long hair, for men, was prohibited in schools, churches, jobs, etc. They preferred that we lie to them, so that we could attend the musical shows that took place on Sundays. Shows where we danced while listening to local groups that masterfully interpreted the rock music they played. At these shows, in order to cater to the underage, there was no sale of alcoholic beverages. They started at 3:00 PM and ended at 11:00 at night. The locations were tennis courts, skating rings, or underground parking lots.

Multiple story parking lots, and some dance halls, began participating in these types of shows, but they did so very clandestinely. The odd thing is that the organizers obtained permits at city hall, in order to have these events this way, the police were vigilant, but did not interrupt the event. Except, of course, if there was disorder on behalf of the multitude of participants, or if the organizers did not have the corresponding permit.

In the afternoons you encountered musicians, beautiful girls, people with long hair and extravagant clothes who spoke of poetry, of liberties that the young ones enjoyed in developed countries. Most of all, in the United States and Canada. We largely entertained ourselves by dancing and learning of things that occurred in other parts of the world. What did not change, was the respect for the family. Being a friendly person, I participated in special parties, dinners, and family meals with a large quantity of families, in and outside of the neighborhood.

MR. LONELY AGAIN
SAD STORY OF AN IMPOSSIBLE DREAM

I watched with astonishment, those matrimonies, good or bad, that educated their children. That was normal. The influence and participation of both parents in the formation of children, with the great responsibility of maintaining their family united. It was respectable, belonging to one of those beautiful families to which I was invited, and well received. But I was not a member of the family. Being a member implied responsibilities, joy, entertainment, and lots of love. I understood that I lacked many things because I did not have a father, or brothers. My mother and I were alone in this large city because our families lived in other cities. Others, in far and away countries. Thus, I was poor for not having a complete family. That, however, did not embitter my existence. On the contrary, it made me admire and appreciate the families. Wishing to, one day, have a family of my own.

I remember one woman, who would wash and iron some of the neighborhood peoples' clothes, as a way to earn a living. We young ones in the neighborhood habitually went to her house every summer afternoon. While she ironed clothes, she told us old stories of mystery, terror, etc. Mrs. Alta was excellent in her narrations. When she finished ironing, it was the end of her stories, this was around 8:00 at night. We helped her carry the clothes, so that we could go with her to return them. This way, she took each one of us to the front doors of our houses. After hearing her stories, we were scared. Every night, she would say that she would not tell us any more stories, because we were more cowardly than a chicken. The next day, however, we repeated the visit to her house.

On the weekends, we had our age appropriate activities to attend to. We had an infinite amount of mischief and adventure with which to entertain ourselves. The days of infancy were getting left behind, and we were changing.

ADVENTURES OF PHILOSOPHIC REFLECTION
SAD STORY OF AN IMPOSSIBLE DREAM

Our neighborhood had a light, hanging from a cable, to light the night. Of course, this was not enough for the whole street, which was about 300 meters. It gave us fear, walking at night. The construction of the buildings was colonial, reminding us of Mrs. Alta's' macabre stories. After the public city works we had 7 light posts. So, the neighborhood was changing, just like us. We left our infancy with that one solitary light bulb that lit the street. During the week, as it got dark, you could hear guitars, playing songs that were popular at the time. Some were played spectacularly, while other were horribly played. It was entertaining, listening to those neighborhood interpreters that made time pass.

By the time you noticed, it was already 10:00 at night. Mothers and fathers called us with furious yells, for us to go have dinner and go to sleep, thus ending the daily entertainment in the neighborhood. It was also the end of comic books, which we were beginning to keep in family bookcases of in a drawer we could not throw them away because they were a reminder of our infancy. The Amazing Spiderman who, even with his super powers, struggled economically and in paying his rent. He hides his secret identity from his aunt, who loved him as her own son I liked him because he was poor and honest. He did not abuse his powers, not even to pay the rent. I admired him, and identified with him, for the rest of my life in wanting to be simple and just like him.

Of course, there were other comics I enjoyed, like The Fantastic Four, Thor, Walt Disney, the entertaining Burron Family, Rabid Roland, Los Supersabios, and many more comics that entertained our infancy, which was rapidly becoming distant, before we even noticed. The adventures we took on our bikes all over the city, and its surrounding areas, were left behind, along with all their memorable dangers and thrills.

MR. LONELY AGAIN
SAD STORY OF AN IMPOSSIBLE DREAM

Such as the games with marbles, whipping tops, cup and ball, diabolo, yoyo, roller skate races, 16 holes, and an endless amount of other games. The city changed. The electric trains disappeared, as well as the "fly trips", where we would hang on to the back of the train, in order to avoid paying. City Mayor began construction on the subterranean train service. Enormous buildings were appearing rapidly. Radio and television gave us sophisticated spectacles with a great variety of channels and 24 continuous hours of national coverage. Everything was changing, just as we were reaching adolescence, with physical and mental changes, which changed the way we understood and interpreted life.

Something we lost, I remember, when we used to play cops and robbers. We fought because everyone wanted to be the cops, the good guys. That's the way it was in those times. We would say that if we became doctors, lawyers, etc. We would help the humble people, even though that meant not being rich. We dreamed of making a better world. Sadly, the ones who accomplished becoming police officers and public servants, dedicated themselves to robbing. Beating and assaulting, even sexually, unknown innocent citizens, the they made the thieves steal for them. They protected the thieves so that they would not be arrested, and be able to continue stealing for them.

Others were able to reach lower positions in government. They stole and swindled until they could no more, without caring that they were harming the poor people. The ones who became professionals never even provided to the poor with a free consultation, charging them the same as they would be rich. They would trick them, so long as they could make more money.

ADVENTURES OF PHILOSOPHIC REFLECTION
SAD STORY OF AN IMPOSSIBLE DREAM

So, that sweet infancy in black and white became a thing of the past, forgetting all dreams of making the world a better place, but not for me. I continued to dream about bettering the world, sacrificing what others wouldn't ever dare consider. Returning to the topic of the shows, listening to radio rock and the nocturnal guitarists of the neighborhood created, in me, the desire to learn how to play guitar. A few months later, I learned. I pleased me like nothing else in life. I continuous with my classes and school work but the rest of the afternoon and night, I would practice at home with every desire of joining a rock band and becoming a professional musician. The Beatles dominated the world wide panorama. I liked them, but not more than my friends or acquaintances. The girls shrieked at the sound of them on the radio.

That was something never I did not understand. During their presentations there was fainting, collective hysteria with endless screaming, all the girls crying from emotion, but it only occurred with The Beatles. It was the famous Beatlemania, which could be neither understood nor explained by scientists or psychologists. I heard, for the first time, the Sergeant Pepper album. I was impressed, just like millions of other people around the world. I could not believe that was The Beatles. I listened to both sides of the album around 7 times in just one day, admiring the quality of the sound, the compositions, and the way they were interpreted. The album was recorded with a symphonic orchestra. The Beatles wrote the parts of every instrument, which was near 60, letting us know that they were geniuses, and that we were witnessing musical history with that incredible album. A masterpiece of rock.

The first live global transmission by satellite was on June 25th of 1967, with the largest audience of the time. 350 million people. It was called Our World.

MR. LONELY AGAIN
SAD STORY OF AN IMPOSSIBLE DREAM

Over 25 countries participated, with the intention of showing something that characterized each nation. The United States broadcasted the birth of a baby. It was marvelous, because there were people who had never witnessed a birth. Other countries showed scientific advances, tradition, art. 17 countries participated live, nothing recorded, and with no political participation. The nation which impacted the world was The United Kingdom, by showing the recording of the song, all you need is love by The Beatles. It was shown by order of Queen Isabel. There, we saw many musicians gathered, such as Mick Jagger, Donovan, Eric Clapton, just to name a few. They gave us a delicious experience.

Imagine the song, simultaneously being sung across the entire planet, with a message of peace, and with the best musical group in the world. I have continued to watch and listen to the video of that recording, and the message continues to remain valid. All we need is love. I was growing and participating in music groups of the neighborhood, but the promised no success whatsoever. They behaved like ordinary drug addicts. They smoked marijuana and made a 4 Minutes song last as long as 3 hours, without sense. It was absurd because you did not learn anything with that type of practice. I went to practice with another neighborhood group that did not do drugs, but instead of practicing to learn and perfect more songs, they were worried with looking pretty. They thought it was enough to simply have instruments in order to be successful, but it was not the right path.

Practicing, trying to play the songs just like the original sound, requires effort, continuous practice, and an excellent ear in order to not confuse the notes that help you interpret the song according to the original.

SAD STORY OF AN IMPOSSIBLE DREAM

Since I didn't have brothers, only my mom, who worked long shifts, I had time to enjoy myself, with solitude as my only company. Therefore, I had time to spare for practicing guitar and listening to discs, while trying to learn the songs. I listened to them millions of times. It was tiring, but not boring. I discovered that even though you bettered your musical abilities, you never finished learning. The better you played the songs, the greater the need to perfect them to the point that you sounded like a professional. So, my world became rock music 24 hours a day. Even when sleep, I was learning and practicing everyone in the neighborhood said that the best guitarist, was undisputedly someone called Pancho. As soon as we battled musically, it was demonstrated that the better guitarist was me. The difference between one and the other was enormous, because he dedicated his time to drinking alcohol and smoking marijuana, supposedly to inspire himself.

It was a shame because he had talent, and he sang well, but was more a criminal than a musician. I in turn, dedicated my body and soul to the arduous task of learning, practicing until exhaustion. I became the best guitarist in the neighborhood with the intention of bettering myself, I began to explore and meet other groups. I realized that the best musicians were at least a decade older than I was. Of course, they had more experience, even about life itself. They were the great groups that played shows and sounded just like the records, of the musicians they were interpreting. Those groups practiced every day of the week because Saturdays and Sundays, they played at 4 or 5 different places. Being the best, they made plenty of money, so they had good instruments and amplifiers, comparable to the international groups I listened to on radio rock. I finally managed to place myself in my own group, which proposed practicing all week from 4:00 in the afternoon, to 8:00 at night, in a room that was located in the drummer house. They hired me for being an unknown musician, yet demonstrating musical qualities. They were a decent to good group, but disintegrated when the leader, the guitarist quit.

MR. LONELY AGAIN
SAD STORY OF AN IMPOSSIBLE DREAM

He told the rest of the members that they lacked the musical quality, as he founded another group with the same name as theirs, The Flowers. Supposedly, he deserved to keep the band name because he was the only one with quality, and he was the leader. The group, with the new name, The Expedition, was formed by; Chava the drummer and leader, Ears the bassist, Ramiro the singer, and me, the new guitarist. I began the arduous task of learning the songs they already played, in order to present ourselves as soon as possible at the Saturday shows where they already frequented. They said I did not have the skills that the previous guitarist had.

That did not bother me. On the contrary, it motivated me to surpass myself and be a better guitarist. I increased the practices. At my home, I practiced from 9:00 at night, to 1:00 in the morning. I would wake around 7:00 in the morning, eat breakfast, and go to school. I got out at 2:00 in the afternoon, returned home, changed clothes, and traversed over to Chavas' house, in order to practice. This was from Monday to Saturday. On Sundays, were helped at the shows were the famous groups played, with the idea that we could learn from them, as well as enjoying just listening to those groups. They were the absolute best the city and musical environment had to offer, for the time being. Three weeks passed. On Saturday, we played our first show in a distant neighborhood. There were 3 groups participating, of which one was better than we were. The other was not very good, and we were a regular group. Fill, a young law student who was involved with politics, proposed being our musical representative. He offered us the guarantee of playing at political rallies. Charging little, but it would be every Saturday and Sunday morning, and he would provide transportation. This was on top of playing every Saturday afternoon at that distant neighborhood.

SAD STORY OF AN IMPOSSIBLE DREAM

He proposed that we divide our earnings in 5 equal parts as members of the group. We liked the deal, and immediately we were playing Saturday mornings at political rallies, and 2 different shows in the afternoons at neighborhoods that were far from downtown, which is where we practiced the audience was accepting of us, beginning our popularity in those far away neighborhoods. We played one or two new songs every week. The singer then proposed that he should charge double, since he was the group attraction, and without him we were nothing. We unanimously decided not to count with his services. Chava was moved to lead vocals, I was moved to second voice, and Ears helped a bit with the voices.

We immediately incorporated three voices into the group, which sounded better that it did when we had Ramiro. We managed to play all of the songs with vocals that had not previously been practiced, while simultaneously playing our instruments. This required many more hours of practice. Previously, we only had one voice to contend with. We became a group like The Beatles, sounding better with more voices. Immediately, that group that sounded better than us at that first presentation, was surprised because we sounded better than them, simply because we incorporated more voices.

We made sure to choose well, the songs we played. We integrated the music and voices of groups like The Beatles, Wallace Collection, Box Tops, Classic 4, Turtles, Marmalade, America, Kinks, Eric Burdon and The Animals, Three Dog Night, Guess, Who, etc. We also explored more aggressive rock, such as Rattles, Led Zeppelin, Crow, Deep Purple, Grand Funk Railroad, Jimi Hendrix, Black Sabbath, etc. Those groups were popular, but we chose songs from albums that other groups were not playing, so as not to seem like just another group.

MR. LONELY AGAIN
SAD STORY OF AN IMPOSSIBLE DREAM

There would have been comparisons that may not have been good for us. Or, maybe they would have been. But, why risk it the group was improved. We played at the best places, alternating with big name groups at all 4 cardinal directions of the city. We had followers that went to our presentations, creating a popularity that was new to us, at least, up until now. Some of the groups we alternated with were spectacular.

They were the same groups we would go listen to during the Sunday shows, like Love Army, Last Soul Division, Factory, Peace and Love, Anonymous Society, Los Leos, La Tropa Loca, The Cactus, as well as many other groups who were not considered some of the greats, but were as popular as Three Souls in my Mind, which remains active to this day. However, they are now known as El Tri of Alejandro Lora, who is a friend and neighbor of mine. We walked different paths, but we were both rock and rollers at heart. There were other great groups, such as The Cousins, The United Nations, Javier Batiz who was teacher of Carlos Santana, White Ink, The Tribe, and many other, who I apologize to for not mentioning them. I have poor memory, and ultimately, I'm practicing my Alzheimer.

Imagine the excitement I felt, alternating with those great groups that were my idols. We had not yet reached their level. We were maybe 5 levels below theirs. At that moment, however, we were at only 3 levels below them, and it would have been a mere 2 if we had better sound equipment, like they did. We had progressed in a mere 6 months. When I started with them, I had a cheap Japanese made guitar. At this moment, however, I had an American made Fender Duo Sonic. We bought it used, and although it was in perfect condition, we sent in out for paint. It wound up just like factory condition, and it sounded even better.

SAD STORY OF AN IMPOSSIBLE DREAM

Having this guitar to compete with the greatest guitarist depended entirely on me practicing more and more, and with more effort than ever. Sometimes, the world is small. Good, because I began to meet many of the great musicians from the bigger groups. My mom had a friend, who became her religious sister, for baptizing her daughter. That lady had a brother who they called Satanas, because he dressed in red almost daily. He was a member of a group called The Herb. They practiced in a very distant neighborhood, where Anonymous Society also practiced. The Anonymous Society had a guitarist named Alejandro, who they called Top Cat. He was Satanas' music teacher, and the one who helped place him in The Herb group. After meeting Satanas, he invited me to his practices. Pleased with the invitation, I went to listen to them in a farmer barn, they played almost every song by Credence Clearwater Revival, an international group of high popularity.

They played the songs well, at about 80% or 85%. They had good equipment, almost like the bigger groups. They practiced in a barn, where they raised goats, pigs, and process milk cows. They owners' son was the second guitar, he provided the instruments and amplifiers, since the family business had a good income and he had plenty of money. At the end of their practice, Satanas and I went 4 blocks down to an automotive shop. In the back there was a small room, which is where The Anonymous Society practiced. Better known as The A.S. We entered the room without making noise because they were practicing I live for the Sun by Vanity Fair. The sounds of the instruments and voices sounded 100% like the record. Wow, how did I wind up there? Satanas was Alejandros' friend and they were practically neighbors, separated by only one block. We would go get Alejandro, so that we could head home together. I lived 8 blocks from them, also their neighbor.

MR. LONELY AGAIN
SAD STORY OF AN IMPOSSIBLE DREAM

It was a pleasure, meeting the group face to face. Dayton the drummer, Panchillo the bass player, Carlos the keyboardist and leader, and Alejandro (Top Cat) the guitarist. It was like a dream being at their practice, when they decided to go over Let it be by The Beatles. They will debut the song at their next presentation, Saturday. When they played it, they sounded exactly like the original record, every instrument, each voice, the piano, all of it was in every detail, just like the song. I was introduced to them, telling them I was the guitarist for The Expedition. They said, surely out of politeness, that they had indeed hear the name of our group, which was beginning to gain fame. Carlos had a beautiful sense of humor. He told various jokes without using any bad words. He seemed like a fantastic person who, even being comedian, was well educated and with good behave.

To my good fortune, Don Nuno arrived, owner of the shop and representative for the band. He invited every one of us, without exception, to have dinner at his house, which was next to the practice room. In his house, we gathered around a large table, to delight ourselves with dishes prepared by the lady of the house. I observed some glances of complicity between Patricia, Don Nuno's daughter, and Alejandro. It seemed strange to me because she had maybe 15 years of age, while Alejandro had 25 years of age, so I found the situation entertaining.

Patricia had the body of a woman and a beautiful face, temptation for any man. Respectfully, as it should be, I dedicated myself to simply observing. Later, we said our goodbyes to everyone, but Alejandro (Top Cat), Satanas, and I walked to the bus stop where we would board, to return to our neighborhood. They carried their cases, which housed their guitars. Me I did not have my guitar that day.

ADVENTURES OF PHILOSOPHIC REFLECTION
SAD STORY OF AN IMPOSSIBLE DREAM

I did not practice because Chava had a doctor appointment, so I took advantage and went with Satanas. Good thing that I did it that way too, because it was the beginning of my ascension, from my incipient musical career. During our return trip, we chatted. Alejandro told me that he lived with his mother, just like me, except that he had three baby brothers and sisters, that's how he referred to them. I enjoyed getting to know him, I was invited to his practices or got to see them in The Cortijo, which was a bull pen located in front of the shop where they practiced. The following Sunday, they would perform there. It was their "home field", since they were the local group. I walked back home very pleased, I was smiling and grateful for the good fortune of getting to know those youngsters, from the group I so admired.

The next day I went to my groups practice, but my partners did not believe I had been with The A.S. in their practice room, but that did not bother me. Saturday arrived and the went to perform at two different places. Since we were making more money, on payments, we acquired a Fender Super Reverb. This way, we were only renting one amplifier for the shows, in order to be more competitive. During practice, it enough, to use the new Fender and any other not so good amplifier for the bass.

Early that Sunday, we played at Fili's political rallies. In the afternoon, I asked if they wanted to visit The Cortijo but they preferred going to Tthe Sport Center Nader, a nearby place where groups that were deemed big and famous played. Once at The Cortijo, I paid my entry fee and went to greet my friends front The A.S.

Carlos and Alejandro were polite and courteous, displaying joy in seeing me. The United Nations also performed, playing songs by Electric Flag. They played them at about 90% to 95% when compared to the originals.

MR. LONELY AGAIN
SAD STORY OF AN IMPOSSIBLE DREAM

While The AS, my friends, were finishing getting their equipment together to begin their performance, Carlos greeted the public and asked if anyone had heard The Beatles album, Abbey Road. Everyone responded with a yes, and started naming some of the songs on the album.

Carlos said he was dedicating, for the whole public, side one of the album and immediately began playing. They sounded 100% identical the record. They played all of the songs on side one, one after the other, in the same order that they are on side one of the record. When they finished, Carlos imitated the sound a record player makes, gestured flipping a disc over, and said they were now going to play side 2. They then proceeded to play all of the songs on side 2, until the album finished. The public was applauding with craze, as though it was The Beatles on stage instead of The A.S. We were impressed. Then, they played Let It Be 100% identical to the record, and said goodbye by playing the reprise of "Sergeant Pepper's Lonely Hearts Club Band" and "A Day in the Life"

At the end of the performance, the public would not stop applauding. They praised them like they were the best Beatles cover band in the world. I included myself in the clamor of the public and ran over to congratulate them, musically showing them my respect. Top Cat (Alejandro) asked me if I lived near The Sport Center Nader. I responded with a yes, in fact, it was 2 blocks from where I practiced with my group. He politely said that they were headed there to perform, and asked if I would like to accompany them, I was welcomed. He asked me for help in either moving the equipment to the truck that would be taking us, or guarding his guitar. Out of cowardice, or to remain alive, I chose to help with the amplifiers.

ADVENTURES OF PHILOSOPHIC REFLECTION
SAD STORY OF AN IMPOSSIBLE DREAM

On the way he asked me why I chose a task that was more difficult that guarding his guitar. I replied by saying that a black Gibson Stereo identical to the one "BB King" uses was an enormous responsibility, and that I had no doubt that someone would kill me in order to steal it. Top Cat and Carlos, who overheard, laughed as we continued on our way toTthe Sport Center Nader. Once there, we used a service entrance that lead us to a cargo elevator, where friends and musicians took on the task of introducing the equipment into the elevator. We then rose to the third floor, which housed the largest reception hall. We immediately hear music from "Factory", who at that time, played songs from other groups such as "Chicago" at about 100%. Meanwhile, on a balcony in front of them, we began to set up the modest equipment. It was not really enough to be considered the quality and prestige of a first class group.

Top Cat was glad that I helped him guard and carry his guitar. He said that if I knew the model and who of international fame had one just like it, which at the time were the only two of those guitars in the world, then surely I would not permit anything happening to "Lola Patricia". It was the name he gave his guitar. As usual, Carlos greeted the public and dedicated the performance to them.

They started with Let It Be, exciting those present with the perfection of the performance. My band mates were watching from the second level. They were mixed in with the rest of the audience. It surprised them, to see me on the balcony with Anonymous Society. I greeted them with pleasure. As of that moment, they did not doubt that these were my friends. Especially Top Cat and Carlos who were my neighbors. Carlos lived only three blocks from Top Cat. Even though I did not have the musical caliber that they did, I felt greater than ever before.

MR. LONELY AGAIN
SAD STORY OF AN IMPOSSIBLE DREAM

I had only known Alejandro for a short time when his mother died. Satanas was the one who let me know. I told the sad news to my mother and she asked me to let Alejandro know that if he needed help in tending to his baby brothers and sisters, he could count on us. All he had to do was let us know. Later, Satanas and I went to the funeral home in order to be with Alejandro. When we entered, the people were sad and crying. They were terrible moments. Alejandro was sad, but he did not cry. His baby brothers were crying inconsolably. It surprised me to learn that his sister was 22 years old, his brother 18, and the younger sister 16, just like me. I there understood that for him, they would always be his baby brothers and sisters.

Someone told Alejandro to cry, let go of his pain, that there was no reason for him to hide it. He responded by saying that if his baby brothers and sisters saw him cry, they would be even more sad. He had to show them strength as man of the house, giving them comfort. He asked why he needed to cry at that very moment, when he would cry for her his entire life. It pleased me to know how beautifully he expressed himself about his mother and siblings. I learned that he was a good son, a good brother, and of course, a good man. I was proud to know someone with such a good heart, and I joined him in his pain. Later on, after hugging Alejandro and his siblings, Satanas and I left for our homes. We were held silent by the sadness that held our mutual friend.

The A.S. rested on Fridays. That first Friday, they asked to come visit us at our practice. When Carlos and Top Cat heard us, they said that we were a better group than what Satanas had said. They told us that we had our own style, that the selection of our repertoire was excellent, contrast to us only being 3 members yet properly filling the musical gaps.

ADVENTURES OF PHILOSOPHIC REFLECTION
SAD STORY OF AN IMPOSSIBLE DREAM

The voices need some work, but sounded good. As if their visit had been some sort of exam, they passed us. Satanas visited us only once to sell us music records because he needed money to go with his girlfriend wife, but months then stop being a musician, looked for a job working every day to have a marriage life forgetting the rock life, I confess to not search for it nor I knew nothing more about him. The situation of our group change because we started to use the techniques of The A.S. by advice of them rested on Mondays so those days I went to the house of Top Cat, or to the place where rehearsed.

The kindly became my master as that perfected my musical style to be a complete guitarist. the love seemed be enemy of the rock as epidemic also contagion to the Ears is got wedding starting to make plans to marry is giving to the group of way friendly. The life weaves tangled cobwebs that cross roads sometimes complicating them other times facilitating them as happened for find the replacement right of the Ears. So just a week before had alternated with The Flowers the group of Chava the fat as you said to the guitarist that I had replaced, before alternating said that musically we were a bad group and that they would give us a beating, he asked that the tardeada was a hand so the winner would take on two salaries, and the loser group nothing. I accept because my colleagues were offended, I agreed because I wanted to be clear who was best guitarist. After we won the hand so the humiliated was Chava the fat and his group because we charge double salary.

Two days later arrived to our essay Chava the fat and Guti with the idea of joining us musically, thinking about the benefit of the group we decided that I would play keyboards, lead guitarist Chava the fat, Guti harmony guitar, and Ears the bass bringing 2 amplifiers by not having to rent equipment for presentations. Following got borrowed a box keyboard jaguar that sounded great. Chava the fat could not with the package giving up at the same day so I went back to the lead guitar.

MR. LONELY AGAIN
SAD STORY OF AN IMPOSSIBLE DREAM

More later Ears our bassist quit knowing that Guti would be his replacement, musically the idea was a positive change Guti was better bassist and incorporate a third voice's quality, so after learning our songs we introduce ourselves playing better since he brought his own amplifier for bass, our musical overcoming brought us the need for a voices amplifier, but it would be later when we had more work and money to invest. The A.S. said the equipment problem was solvable by proposing something that we could not refuse, which opened us a successful path in our short musical career. They had too much work and several places for presentations, but they did not have a great equipment, we didn't have both work as them and not a great equipment, so if we presented together, they would get us contracts in their presentations so we will unify the equipment, so both would have good equipment for presentations, and us will take competition with groups without having to rent or ask to borrow equipment.

There in forward us presented together in 2, 3, or 4 places Saturdays and Sundays. Our places of essay were small for to them two groups rehearse, but musically got both that went them benefited by be with them teaching us that we climbed to only a level of distance of the best groups of that time not importing that only were 3 elements.

As mention to the gather the team it battery is developed in a double set that only the great drummers it could use and believe me when Chava it used it did so rather than climbed their bonds musically, he was also a breaks hearts with the girls in our presentations. By its regular our presentations were before the A.S. after them we went out practically flying to the following presentation, so together with helpers that transported the equipment, the responsible in Chief of the logistics of the transportation, installation, verification of sound you called "Secretary" why? I never knew, our secretary was good friend, intelligent, great collaborator called Lalo.

SAD STORY OF AN IMPOSSIBLE DREAM

Believe me Lalo was an important part of the group so much that the handled a budget dedicated to pay transportation, loaders, maintenance of equipment as all electric, strings for guitars, drums leathers, microphone cables, making a number of minor repairs, it is best that he mixed with the crowd to listen to us, giving the correct modulation and volume to each instrument and voice of the group. His affection and loyalty toward us did develop a plan for the special condition that we had in the group, Chava was sick had an estolitica amoeba in the brain causing attacks with seizures with duration of between 3 to 4 minutes during which was left unconscious, the attacks were not frequent but unpredictable to know when would be the next. Lalo after install the team is charge of the modulation and volumes, it was during the first song of our presentation, after is sat beside Chava very close to the control central electric where the connected all the amplifiers, when Chava had an attack Lalo cut the electricity so the equipment is turned off immediately placed to Chava in the floor with a pillow under the neck.

It covered with a blanket prepared for the time, all it was beside the battery by the side inside where the public not could observe them, also he placed a pencil in Chava's mouth so not bite his tongue without leave of rub him saying words that it kept in calm, meanwhile us acted surprised because it electricity is had interrupted doing that it attention of the public was with me and not with Chava. Little after Chava sitting on his bench and while fully retrieving Lalo turn on electricity, I offer apologies said that it was something out of our control but that our sound technician already had everything under control, moments later Chava gave classical music count, one two three four and we play the same song that we had interrupted. that us occurred on average 10% of our presentations.

Lalo were so efficient and good friend who, up to that special situation, always had it under control. Lalo was the forerunner of what later sound engineers.

MR. LONELY AGAIN
SAD STORY OF AN IMPOSSIBLE DREAM

Were called at the time people without musical quality or any knowledge is auto named sound engineers, but knew not modular, and had heard musical, qualities that Lalo natural and huge had it applied in modest way as it always was. The universe pounding to my favor because to the not have brothers always was alone, but gave me friends special that have reminded along my life, have been too many perhaps without deserve it, Benito, Gutierritos, Gerardo the handsome, Lalo the gangs, Lalo and Chava companions of the musical group, Villicana, Alex, Alejandro Top cat, Carlos director of the A.S. the bell, Maria finger girl.

Luis and his brother Beticus, Gerardo Borrego, Arturo Chivo, Daniel left handler, Mario, Nacho Perico, Juan Concho, Conchita, Juanis Jorge the Pinocchio, Lupita, Arturo Fernandez, Andy, Carito, Marcos and Tono Avandaro, Irma, Marisela, Laura, Trini, and many more, all the characteristic which I remember with affection and respect is that they were excellent sons and daughters, I learned that love to your father or mother or both if you were lucky to have them is basic that will guide your life for the rest of your existence, I say thanks to all of them for gave me, how much that I taught, what we share during childhood and teenager times.

Our musical group starting a second year together during which reached the recognition of be group of second level and near to the first level, enjoyed without give me has of be all the week with my group companions, in them trials, in the presentations, dressed equal, in them tours musical ate it same and slept together, as if were brothers, so with them learned to live with the relationship daily of brothers even us, we fought but never to hurt us, we protected one another.

Chava protected me as if was my brother greater therefore is won my sweetheart, so not returned to be alone. the life when going well is alters so not eternally goes well, or so I seemed in that time.

SAD STORY OF AN IMPOSSIBLE DREAM

My mom as adults of that time most opposed to rock music, men with long hair, to rock bands, school holidays were about to finish having to return to school, my mom had plans that I gave up entirely to my group to concentrate at school, I opposed leave the music, but she said that had two options, first I was living in her house and go to the school, not more rock and roll group, or go out of the house as a second option. I loved the music, the group that was my universe so chooses to get out of the house, by the time Chava and her family gave me accommodation, had a bedroom available for a sister's girl had escaped with the boyfriend leaving his family plunged into sadness, demonstrating that the epidemic of love could get at any time, the family I try well, enjoyed of it company of Chava sharing as brothers, I liked but also worried because I became in a load economic for the family.

So which I dedicated myself to find an affordable place, that would give independence to me to devote myself to the band, also let grow my hair to the style of the rock fashion. Alejandro and his siblings lived in rooms near the roof of a building where his mom was in charge of cleaning. one of the rooms conditioned it as cuisine had other three rooms which were bedrooms them, had other two bathrooms with showers that are shared among a total of twelve rooms which were the total of rooms on the near roof. For my good luck a room was vacant, so Top cat speak by me with the person that rented the rooms and by an accessible price, Mrs. Trastupijes let me rented including the electricity and furniture. she not is called so, but Alejandro it had named and I also without she is joked. that joy was the have to Top cat of neighboring, so of the night to the tomorrow I became in musician professional of full time since my income came as only of the presentations of the group.

A once installed in my room, my life change positively both musically and in my behavior, at 11:30 in the morning woke up, took a shower, and ate breakfast with my neighbor Alejandro, her older sister was cooking more than exquisite.

MR. LONELY AGAIN
SAD STORY OF AN IMPOSSIBLE DREAM

We studied the songs to play each one with our own group until around 2:30 in the evening time that we stopped the practice. Preparing to go to rehearse with our groups then practice where of 4:00 to 7:00 if I ended first was in seeks of Alejandro until its place of essay which enjoyed in large by listen them, learn and with like greet to Carlos, others times Alejandro ended first and I sought in house of Chava where was our practice room. Around of them 9:00 of it night had dinner by its regular in a modest Chinese coffee where the food was cheap and like homemade, others times had dinner in his house so to them 10:30 of it night rehearsed and talked until them two or three of the dawn for after go to my room to sleep. to the day following is repeated the same cycle. The Saturday and Sunday was when we were working on the presentations of our groups, sometimes together, other times each who covering by separate them presentations by have contracts in places different, at the end of the day already in the night around the 1:30 of the morning came back to meet us in the Chinese coffee to had dinner and ran to the house to sleep. Then musical practices with or without group were of 14 to 16 hours daily It also had wordship and teachings of Alejandro, my progress was accelerated to giant steps so each day I turned in better and more full guitarist.

In it reference to voices and arrangements musical I asked to Carlos and as always I said kindly. certain day I ask to Alejandro that because the nick name of "Top cat" smiling me wonder that if saw the cartoons of "Top cat and his gang" in the television? sure that if I replied also still me remained liking were fun, he mention that when started playing in his first group, some friends who wanted to be guitarists followed him to his essays, carried him the guitar being his assistants and they followed him everywhere, his group and other groups when they saw him followed by his aides say there is Top cat and his gang. Then Alejandro joined others increasingly professional groups which did not allow strangers in practice so they had to unfollow but not hide their sadness.

But the nick name Top cat stayed forever, their friends we called him Alejandro, I was his best friend and mine. He mimicked to perfection Cantinflas and made me laugh when he said things to the special way of Cantinflas, but it was curious that only made it with me to make me laugh because everyone who knew him did not know that, towards this as perfect imitation, but to me it amused me and if I was a little sad did to make me laugh and forget the sadness. To the start of third year with the group had contracts by all the city, our income where great and the group sounded well, the public us compared with the greatest groups of that time. The A.S. bought in payments 4 amplifiers brand "Kustom" that were really good and sounded great, with columns of speakers were cushioned in very special way to see elegant because they were black, were 2 amplifiers 200 watts for the guitar and keyboard, another 400 watts for the bass all with 2 columns each, the voices amplifier was 600 Watt with four columns using 2 of them behind them next to the amplifiers and the other 2 to the front for the public.

With that equipment The A.S. sounded better than the original groups interpreting, when we presented together they allow us to use their equipment and we sound like any great group of first level, were the best times in both groups. visited my mom every 5 weeks, 8 weeks sometimes because we traveled to present us in faraway places, but it was called her by phone. I followed with my musical career leaving out of going to school because I was a full-time professional musician. The A.S. reach to a level where earned a lot of money that the drummer and the representative made handling illicit from the money for them two win more money that the rest of the group.

The A.S. that decided to let Dayton go without use his services, replacing it with Jesse a veteran drummer that came from Tijuana, musically was best than Dayton so The A.S. sounded of it best. Their economic problems by its debt collapsed by the purchase of the super equipment and others things more.

MR. LONELY AGAIN
SAD STORY OF AN IMPOSSIBLE DREAM

Then led to the limit of its capacity, the representative stole already of form blatant taking all the presentations money. He took the equipment because it bought to his name so return, part of the equipment, he renegotiates the debt and stayed with three amplifiers one 400 watts and 200 watts also with the 600-watts-voices, but only two columns, total of 4 amplifiers and 10 columns of speakers I only keep 3 amplifiers and 6 columns of speakers and with the debt which remained large. Not having a group that represent need one to use the equipment to continue making payments and earn some money for it, but its bad reputation made him looks like someone not reliable, I don't know what happened to him or the equipment. The A.S. was without equipment, which had it gave as a down payment to buy the gigantic equipment so rehearsed and shared our equipment when presented together, in occasions had presentations by separate so they had to rent the equipment, others groups also helped them let in use the equipment during presentations in the same place, already disappointed of the situation, opted by separate is being a hit hard not only for them also to me because were my idols.

We got a keyboardist which buy in payments a keyboard Box model Jaguar that sounded of it best, but us lasted little the taste since his father and the big brother of Gerardo forced him to quit of the group by religious reasons and that not playing ever rock and roll in all his life and that sadness that so was. Carlos helped me learned it basic for can use that keyboard, meanwhile Alejandro not is wanted to integrate to any group loved be independent so is dedicated to take palomazo as is said in the environment musical that not was another thing more than what is met as "freelance" Participating with some groups but not on a permanent basis, sometimes presented with us sure as lead guitarist, I was second guitar and keyboard player, with Alexander we sounded like the same A.S. so we jump ourselves in the taste of the people as first-level group, when Alejandro was going with us we rented a Twin Fender Amplifier for guitar and voices;

Using the Super Reverb Fender amplifier for the keyboard or the second guitar and vocals, Guti was using his Golden Gate amplifier copy of baseman Fender that sounded beautiful so finally we were the group that dream to be. When Alejandro had another presentation, Carlos was going with us as keyboardist and vocals so we rented the Twin Fender amplifier, but for me as a lead guitarist and we sound like The A.S. in its best times. so time pass several months, I was going visit Carlos home him and his mom were originating in the North of the country, were he learned English at an early age and wanting to be a school teacher, is why moved to the capital city for enter to the normal school of teachers in which he graduated but not never work as a teacher because his passion was the rock music, his mom supported, so when Carlos not had group or contract for presentations his mom help him which the home bills the mom baking, washing and ironing clothing to customers that delivery and pick up clothes to her house.

When Carlos earned money he paid expenses, carrying his mom to lunch, he bought clothes, shoes, etc. they lived humbly in roof rooms like Alejandro and I, I stalked me sadness to be distanced from my mom, she did not support me even knew that it had progressed musically because group we had, the instruments and our wages were obtained thanks to the musical presentations where the public paid by hear us and see us, but repeat my mom not had idea of the achievements reached with my own effort. To the begin the third year as group had both work that ran of a presentation to another by the four cardinal points of the city, the presentations were successful with Carlos or Alejandro.

Unfortunately, by conflicts with our representative and then with Chava, we opted to disintegrate the group when we were at our best moment. sold out the equipment, so I kept as owner of my guitar Duo Sonic Fender, a wha wah Box, my distortion Boston, and a volume Shure microphone.

MR. LONELY AGAIN
SAD STORY OF AN IMPOSSIBLE DREAM

I take to go in my own way becoming "freelance" as Carlos and Alejandro, with them travel to other cities in touring, sometimes in palomazos with groups throughout the city, I me fit to play guitar, keyboard or bass. Alejandro I presented as his cousin because that way the musicians of other groups trusted and gave me more work and don't let down anyone because I was actually a good musician with great capacity especially when improvising was our best feature. After Carlos founded the A.S. with new elements, little time after also I went recruited that amounted to a graduation professional, they were the group that admired to the convert me in the lead guitarist occupying the honorable place of Top cat, so by a time not it could believe, lived a dream wonderful. had lack of equipment spending part of the gains in rent amplifiers, so the economy we smothered so had that break down the group. Carlos was owner of the name "The anonymous society" register with "Capitol Records" of the Mexico City, in gratitude that I admired them so much and I was so loyal with them took me to the Capitol records label for naming me the new owner's name, out of respect I do not use the name with any group in Mexico.

Presenting me with several groups on my own, sometimes with Carlos, others with Alejandro and rarely all three together with a drummer to complete us as group, were unforgettable times where I learned the art of improvisation with the best musicians in the rock music so it did keynote presentations most often without even practicing or know the original songs tunes, but they were wonderful Alejandro was the best guitarist of Mexico beating to musicians as Javier Batís that was the teacher of Carlos Santana, but he not had the fame international nor won the money that they because? Alejandro was very simple and modest that he was enough with enjoy his guitar it others lacked of importance. We taught the art of keep your guitar in perfect conditions, like octaves it, change the old frets of new German silver, rewired tablets of sound to increase its ability to sound, the first lesson I got from him was cleaning the instrument as the basis for so to be good musician.

We involved in the tours with artistic caravans of the main brewing companies of the country as Moctezuma, Corona accompanying to famous singers, by emergency of calendars in their presentations not had time to rehearse, but went well and the public enjoyed to the presentations for songs that don't give us time not had touched or practiced together those songs, others times had minutes just to know the other members of the group. The rock in their early 50's is interpreted songs foreign with lyrics in Spanish therefore them artists is developed in pioneer's e idols of the rock in Mexico, I even had born. to beginning of the 70's when happened my history.

Those famous musicians made their great returns regardless of the great successes and great performers sing in English, but they had their loyal audience that had not forgotten them performing successfully as in its best times, but resorted to musicians as us without having to re organize their own groups. Also did presentations of our group playing rock in English than our audience liked in addition so were the way our contracts in these artistic caravans. We accompany musically to artists such as; Enrique Guzman, Cesar Costa, Alberto Vázquez, Manolo Muñoz who was the best voice of the country, in presentations of them I had to do second and third voices as he is required even in infirmities I was singing for them in the end I became an important part group for ease of singing in both languages, presenting us in Palenque's, national fairs, classrooms of dance casinos, and in the newly opened Terraces Casino accompanying to Roman that was a fourth place of the international festival OTI certainly will tell you that master crazy presentation.

The singer Romano hired Alejandro and I on a Wednesday day, gave us records with the songs that we will perform, among them was the famous theme from The godfather sure he sang it in Spanish. we realized the task of studying and learning the songs that day Wednesday, the Thursday early morning traveled to Cuernavaca in Guerrero, Mexico.

MR. LONELY AGAIN
SAD STORY OF AN IMPOSSIBLE DREAM

Where we would meet in the afternoon with a keyboardist and a drummer to complete the musical group, in that occasion I would play the bass. They were 6:00 afternoon when we met in the lounge of the presentation for rehearse the drummer came not appearing keyboardist, of emergency seek a keyboardist or a bassist, but we not got to nobody. That night learned and practiced the harmonies and figures of all the songs in a keyboard "Hammond" of double keyboard wonderful instrument. It was in the Hall to our service to use it, had more than 200 keys of sound that when you mix are more than thousands of sounds, had pedals for bass sound. The night of the Thursday and the dawn of the Friday rehearse Alejandro in the guitar, me in the keyboard the whole of the songs of the presentation.

Friday at noon met with drummer and Roman to be tested until night all songs being adjusted figures and harmonies, still had the problem of not having a bass player, keyboard pedals sounded perfectly like a bass but timing for using them was difficult since all the groups of that era used simple keyboards without pedals and the bass was played by a bassist player, in this case we had to do the bass with pedals more double keys keyboard.

Using my left foot for reach and to touch the half of the pedals of the right side, Alejandro with his foot right played it another half of the pedals sounding the bass of way excellent, believe me in the morning of the Saturday rehearse the bass with our feet, in occasions Alejandro stepped me on, in others occasions I stepped him on. That Saturday night and the night of the Sunday that were days of the presentations in front of the public, nobody notice it absence of the bassist, by fortune not did wrong with so many harmonies and figures with the two set of keyboards, not confused with so many registers of sound, Alejandro play the guitar beautifully as natural of his way, at the end of the presentation we finished with feet and pimples hit as if had played it end of a championship of football.

SAD STORY OF AN IMPOSSIBLE DREAM

We were so sore that can't walk we have sick legs, Roman was happy and surprised music quality and ability that we compensate effort paying us both of them the salary that would have been for the bassist and other money extra congratulating us by the magic of our improvisational to perform with good of the big commitment. Two days later went to visit Carlos that was prepared for a presentation at a hotel where would be the keyboard player accompanying a singer of romantic music, his shoes were polished well, but Carlos placed a piece of cardboard inside to cover the hole in the soleplate, that was because they were worn out from so much use, but above it showed nothing, his mom iron he a pretty jacket which is hung a little bit the left sleeve by the inner liner which had no remedy or patching it, be broken and that the jacket had more than ten years of use. Carlos it looked good, super ready for interview regardless of the pit in shoes or old jacket, he and his mom were happy to have a chance to get a good music contract. to observe them, believe me that I thought that if there were a God I would like to be like them.

Happy and optimistic at times difficult. both we said goodbye to his mom, the hotel which was near his home, on the way Carlos said that the singer was nice and pretty and like to go out with her. We arrived to the bar of the hotel where quickly Carlos integrated to the group began the rehearse, meanwhile I left fly my imagination wishing to be as Carlos and his mom because they had a relationship pretty of mutual understanding that any would envy, I promised in silence that, if could live of that way with my mom, would be the happiness for me.

So time later I was playing in Tijuana with Alejandro, something as well as 6 months with different rock groups Mexican and North American by the proximity of San Diego, California started to feel that was far from what wanted in the life because loved the music, to difference of Carlos and Alejandro I not enjoyed my career musical if be beside my mother I said Alejandro and him understood.

MR. LONELY AGAIN
SAD STORY OF AN IMPOSSIBLE DREAM

Because that day after playing told me that if he where me break toward the capital city looking for mom and begin study in the University, actually said he was surprised that having the scope to be professional graduated from University was away from the studios, and told me that it would be what would you do if you return to studying. Early after Alejandro bought me a ticket for travel of return to my house, he took me to breakfast after we went to the bus station for start my return to the house with my mom, Alejandro said that he will miss me but he wanted the best for me, although was sad only with the memories would be enough for be happy by me and by him, for guiding me in the way correct. Already aboard of the bus through the window I said goodbye and saw him clean tears of his eyes, that was a great honor for me because when his mother died not he had tears, but in my farewell it made, is it thanks eternally.

On the return to the capital city leave my room and return home with my mom, I sold my guitar and my equipment, with that money use it to buy books and clothes to enter the last two semesters of College to later enter to the University. Not returned to visit the home of Alejandro or Carlos because there was the temptation to return to the music so that I walked away from them without any problem between us only that was the best thing to devote to study.

Coincidence or whatever Carlos and Alexander were good kids and good people followed his example and I wanted to be a good son, them and I didn't have parents to our side, but had much mom took us along in our careers and were a source of joy and pride. I taught countless of musical skills, but I taught to be good son which until my old age enjoy it and thanks them, as older brothers that not had. Not I have words to thank them, but sure know that you miss them as people rather than as musicians because teaching had come to an end only music was daily practice be good son it is practical of lifetime.

I take to study and recover the love to the studies as did with the music, was nice convert me again in student, I liked be in the school with companions and beautiful girls in the end I involves with joy and student vocation. Between to study to the vocational number 4 of science physical mathematics, so the studies required great concentration, knowing a world different since the school was in the road that you wore to the Ajusco, back of it school had a series of caves inhabited by people that, as the stone age of the cartoons, they had light electric, refrigerators, televisions, but within caves that they dug and made more rooms, was as a tale of fantasy, but were real.

We had classes of workshop during 3 weeks each semester participating in activities all the day of 8:00 am to 8:00 pm with a break of 2:00 pm to 4: pm in the afternoon for eat, so us imbued to the caves because is dedicated to prepare food homemade indeed to the house that where you said the "Dennis" as restaurant of international chain, where dining economic, clean and mostly to a step of the school that was an experience unique in my life. I stayed studying for 6 consecutive months until finished the semester to rest two weeks to start the next and final semester, Saturday and especially Sunday walked the streets of the city that did not have the bustle and traffic of the days of the week, so it was delightful to walk throughout the downtown of the city. I was inactive because on Sunday were the most active days during the time of the group so it premiered activity musical, but I dedicated to continue with my career and above all regain the relationship with my mother. Walking a Sunday, I met a friend who we were in the same high school, he was younger, so I was in one grade lower than me, I fell well because it was controversial, problematic, etc. during that school times got into fights with a member of the Izazaga gang behind school which where the terror of the surrounding area but they are my friends therefore remove it troubles because otherwise he would have spent it very badly so that did a bit of friendship thanks me for my intervention to save his skin.

MR. LONELY AGAIN
SAD STORY OF AN IMPOSSIBLE DREAM

By those times I remembered with appreciation, but what the musical group, he heard us for several occasions, he was fascinated by the idea to have one day his own group. So that we stopped talking for nearly 30 minutes or more inviting me to listen to musical church choir as they played Catholic songs, but they were really modern ballads sung by pretty girls, the young among them the accompanying them with guitars, so it was all a musical show. After insist I accept that I would come to listen the presentation of the music in the church choir the next Sunday. Because they imagine that by I not having music presentation to the following Sunday I became present in the Church listening to the pretty girls and improvised guitarists that did not bad at all, sang regular but not put in the correct path, vocals and above all that there was used not correct way the voices for the presentations masterfully, human material had it I recognized it instantly, but they had to educate the voices.

At the end of the mass and musical presentation we met in the hall of the church where I was presented by Gilberto to his girlfriend and sisters who were members of the musical choir, I was introduced to his sister more simple and cute person she not sang only going to mass and accompanied her sisters so they could participate and see Gilberto because as they were daughters of family old fashion went always accompanied or wouldn't let them leave. Them were girls of 17 and 18 years old of age equal that Gilberto, I had 20 years old the sister greater had 30 years, worked in a bank being a person that helped in them expenses of the home being single until that time. then talks where my knowledge musical where enhanced by Gilberto us lead to the offering for me involve like the director of the choir, I accept only for three weeks with tests of 3 days per week to locate their voices and attach guitars with voices so not needed long solo effort by them and they truly accepted knowing more than the agreed deadline. That week rehearsed for three days at the rate of two hours per day placing each voice on site, the following Sunday waiting for a presentation with the voice quality.

Settings and incorporate the use of sound to enhance bass lower voices before not using because they had no idea of what was singing. That Sunday everyone with their tessitura of the voice. were heard fantastically people notice the improvement, as well as they themselves hoping to improve more during the next two weeks. That Sunday I was introduced to another beautiful sister who was my age and went to church just to get to know me, trials did not go because he worked in a commercial store with the three older sisters who helped home support as well educated members of family. That day during the four hours that were together not us separate and talked of thousand no sense with the idea of know us, she chose me as someone special or so I felt and she invite me to pick up her at the exit of her works and together walk towards her house that was the day after day plan.

Was so pretty that said she wanted to go by her to her works but not could because my classes were by in the afternoon and came out around them 7:00 pm night in addition the return time to the house that would be around 8:00 pm night, but were of see us to the following Sunday, I assumed that before go to the school I present to her work in the books department and exchanged reviews of authors that enjoyed of their works as Edgar Allan Poe, Julio Verne, Oscar Wilde among others, then I said goodbye and left road to the school. Weeks in which we share time together, I turned my training with the choir of the church not accepting to stay as director in final form because that would result in take me out of the removal of the music that I chose as my new life where there was only the school as a goal and the romance which was to become a sad story.

Our relationship was something more than special because us met newly out of the adolescence entering in the age adult where should mature together. Living a stormy love that lasted a decade and never mature, when girlfriend and boyfriend went in group with her sisters, friends, and couple of them because it was the only way permitted to leave.

MR. LONELY AGAIN
SAD STORY OF AN IMPOSSIBLE DREAM

Because they were members of a family educated like old-fashioned, so it came together or not left any. The fun was out to talk, it did by hours because actually we felt happy being together. Virginia was a young girl extremely beautiful, with a touch of distinction that made her unique, walked of a special way that only of see her come towards you could fall in love madly as happened to me, I was feeling happy and lucky of she was my girlfriend. Sunday got together in the church, and then of the mass were to a singer music coffee, or just to walk, but always talking with hands entwined, or embraced, in end was beautiful pass that day together. She worked at the same place with major and minor siblings, I was going for her to leave, and we walked up to his house, sure did with the intertwined hands, talking of thousand things with or without interest, just to enjoy mutual company. In occasions, I came out afternoon of the school or I gurgled in the traffic so ran as if would like to win a marathon, running as crazy by streets and streets to get with her, to tell truth, I was lucky to be not kill me a car to be run like crazy in a big number of times.

That didn't care since I was desperate to get beside her, really we wanted, because she hoped to me with the desire that came to perform our daily walk hugging each other. To the time, we respectfully told his father that we were dating and with his consent we stayed at the door of her house talking to about 9 or 9: 30 at night time when I was leaving for the neighborhood to talk with my friends, or simply go home to do my homework which were enough.

I make a parenthesis to tell them what happened with Gilberto was responsible for having met Virginia. As I mentioned them I was young but did not see beyond her eyes, he was irresponsible, spent the money from tuition fees in drug and follies which did not lead it to any positive way. He worked them end of weeks beside his father that had a business of groceries to the wholesale winning money to hands full. Gilberto stole the father each time.

ADVENTURES OF PHILOSOPHIC REFLECTION
SAD STORY OF AN IMPOSSIBLE DREAM

He was going to work becoming fool inviting all to all to be popular in the neighborhood and especially with Teresa his girlfriend. He didn't know it wrong that was, that could be popular, but by their positive actions, also if wanted to steal was well but that save because never know that can pass, by supposed that not understood continuing his life with drugs cheating to their parents. Shortly after his father died leaving him his business to the eldest son of his first marriage the family of Gilberto with scarcity where his mom had to maintain them and educate them both to him as his brother and sister younger than him leaving. Without money stopped being popular in the neighborhood, discovered that Teresa didn't wants him since end their relationship with, when he had no money, became mad with sadness and attempt to commit suicide for her, the only one who came to comfort him was me because I knew that it was a result of their irresponsible actions, try to comfort him telling that there are hopes to achieve and try to achieve is the beautiful thing of life.

With down head mentioned that his biggest dream was to belong to a rock band, but when he likes to do with me repeatedly replied that I was retired so I could do nothing for him not tell me. Crying said that I was retired after having achieved the dream big of a music of rock, but the knot and that would be happy again if I not helped to achieve that dream. After think it carefully felt that he needed as a friend and as musician so I said that of guitarist is would die of hunger, but could be a good bassist. That would have to follow my instructions and rehearse with dedication absolute and the possible soon be ready to begin a new stage of his life and convert in musician as his dream. He promised to follow my teachings to initiate instant so I decided help him. As he was a guitar player wise tones I didn't speak with an ignorant musically, also loved the music of the Beatles, we started rehearsing with two acoustic guitars but used to play bass, learning songs from the Repertoire of the Expedition.

MR. LONELY AGAIN
SAD STORY OF AN IMPOSSIBLE DREAM

So he had a basic of how everyone is rehearsing his part and that soon we practice with a drummer trying as a member of a group. While I was in school he practiced records, but formidable way with a dedication not known, in just eight weeks was ready in each one of the songs from the Repertoire of the Expedition group. I began teaching improvisation that was a technique with exquisite skill, believe me I had wanted so much to become him a musician that achievement it and based on their own efforts reminding myself when I start that music way I, believe me I liked the sound achieved by both and as he voices fits he needs to make second voice, we sound very acceptably receiving congratulations from listeners in the neighborhood.

Thought Gilberto was ready to perform it in public and see as is entailed, would have that dominate to the monster that clapping and love you according to your presentation. Call one of the halls where we introduce ourselves before the Expedition with letting them know that we were back, but we wanted to try the new bassist without having to carry equipment used only the equipment of the group who were playing only would be guitar and bass.

The organizers showed their joy for the return of the group saying that they provide all the equipment including guitar and bass, only we should introduce ourselves around 8:00 o'clock in the evening so we were at peak times so it was a schedule of luxury. Talk by phone with Chaval who said with pleasure it would be to relive those unforgettable presentations, of course that wonder if bassist may be good enough to perform well, I told him yes, he was ready to play all the previous Repertory of the group.

That Sunday Gilberto carried Virginia, Teresa, and other sisters, neighborhood friends who were excited to listen to the group again, of course it Lalo was also to help modulate in a few minutes during the first song as I used to do it before.

ADVENTURES OF PHILOSOPHIC REFLECTION
SAD STORY OF AN IMPOSSIBLE DREAM

When climbed to the stage the people applauded because pleasantly us remembered so started to play, Gilberto was so well coupled that not is noticed that was new with the group. We arrived in a part of the song where singing without music then continue with music and voices at the same time, I confess being fearful of Gilberto not sing or that it escapes from the tone, but to the surprise of all the voices sounded masterfully so from that moment the public we surrendered and every song we interpret applauded them as in the best times of the group we had. We did near 10 presentations and a XV years party celebration of one friend of the neighborhood. Mention that only was matter of time so I back to my retirement from the music, I so should them get a guitarist for continue with the presentations without me.

Chava showed disgust saying that if I am out he also would quit, because he returns only by me. Was a super singer know me saying that knew of my musical return and with others musicians had a group quite good called the Odyssey, that they wanted me as guitarist offering instruments and amplifiers. I did accept with the condition of carry my bassist they gladly said yes. That week we introduce ourselves to rehearse, learning from the Repertoire of them and they learn from our repertoire so after two weeks, we put together a very competitive group performing with success, my singer friend the Bell sang super well so on the aspect of voices we were well organized, the music was formidable because Mario was terrific on the keyboard, his brother George was versatile since it was on the verge of being the bassist, but for take Gilberto became in the drummer playing in a way more than acceptable, we were a second level but one step from the first level group. Kept with them near 6 weeks saying by the school time they would have search a guitarist to replace me again, two weeks more and got my replacement, Gilberto wanted to quit to go with me, but I said now you are secure in a good group with quality, instruments, also the way to make his dream musical career.

MR. LONELY AGAIN
SAD STORY OF AN IMPOSSIBLE DREAM

Obeying me by his well accept stay and was the start time of his career that was successful by near 40 years until the day of his death, because he never cared to be healthy and continued being active smoker of marijuana, cigarettes, alcohol, and more, but dies being happy doing what he liked because was proud to be 100% rock and roll musician.

Returning to the history of love that was stormy, because wanted be together more time, but not fixed the problem, because the only way was marry us, but she does not like my propositions because we were young and not ready for something so serious as marriage, so we continue together, but suffering by only see us as boyfriends. That was not mattered in fact because we enjoy the little time that were together it used to the maximum, discovering so many things of us themselves and falling in love with us each time more.

Being at the University, after seeing Virginia was returning home at night, lived in the neighborhood with friends enjoying smoking marijuana and talking until one in the morning to go to rest and be ready for the next day activities. During the evenings neighbors thought that we are growing up to become the successors of bad kids who abused residents and up to the business of the area because the generation previous so it made but to his pleasant surprise us only we have fun and noise because sang songs of rock and roll but respected to all them neighboring and passers-by of the neighborhood, as well as the business, so they let us hiding in their houses when arrived the police and wanted to arrest us although not were offenders.

In meetings at night we engage with all kinds of relation reason why I was involved in a car crash when we went back to the distributor of cars where Jaime was working and had borrowed the car as he and Cricket were going to collect money they owed to me, so that Jaime would pay me the loan I made which I needed to pay school costs.

ADVENTURES OF PHILOSOPHIC REFLECTION
SAD STORY OF AN IMPOSSIBLE DREAM

For my surprise wanted to assault a shoe making, thinking that I by be intelligent could disconnect it the alarm, but already angry remove the keys of the auto to go back and return to it dealer of cars after go to my house, by assumed that was angry they said that in the trunk had two kilograms of marijuana for deliver it and that he would pay his owe, do not listen to them and follow road to the dealer.

An auto that past the red signal running fast hit us, after the scare try to drive far from that place, but the auto stopped, immediately Jaime and the Cricket came out fleeing without wait for me so I ran in opposite way, after a persecution of 12 or 15 bloks not remember exactly achieved escape of the police, running all the way to the business of my mother and her partner, a restaurant bar. Jaime and Cricket to be saved according to said that I was head of the band forcing them to steal and distribute drugs reason why I became a fugitive.

Abandoning the town sheltering me in a distant small port city dedicated to work and play football like I used to. Virginia and I stayed submerged in the sadness, she believed in my innocence, but should be away one of the other, our love is increased continuing the romance during 12 months so us wrote almost to daily, sometimes I called by phone saying that would be together soon.

Later authorities found that the driver of the auto with that impact us was drunk, and drugged, a video showed that he never saw the red signal causing the accident, the car dealer showed that the auto that I drove not was stolen only use it without permission of the dealer, Jaime and the Cricket confessed that I not had nothing to do with the drug found in the auto. Acquitted of the charges I can go back home and continue with my studies and romance. Was very sad know that Virginia refuses marry with me because she does not like to be far of her family, so I need to let the place where I had a good job and an economic secured future.

MR. LONELY AGAIN
SAD STORY OF AN IMPOSSIBLE DREAM

Already back in the big city continue the romance coming to the sexual stage, we loved so much when she got pregnant and let me know that, it was pretty news because we could get married and be together forever, she only said that she wanted to abort reason why I decided to respect her decision because it was her body, sadness me however because it was the second time that rejected being my wife. We went to a clinical of abortions making us a couple more than it statistics of abortions in the country, as I wanted took responsibility of the expenses, I stay with her all time without release her hand. After sleep and rest some hours we back to the house with her family that learned that was sick and I accompanied to the doctor. I went to my house and cried because had been happy of turn me on father.

Discovered that when a couple leads to out an abortion for cover social appearances the emotional damage feels by life, something it dies within the couple, I not I recover of have killed an innocent creature. I became in a criminal paying so carried out the crime, hiding that evil action four decades until today. Their sisters Teresa and Georgina search freedom and they were changing of work to work in several banking branches, so began to enjoy to meet friends and new friends of another branch making a relationship, exaggerated freedom where began to smoke, drink alcohol, and more bad habits, they did not do before, of course the family do not know, but they do more and more frequent.

Affecting our relationship because Virginia, also went to work to a bank branch to follow their sisters and friends, behaving as them, reducing the time to be together to the minimum.

She involves in all their activities out of the work, trying to me as if I out little thing, as if those people of the bank were superior to me, never knew that aspect. Taking advantage of the time extra that she gave.

Finish my studies working in the National Tourist devoted to the design and public relations activities. Started to handle my own money that turned out to easy of win, because had time and ability to perform infinity of tourist events inside and out of the country, starting to travel to the foreign countries and need learn languages, first French, then English, indeed, to Virginia I invites to study English with me and pay the course for both in the Anglo Mexican of Culture a College quite recognized in the teaching of the language English. We went the first and second course, but no more because Virginia chose to go with Teresa, Georgina and friends to have fun. Meanwhile, I kept growing me intellectually and economically, Virginia rather than be proud of me, it felt offended, because for graduates and smart no one could compare to his brothers, I never knew what was the problem because I was not competing with them nor with anyone, only myself to try to climb positions in the National Tourist Council as a result got first level relations, useful in all work.

Our relationship exceeded them seven years being each time more stormy for both, her father said that was time to formalize our relationship, and as Virginia always obeyed to her father decided to marry with me although not was of its pleasure or in the time just for she, since not wanted to marry with me but accept because believed is pregnant and not wanted to pass by the pain of another abortion, when married returned to the normally not having real pregnant but already was married not liking her the sacrifice vain of join is to me by life. Because of the wedding, by means of an economic arrangement, I paid to her family to be in the destroyed condominium that was the family residence and that would be our home. I took near two months to remodel it and repair it, because those ceilings are had to install new, as well as the floor, including doors and windows, to leave it in conditions to be inhabited. Then the painting, the furnishing and the decoration that included forty-seven pictures of art.

MR. LONELY AGAIN
SAD STORY OF AN IMPOSSIBLE DREAM

All them framed in aluminum and with crystal anti reflective for an investment total of $60,000 dollars approximately. Only two pictures were work mine and send to make an art and craft the style Huichol made by an artist originating of the Nayarit state that it made with string and wax as great, thence made other 5 pictures more to give like special gift to different personalities between them to the reporter in chief of the first morning news program Mr. Guillermo Ochoa and Lourdes Guerrero presenting to the ingenious artist in national network being a tourist and cultural promotion for the Nayarit state. Also had a TV segment weekly from 15 minutes to present tourist aspects from Mexico during 12 months.

Were 43 pictures of artists like, Vasarelli, Stewart Moskowits, all them representatives of the modern art contemporary with fame international, my goal was go replacing each copy by original as a gift to Virginia and heritage for our children. Was a dream difficult of achieve, but not impossible because the price of the pictures was accessible since saving could buy one or two by those first two years, after taking more contracts and experience perhaps 5 by year. Seemed madness, but I not had pictures of Picasso or of Miguel Angel so would be an adventure beautiful, achieve the serious show the love to Virginia by all the time that would have spent together. In the apartment, I went to live and work, because I installed a Design Studio with which obtained income, since I began to have more and more contracts with the National Tourist Council taking care of international events traveling abroad frequently.

When us married, Virginia make copies of the keys of the house and gave a set of keys to each member of her family, something as well as sixteen sets of keys. The honey moon in California was a fast trip, since asked only three days in the bank, because for her was important back to the work soon as possible. In San Francisco and its surroundings, us are dedicated by three days to buy gifts for each one of the members of her family, making our honey moon in a shopping trip.

148

ADVENTURES OF PHILOSOPHIC REFLECTION
SAD STORY OF AN IMPOSSIBLE DREAM

Without visit a romantic place, dinner or dance, only shopping for the day and nights to sleep by the exhaustion of choose gifts. A time already installed in the apartment, I was happy dedicated Monday to Friday early mornings to prepare her the shower so when she is awake had list the hot water for bathing, I cooked the breakfast and kissed her when was leaving to their daily work. Virginia decided to continue working, because was very clear when said that she never would depend on of me, as an offense to depend of me. Already married the afternoon, or the evenings, if I wanted to eat with Virginia, it was possible if I moved to the restaurant that co-workers had chosen to then leave and continue each person with our own work. By the nights the apartment was filled with the presence of their sisters, boyfriends and friends that entertained smoking and talking until the hour in that passed Irma with her car to give a ride to their house.

The weekends, we translate from Friday to their parents staying until the evening of Sunday, without having outings to the movies or to dinner, except if Teresa and Georgina wanted to go to the cinema, dancing or dining, then Virginia wanted to go out with me or without me, always was the same, so I choose to let her go with her family from the Friday night, leaving me in house with Kicho and Kimba my two Siamese cats, going to eat at the house of my mother that lived to only two bloks of the apartment. When I traveled and returned home, the apartment become in private party, course were Teresa, Georgina, friends and boyfriends of the bank, without scare nor remorse, saw me and say good bye leaving alone with Virginia I never said anything because not knew what think, or that could tell if was clear what passed in my absence. The apartment always I was taking care, paying all the expenses, including the cleaning services, washing and ironing clothes that were a day and delivered it the next day, toward the pantry shopping because it was still cooking breakfast for her and cooking for me because I ate and dined alone.

MR. LONELY AGAIN
SAD STORY OF AN IMPOSSIBLE DREAM

Since Virginia was eating and dining as always with her sisters and friends of the bank. That was my marriage life by the twelve first months. I remember already married to prepare an event with Aero Mexico Airline at the luxurious hotel City of Mexico, where I prepare its annual report activities and a gala dinner, involved the government, private industry with the personalities of the tourist environment of the country. Was invited Miss Aero Mexico, Miss city of Mexico, Miss Latin America, and many beautiful women. giving aspect of beauty contest. Virginia accept to go and wore an outfit elegant as was her way, she shows with so much class and so pretty, I remember with pride as all looked at her overshadowing in certain grade to several of the beauties present. Every one congratulated me, because had for wife a beautiful woman was something wonderful, but we returned early to the house, because the following day, she had to go to the bank to work.

Later, did friendship with the husband of a friend of Virginia that worked in the same branch of the bank, with them enjoyed a bit the life in couple because they invited to go out, so nice meet that couple of wonderful friends. Him and I, played football on Sundays with one of my brothers-in-law, so went out on weekends to ride, lunch, dinner, etc. and the Sunday morning were the four to the game of football, and only to the end of the game went to the home of the parents of Virginia, so we stayed together on weekends. The friendship grew between us, our wives went to the women's team of volleyball, from the bench, we, supporting them, training and course to the games where participating. Virginia, at home I helped to train, they played so well and increasingly better which were crowned champions of the tournament, which was beautiful an almost incredible achievement because they started very bad, nobody believed in them, except us and at the end were the champions, "wow that beautiful memory". Of course we went to celebrate the four, so our married life was better than in the beginning.

ADVENTURES OF PHILOSOPHIC REFLECTION
SAD STORY OF AN IMPOSSIBLE DREAM

A player of the football team, I did don not know that Virginia was going to have a baby, already he congratulates me I thanked acting as if I knew the news. At the end of the game, I went to her parent's house, finding me out that everyone knew of her pregnancy except me, when I asked her why I wasn't the first to know, responded with anger that was subject of her and no matter what I think. She became with pregnancy because his father told her that when will have a grandchild, so it would give him because was due as good daughter who was. Each month or before, I accompanied her to the doctor to see that all was well, cause of the pregnancy, Virginia spent more time in house of her family. So I went to visit her as when you visit a sick friend but was not my friend, nor was sick, was my wife! I kept working and traveling, the distance grew to such grade, that lost the notion of the reality or not opposite the reality that two of us near a pastry, mention that, if could have a cake for her birthday, I answer yes. We immediately bought it, we went to her family house with the cake and celebrate her birthday.

There was a time in that had given my life by her and, however, that time not remember that was her birthday, was sad, because was the signal of that began to the final. Time before birth the baby, Virginia told me that the baby could not be in the apartment unless they were not cats, already I imagine if wanting the baby at home, I went to visit a friend who begged and begged that he wanted my cats, so to his pleasant surprise I give him with their toys and bed, so kicho and kimba were to give to the stranger house, imagine that cry as small child, feeling me in a way that not knew it was good or bad by what did, of there in forward ate and dined only, because not were with me kicho and kimba. I went to the hospital where would be born the baby, her family was present, as well as my mother, after long hours of waiting, we were informed that the baby had been born and was a boy, everyone rushed to see the baby to the top floor, I asking how was her, because I was concerned, since I felt happy when they said that she was well, only slept because of the anesthesia.

MR. LONELY AGAIN
SAD STORY OF AN IMPOSSIBLE DREAM

Running went to see her, was asleep, but she looks so pretty that taking their hands and kissing her, I thanked that perhaps without deserve it she had given me a son, then went the others seeing to the baby through a crystal, being amazed by it nice that was. Next day, I went happy to the hospital to pick up the baby and Virginia, but her family will take both to the family home because they would take care of them and were better than me. I went to pay the hospital bill, almost had to fight with one of his older brothers because he insisted to pay the bill, explain that it had saved the money long ago, I knew that it was my responsibility and I didn't see well because they had to pay so, without listening the protests, pay all of the costs. They carried Virginia and the baby, as well as those floral arrangements, abandoning in the hospital the arrangements giving by my mother and me. I went to visit her to their parents' house, they offered I can stay with them all the time that I would like to, but do I not accept, because I had to be in the apartment having work to do in my design studio. the big sisters Cristina and Yolanda, signed by me and gave me money to buy photomechanical camera, to grow my design business.

After few time I paid thanking for the help, the problem were the younger sisters that by lack of freedom in their house and by the excess of debauchery to which is accustomed, took advantage of the excuse of that came with Virginia and that were in the apartment, but not said that was their refuge loving involving it smoke, and drink alcohol, went I return of my business travel the house was converted into a private bank's party. The soon, Virginia returned to work at the bank, but remained living in her parent's house, so I visited the baby while Virginia was working, when I was in the apartment with the baby, because she went to the doctor, so we finally were together the baby and me, had to go to the National Tourist Council so taking diapers, bottles and the baby I went to work. In the offices of the National Tourist Council all were happy to see me with my baby.

ADVENTURES OF PHILOSOPHIC REFLECTION
SAD STORY OF AN IMPOSSIBLE DREAM

With the visit of my baby, returned to house and later in the evening she went back to pick up the baby going to the parent house. By second occasion happened it same Virginia was to the doctor and leave the baby with me, I having that go to the National Tourism Council, take to the baby with my Mom, already as imagine my mother turned crazy of happiness with the baby and I went to work, meanwhile Virginia was angry to pick up to the baby. I ask, that when do the official baby name civil registry, let me know in advance because as I was traveling I wanted to know when we would do so, I expressed to her my desire to do together, she answer that there was no hurry and that it would make me know when, few days later travel abroad and upon my return, I found out that she took the baby without me so, on his birth certificate, was not my signature as it should be, by assumed that you claim, but got by response, that was her son and with her signature enough.

I lost the interest of track involved in a fake marriage, so I told her that we had to fix the situation or get a divorce, she chose divorce. Mention her that, to get married, we speak with her parents, so for the divorce, we should talk to them. We met in house of her parents, his father, Virginia and me, acting the father as mediator. I told him everything that happened in the apartment in my absence, of course was upset and he does not like to know something so unpleasant in her minor daughters, although he already had evidence of their behavior. Virginia said that I had the apartment full of friends, answer that not was true since had employees, schedule work from 9:00 am to 5:00 pm of worked in my study and sure were friends of mine, one of them, was boyfriend of Teresa friend of their sisters and by him we met us, the other was the best friend of Alejandro one of their older brothers of her, in addition he was friend of her family the parent of her knows him for long time ago and he is a good person is because after work together we became in friends.

MR. LONELY AGAIN
SAD STORY OF AN IMPOSSIBLE DREAM

Virginia said that I was a useless and that "I not served her as a man" at that time no I was not answer her, because the only thing that could answer would have been "compared with whom" so I choose to understand what she meant and I told her father I wanted to divorce. Her Father said both fail, because we do not respect the apartment that represented our home, which we should think about things before you get a divorce, but that there was no other solution, he guaranteed me divorce and my freedom because it expresses that just wanted to be free and not be tied up in a union without sense. Virginia continued offending me threatening that she would never let me see to the baby or my mother, that divorce would give me with the condition that disappeared forever, I replied yes sure I will disappear forever.

Something dirty, was that had the brazenness of losing me, ask to leave the apartment because Jorge one of her brothers that took fast wedding, and lived with their parents, needed the apartment, so would have that get me, without import what had spent in remodel it, furnish it, decorate it etc. by a value approximate of $60,000 dollars, so I would have that be the involuntary sponsor house for her brother, which never thanked me, or returned the money that I invested. After the birth of the baby, Virginia was with her parents and as magic suspended the parties in my house, so was clear, it planned in advance and she only likes that I leave. Picked up my things from work, clothes, and records, leaving my ring of marriage, in the drawer where kept personal things. Went to the business of her father, and delivering him the keys of the apartment, he did know that not I never back again.

I went to live to my mother house, meanwhile Jorge the brother of her and her wife were to live in my house, prepared my split final of the country, since live in the same place not would be suitable, went the loser in that romantic history.

SAD STORY OF AN IMPOSSIBLE DREAM

Alone, without wife, without baby, without house, without place for work, even without my beloved kicho and kimba. I continuous traveling, preparing my output of the country, but to my return, visited to the baby carrying him gifts, clothing, and money, Cristina her sister more I saw and was well, because knew that was nice that visit the baby and be responsible. Sometimes I went to the bank, to leave Virginia with money for the baby, because the bank was near the National Tourism Council, she accepted the money forces mentioning that her didn't need anything from me, in the end, it showed a hatred never seen on her face, or at least so I felt it. Weeks before my final departure, the couple of friends, looking for a way to reconcile us, were a weekend, by Virginia and the baby. Then passed by me so together we were, went shopping, to eat, buy dinner to go to their house to spend the night. All the time did I spend with the baby and buy things for him, I was not rude at any time, but avoided talk to Virginia That night we lay, but the baby lay down it in the middle of the two us, by common agreement and talk about things that already had no remedy, because we were two strangers.

I mention, was ready to go, with the wish of remain in the United States and not return more than of visit. Virginia said that if I wanted to, she would go with me, but I did not believe her, I replied that she could not be away from his family. I thought for sure the father had said that it had to be with me and as she obeyed told me, but didn't make it, so sure she would leave me at the first opportunity she had, not to mention more we slept that night as enemies.

If she must want to be with me, why not said don not go, let's go back to our apartment to continue with our marriage. Sure that no way to do because there lived Jorge his brother and her sister-in-law. Follow me, was to be sure is of that came out of the country and then leave me. To the dawn, our friends were surprised because expected wishing that had arranged our differences.

MR. LONELY AGAIN
SAD STORY OF AN IMPOSSIBLE DREAM

But not happen like that so I ask them that please take us to our respective houses. In silence we went first to my mother house, dismissing me from her, as well as of the baby knowing that was the final goodbye. Days after, wanted to dismiss me from Virginia and the baby because my departure was scheduled for the next day, talk by phone according to meet in her parent's house, when I was there, I asked her to go out of the house, because the last time we were inside behaved rudely humiliating me, but she sent to tell me with of his brothers-in-law, that she not talk with me outside of the house, replied that would expect outside and that of not exit I would understand and go without disturbing her. Don't know how much time wait, perhaps 30 minutes, not remember exactly the time, convinced of that not would be outside I leave, after that makes many years, during which not returned to see them, even in the few occasions that returned to the country for visit my mother, or when went to pick up my mother to bring to live with me. Never visit them, because I saw in Virginia a hatred so large that it was hurting my feelings, I couldn't believe, that she was the same sweet person, only I saw a person with destructive hatred. I was sure, that she had married and the baby it had deceived with that I not exist.

And the husband of her was his real father, I thought not to destroy the life of the baby, he had father and mother, as well a family, was preferable meet the wish disappearing of their lives, also his father gave me freedom because to the house of my mother, came an act of divorce at the time left the country to live in a foreign country. I remembered both on their birthday, mentally sent them hugs and kisses, wanting and believing that they were well, I knew that there was no need, so made me feel it, was my mistake by accepting their status as disappear from their lives, I was stupid and inexperienced in everything that happened between us. Not all was bad in our relationship, I think that had married three years before when I was asked her, or never marry and forget about us because in real we were wrong to marry without real love.

ADVENTURES OF PHILOSOPHIC REFLECTION
SAD STORY OF AN IMPOSSIBLE DREAM

By assumed that I behave badly, since smoked marijuana, in the house during the time that Virginia was outside working, or in the house of her family, at the end, thought have perfect excuse, but not was so simply me sinking in that addiction and in sadness that not was justification, but for me in that moment of clumsiness it was. in my work and contracts, I behave professional, not presenting me with the bad habit, not in those events or exhibitions, inside and out of the country. She was with their sisters Teresa, Georgina and friends of the bank, and I with the addiction, we went walking every time more far one of the other until our separation end.

Already in the foreign country, with little money, without work, not counting with the permanent residence only with a tourist visa, had a start difficult, also the sadness of having it lost, as well as to the baby and far away from my mother. Was painful, because after live with Virginia by ten long years, not knew how be without her and without to talk her, learned to walk in the rain, because nobody notices that crying. Not blame to anyone, not me whining with no one, only wait to the things change. was trapped in the time in what lived with her, movies, music, all it of that time around me, to the grade of that had The Beatles room, where had books that she gave me because are part of that wonderful life that lived with her, remember as ran desperately for get full-time and see it out of their work with their older sisters, remember those Sundays where talked as lovers, those walks with hands intertwined, trapped in those times but was my decision.

Here comes the sad thing in this story, I was linking every detail of our relationship by discovering the truth which conceals up to today where I will say the truth that I am furious throughout my existence. When we got married she was crying while I was happy why? because she doesn't want to marry me, but fear of abortion again for that reason continue with the lie and marry me. Do not stop working was that she doesn't want to engage with me economically.

MR. LONELY AGAIN
SAD STORY OF AN IMPOSSIBLE DREAM

All her sisters when marry, never work again, but she does not. Honeymoon was only three days because she needed to return the bank to demonstrate to her boyfriend, that married with me only to cover appearances. Register in the civil records the baby in my absence was that not wanted my signature by not be the father of the baby. to only 12 months that was born a nephew called Jorge Alberto however our baby she called Sergio Alberto, why another Alberto? because in the bank had an Alberto waiting my disappearance to say he was the real father. In the hospital chose cesarean section surgery because of that way I not enter to the operating room I was not the indicated to be in the birth of her son because was not mine. her family knew the truth because that's they wanted to pay the hospital bill betrayed as something was wrong. took her and the baby to their house almost to hidden betrayed that had fear that I will find the true and vandalized or something by the style.

In reality were so many signs that I knew immediately, I wanted to be a gentleman and I said nothing, but as soon as she recovered she ran to the bank to follow her romantic history in which I was outside, later asked me the apartment because she wanted to eliminate me from the scene but hypocritically and to cover themselves to society, I left her I was to leave home, leave to the baby without father, sure that so not was but is what the family is commissioned of manifest to cover their dirty way of acting against me. The only time that she invested money in the apartment was when bought a book shelves wall to wall for the books of their brothers as preparing the moment that already not would be in that house.

May list more situations that checked that dirty maneuver of she and her family against me, imagine betrayed in what could be reason for me suicide, she stole my apartment where I lived leaving me in the street, there same had my study where worked so I was without place for work ruining my economy.

ADVENTURES OF PHILOSOPHIC REFLECTION
SAD STORY OF AN IMPOSSIBLE DREAM

Was a conspiracy family making me know that were very united until in it bad and miserable because were dirty and not the earned be a family respectable, I not did nothing to unmask them because primarily I was a gentleman and I took pride to be better than them because they did so dirty action. I had a hard life because it was broken by separation and so elaborate treachery against me and creating the story that I was bad and that I left my son. I take to travel by the Mediterranean Sea dedicating me to interpret music of The Beatles, Joan Manuel Serrat, July Iglesias, Mocedades, etc. in Ferris and cruises that were my refuge because had home, food, work traveling by Africa, Europe discovering places and people extremely interesting so was my distraction live so during my first 10 years after divorce. Later I return to the National Tourist Council national as representative for tourist and commerce of Mexico in the foreign countries with diplomatic missions around the world by 25 years until get to the removal early in Houston, TX and return to my activity musical for enjoy the last years of my life doing what more I like providing satisfaction to my life.

During all that time suffered because I miss Virginia looking to be happy and that my sacrifice would have been the best for her and her baby. would there is a song by the Beatles which is called "when you have 64" made me fantastic reaches that age, but I thought why the number 64? "? As well 6 and 4 are 10 one and zero are 1 so thought that it came to that age serious the moment of discover my painful penalty that loaded to my backs for almost 40 years. I discovered that the number 1 was where should discover that sad history for abandon it for always and be happy by the rest of my days, that is why I am narrating to be written and shared as the sacrifice of a simple human with goodness, worthy of respect because the people I met as a person honorable although my look always was sad but provide joy to all them people and more to perform the music with all the quality obtained with prior so many musicians that filled my life music with joy and fun anecdotes.

MR. LONELY AGAIN
SAD STORY OF AN IMPOSSIBLE DREAM

Then I did a pause while the mirror man wiped tears from his face that reflected a deep sadness but which finally had been stripped of that truth which gave pain for so many decades. He apologized by have shown weak, but smiled and said that the truth leaves of hurt it because actually Virginia and his family could shame, but not him, the honor and respect shown during his existence was more valuable that all what she had stolen. He said, if I liked the story, had his permission to write it, but without mentioning his name, that from the beginning I knew that should thus be to not provoke an image of man suffered, because he was all suffered less, suede my eyes a victim does not revenge, no grudges against anyone so it was respected as a person and all a good man.

They were beautiful weeks during his interesting story, I wonder elegance with their raincoats, jackets, bags, and their hats Italian style berets that gave a touch of distinction, in the end, we say goodbye knowing that was the end of those meetings and that it would never see like all the characters in my stories, so after a hug we walk opposite paths. Already at home with the new complete story to add it to my book as the last chapter having as a goal post it once and for all. At front of the mirror I took off my elegant wrap, Italian style beret who wore that day and watching my figure who still showed far elegance by the age I said goodbye to my life being happy with my memories.

Is beautiful not grudge anyone regardless of all the bad things you do with or without reason, when you love someone are able to make you aside thinking that it will be happy, by the way, the friend who introduced me to Virginia let me know that she never married and her romance was not happy being alone like me, so nothing earned her perverse action because she did not deserve to be happy.

The happiness is gained based on sacrifices and will that never was, to me that was easy because it became my way of living day to day.

END OF VOLUME I

The people them saw smile, Kissing and go lovingly embraced by them corners of streets, trails, villages, and city, sharing their lives alone to the rhythm of the love that was the chain for live happily condemned to the romance splendid that never them abandonment. dedicated to lovingly raise their children who were fearful of flying as all children birds with broken wings, but they sheltered them with their love becoming the wind that pushed them to be birds flying height faced all his fears recalling loving parents example.

Even alone in the twilight of their lives continued awakening with the golden sunrise bathed with intense yellow tones reminding them that they were together to start another day of happiness and shared struggle to wait for the sunset where the sky turned into a show full of colors of honey with blue announcing the arrival of the nights on which gave rein to the love that brought together them until the end of their days. it was not the real end of this story, on the contrary, was the beginning of my eternal loneliness waiting for her with the same emotion that when we played that we loved. I will remember her beautiful eyes, her smile with that shine carrying me to the world of the most sublime emotions a human being can feel, I know that I love her as I cannot love anyone more.

She dangerously beautiful live in me until the last beating of my heart, her beautiful memories will keep shining my eyes, will I still be Mr. Lonely Again to tell stories and adventures. Love is a soul in two bodies that is looking madly for love is without conditions, joining is as an only one body, an only one spirit condemning is mutually to live and suffer by their love, following the rhythm of their hearts because the universe conjures and is leans with respect in favor of which is love.

End of the Volume I
Volume II in the summer of 2017

Don Triste Otra Vez

Aventuras De Reflexion Filosofica
Volumen I

Nino Plazola

Traducciones De
Albert Nino y Rega Lupo

Correcciones Y Prueba De Lectura
Patricia Miramontes

AuthorHouse™
1663 Liberty Drive
Bloomington, IN 47403
www.authorhouse.com
Teléfono: 1 (800) 839-8640

Titulo Original
On Time With Mr. Lonely

Primera Edicion Volumen I
Invierno Del 2016

Audio Libro
Invierno Del 2016

Certificado De Registro
TXU1-167-111 OFICINA DE REGISTROS DE LOS ESTADOS UNIDOS DE AMERICA

2004 Registro Y Derechos De Autor
Nino E. Plazola

2004 Registro Y Derechos De La Traduccion
Albert Nino

Impreso En
Estados Unidos De America

Publicada por AuthorHouse 09/14/2016

ISBN: 978-1-5246-3942-6 (tapa blanda)
ISBN: 978-1-5246-3940-2 (tapa dura)
ISBN: 978-1-5246-3941-9 (libro electrónico)

Numero de la Libreria del Congreso: 2016915115

Información sobre impresión disponible en la última página.

AGRADECIMIENTOS

A Mis Queridos Hijos.................................... **Albert, Allen Y Alvin**
A Mi Comprensiva Madre .... **Arminda Plazola**
A Mi Querida Tia .... **Irma Medina**
A Mi Querido Tio .... **Mario Alberti**
A Mi Amigo De Toda La Vida .... **Villi Ardavin**
A Mi Adorable Bella Dama ....**Yadira Vargas**

A todos ellos les agradezco el haber puesto sus talentos, en rescate y ayuda de alguien que no es escritor, por darme el valor de realizar y producir un formato único de comunicación en dos idiomas por medio de la escritura.

A todos aquellos seres culpables o no que han perdido su libertad, a los que han perdido a sus seres queridos, a los que han perdido sus bienes y fortuna, a los que han caído en las drogas y que no han podido recuperarse, a los desamparados que no tienen un lugar donde habitar.

A todos los enfermos desahuciados, a las madres solteras, a los ancianos solitarios, a los pobres, a los que trabajan limpiando calles, a todos aquellos seres que día a día luchan y sobreviven sin preguntar ni saber que les depara el mañana sería agradable que este servidor tenga un día la oportunidad de leer este humilde libro a todos estos seres maravillosos como muestra de cariño y respeto.

A todos ellos les dedico este libro

SOLO UNA NOTA

Cuando hablamos de Mr. Lonely, su traducción correcta sería Don Solitario, pero suena como nombre de asociación musical o nombre de luchador, por lo que decidí llamarlo Don Triste para facilitar la idea del personaje. La traducción de Don Triste al idioma inglés sería Mr. Blue, pero no es el nombre que se le quiere dar en esta historia, no quiero confundir a nadie con estas traducciones, solo quiero informar porque se le llamo intencionalmente Mr. Lonely en inglés y Don Triste en castellano sin ser éste un error de traducción. Gracias por su comprensión esperando quede claro este enredo de traducción literaria.

Pensamiento

La obscuridad no existe es solo ausencia de luz, el frío no existe es solo ausencia de calor, lo negro no existe es solo ausencia de separación de color, la ignorancia no existe es solo ausencia de conocimiento, la intolerancia no existe es solo ausencia de comprensión.

Así mismo el mal no existe es solo ausencia de dios, no lo culpes a él de los males que te acechan, no lo culpes de los crímenes ni de las tragedias de la vida, es solo la ausencia de dios lo que afecta nuestras vidas esto lo dijo Albert Einstein cuando era joven.

Don Triste vivió en un mundo donde la ausencia de Dios era marcada y acentuada por lo tanto él no creyó en Dios, nunca rezó, pero solo fue por ausencia, será una lección para que no te pase lo mismo evita estar del lado de la ausencia.

INDICE

Introduccion.. 171

Benito Barrio De La Amistad................................. 173

La Ley 177

El Trapero 183

Artista O Ladron.. 186

El Sabio Perkins... 191

El Boxeador 203

Una Luz En Los Ojos 207

La Busqueda 214

El Muro Y La Fe..220

Las Botas Amarillas...226

El Fenomeno Del Uka Puka...................................239

La Verdad Y Solo La Verdad..................................245

Historia Triste De Un Sueño Imposible......................271

INTRODUCCION

Durante siglos el hombre ha buscado por todos los medios; felicidad, riqueza, salud y juventud eterna.

Las guerras, enfermedades y desastres naturales han contribuido a obstruir la búsqueda de todos estos ideales, pero a pesar de todo y contra todo, grandes hombres y filósofos los han encontrado, en ocasiones los han dado a conocer como descubrimientos para bien de la humanidad.

Esta es la historia de un hombre sencillo con una visión filosófica cercana a la fantasía, pero con un punto de vista único y especial que nos hará recordar épocas de nuestra vida que nunca se repetirán, pero estarán siempre presentes en nuestros corazones porque él habla de amistad, fe, amor y sobre todo de esperanza para todos aquellos que han perdido el único camino correcto a seguir, el de la felicidad.

Don Triste y su magia nos transportarán al mundo de lo inesperado, con situaciones dramáticas y en ocasiones divertidas pero extraordinarias en todo momento, con soluciones y equívocos que nos harán reír y pensar de forma diferente, porque estaremos viajando por el mundo de Don Triste.

Tengan listos sus pasaportes para viajar por caminos misteriosos, llenos de personajes increíbles por su maldad y otros por su bondad que identificaras con conocidos tuyos, pero recuerda cualquier parecido con personajes reales es coincidencia pura, o pura realidad.

Pensamiento
Viajar es la oportunidad de ver la vida con los ojos de otros, pensar y desarrollar ideas con la mente de otros, descubrir el mundo y sus variedades con el asombro y conocimiento de otros, pero recuerda lo más importante, nunca cambies sigue siendo el mismo para ti y para asombro de otros.

BENITO BARRIO DE LA AMISTAD

Dónde y cuándo nace Don Triste, fue hace demasiado tiempo, en "Benito barrio de la amistad", esquina con desesperanza, del sector del espanto en el país de la fe, continente del sueño, Don Triste nace como un miembro más de una familia de pescadores y restauranteros dedicados secretamente al turbio negocio de la mafia. Sus padres viajaban mucho, en especial su padre que era un diplomático contratado por un país extranjero que rápidamente le concedió la ciudadanía, por ese motivo trasladaron su residencia a América, su vida era divertida, sana y serena todo gracias a la sabiduría natural de su progenitora la cual procuró siempre darle lo mejor de todo.

Cuando Don Triste tenía dos años de edad su padre fue desaparecido, posiblemente asesinado tan solo por venganza política relacionada con su trabajo, razón por la cual su madre decidió darle a Don Triste educación en su país natal regresándolo solo por los veranos a su lado, mientras ella permaneció en el mismo sitio con la esperanza de que su esposo apareciera y todo hubiese sido un percance menor, pero no fue así ya que él desapareció para siempre. Don Triste viajaba de América a Europa y viceversa desde la temprana edad de seis años. Su infancia fue divertida y normal residiendo con su tío en diferentes ciudades, escuelas e internados, tanto religiosos como militares. Así transcurrieron sus primeros diez años de vida estudiando cultura y religión. Creándole el temor a Dios como un ser supremo, castigador y revanchista.

En los diferentes barrios y escuelas fue popular, admirado, repudiado, envidiado por propios y extraños tenía agudeza mental y una especial habilidad analítica para; deportes, cultura, travesuras, etc. Usaba el cabello corto y su delgadez le daban un aspecto simpático y divertido al mismo tiempo, él era un niño y el sexo opuesto llamaban su atención a tal grado que participaba en ceremonias y ritos religiosos solo para estar cerca de las chicas más bonitas, que asistían a tan aburridos eventos en la iglesia.

DON TRISTE OTRA VEZ
BENITO BARRIO DE LA AMISTAD

Don Triste se robaba todas las flores de santos y vírgenes haciendo negocio vendiéndoselas a las chicas no muy bonitas y regalándoselas a las chicas bonitas, obteniendo sus favores y caricias descubriendo el extraño encanto que las flores ejercen sobre las mujeres. En su diario convivir en las iglesias descubrió como los sacerdotes manipulaban siempre a los feligreses, mostrando facilidad y habilidad con la que les mentían y estafaban, supuestamente todos los sacerdotes no debían tener relaciones amorosas, pero en realidad tenían amantes e hijos que según protegían por bondad, negando y ocultando su paternidad esto confundía a Don Triste.

Todo en la religión eran intereses, dinero, así como política, estafas e hipocresías, a, pero eso si todo en nombre de Dios y siempre amenazando con enviarte al infierno si no seguías las reglas, reglas que ellos hacían, pero no respetaban, en fin, era un juego sucio que había que aprender a jugar o callar, Don Triste optó por jugar, pero con sus propias reglas. Dedicaba parte de su tiempo libre a investigar las actividades ilícitas de los llamados sacerdotes, sus actividades tanto dentro como fuera de las iglesias comprobando como asesinaban, robaban y se involucraban en política con ministros de alto nivel para decidir el destino de la ciudad, el estado y el país siendo todo esto una actividad llena de atrocidades y miseria.

Después de investigar todo lo relacionado con religiones, Don Triste se aficionó a investigar y analizar a los gobiernos, maestros, escuelas, instituciones, empresas, políticos, etc. etc. Su mayor desilusión fue que la historia, los grandes libros escolares y culturales son solo escritos y aprobados por los mismos vencedores y conquistadores con intereses personales. Don Triste permaneció estudiando en Europa con su querido tío y durante los largos veranos en América con su mamá, ocasionalmente estudiaba en América y regresaba en el verano al lado de su tío, en fin, era un eterno viajar entre el joven continente y el anciano continente, la relación excelente sobrino-tío se volvió fuerte.

De mucho entendimiento y comprensión, siendo un verdadero gozo vivir bajo la protección de su tío Mario Alberti. La isla en la que vivían estaba dividida en cuatro sectores, cada sector era dominado por un protector, a su vez los cuatro protectores eran controlados por el padrino, máxima autoridad de la mafia, el padrino compartía y recibía poder ilimitado de las autoridades gubernamentales, así como de la Iglesia Católica, conformando una tripleta sumamente poderosa que controlaban el país, influyendo en actividades licitas e ilícitas en todo el mundo.

La sucesión de el padrino tema controversial inclusive tema de películas que no era tan complicado en realidad, ya que uno de los protectores el mejor se convertía en el sucesor siendo el nuevo padrino. Don Mario Alberti tío de Don Triste era el protector en el sector de la capital, siendo éste el más importante de los cuatro sectores, y el candidato más fuerte a suceder al padrino. La familia de Don Mario Alberti era grande, habitaban una casa de dos pisos que ocupaba toda una manzana, era tan hermosa como grande contaba con veintidós recámaras, diez baños, seis cocinas todas con sus respectivos comedores, cuatro salas, seis enormes estudios y un grandioso salón de reuniones.

El centro de la casa había un patio grande con un estacionamiento donde en promedio había veintiséis autos de todo tipo; deportivos, camionetas, modestos, lujosos y una limusina, la casa era resguardada por doce perros y un fuerte grupo de seguridad compuesto por gente leal a la familia por generaciones, en una esquina de la casa se encontraba ubicado un semi lujoso restaurante que por generaciones fue el negocio familiar llamado mi familia. A Don Mario Alberti era fácil encontrarlo en la oficina del restaurante, la cual era su centro de operaciones para todos sus negocios, los miembros que conformaban la familia poseían todo y para todos, por ejemplo.

DON TRISTE OTRA VEZ
BENITO BARRIO DE LA AMISTAD

Don Triste podía usar cualquier automóvil en cualquier momento, pero no decir o pensar que le pertenecía solo a él ya que les pertenecía a todos. Cuando un miembro de la familia se casaba su cónyuge pasaba a ser un miembro más de la familia, viniendo a residir en la casa, teniendo una recámara independiente pudiendo cocinar a su propio gusto en cualquiera de las cocinas, podía trabajar con Don Mario o recibir dinero para comenzar su propio negocio, o simplemente trabajar en el restaurante y tener un sueldo cómodo como todos, también podía hacer uso de cualquier automóvil del estacionamiento.

Pensamiento
Los familiares pueden ser tu felicidad o tu desdicha ¿cómo saber quiénes son los buenos para ti y cuáles no? No te atormentes con la elección, solo sigue tu corazón el resto es trabajo mutuo. La verdadera familia hace todo de común acuerdo el verdadero respeto y cariño se reconocen mutuamente.

LA LEY

Como es sabido por todos, el gobierno, y las instituciones que conforman la autoridad que rige, corrige, regula y orienta a la ciudadanía brindándole todo tipo de apoyo y protección, así como un sin número de servicios, pero esta ley tiene un precio por lo tanto se vende y se compra habiendo postores sin escrúpulos, en fin, esa es la impresión que le causó a Don Triste cuando involuntariamente enfrentó por vez primera a las autoridades. Don Triste acostumbraba caminar muy tarde solo no importándole que era un menor de edad, cierta noche en que iba camino a casa lo detuvo una camioneta oficial cerrada de color gris, supuestamente dedicada a proteger menores de edad recogiéndolos y trasladándolos a centros de protección, brindándoles abrigo, comida, educación y en el momento apropiado darles una familia, en pocas palabras se convertían en sujetos de adopción para no deambular por las calles solos y desprotegidos.

Don Triste les mencionó que tenía familia, así como un hogar, mostró identificaciones y sus libros escolares, pero aquellos representantes de la autoridad no escucharon y lo introdujeron a la sucia camioneta trasladándolo hasta un centro para detención de menores llamado hospicio. Ya en el centro de detención después de quitarle su dinero, reloj y todo lo de valor, se limitaron a enviarlo a un dormitorio con quién sabe cuántos menores más, diciéndole que se durmiera y al día siguiente aclararían su situación, en fin, ya muy cansado más que sorprendido, optó sólo por dormir donde pudo y como pudo. Serían cerca de las 6:00 a. m. del día siguiente cuando fue despertado por otro menor llamado Benito, diciéndole que se levantara, tendiera el sucio catre y se preparara para la ducha, Don Triste hizo lo que se le indicó al mismo tiempo que Benito, pero este último con un gran temor reflejado en el rostro. Entraron en el dormitorio seis jóvenes entre dieciséis y diecisiete años de edad, uno de ellos que parecía ser el líder ordenó a todos los pequeños quitarse la ropa, formar una línea y entrar a la zona de regaderas.

DON TRISTE OTRA VEZ
LA LEY

Todos ellos obedecían, pero llorando, uno tras otro fueron entrando al famoso baño siendo empujados salvajemente al interior de un pozo con agua helada en el que era imposible nadar, solo podían agarrarse de las orillas que eran resbalosas y para colmo los jóvenes encargados de cuidarlos continuaban castigándolos a cinturonazos. Apresurándose a cruzar el pozo como podían los grandes ayudaban a los más chicos, luego al salir del pozo llegaban a las regaderas. En donde continuaban recibiendo agua helada y al mismo tiempo el castigo de cinturonazos a diestra y siniestra, después regresaban al dormitorio para vestirse, pero a veces sus ropas desaparecían y para colmo sin secarse porque carecían de toallas, continuando el concierto de los cinturonazos encaminándolos hacia un feo patio para por fin desayunar.

Nuevamente formaban una larga línea para recibir charolas con pan y comida eran proporciones raquíticas, pero podían pagar y recibir comida extra pagando con botones de la ropa convertidos en moneda oficial. Don Triste entendió por qué todos carecían de botones en la ropa, los jóvenes encargados ostentaban largos collares con botones de todos colores con los cuales compraban cosas, recibían favores o evitaban castigos, Don Triste recordó que su sweater tenía botones metálicos dorados los cuales eran valiosos en ese lugar. Así que Benito y él comieron raciones extras ya que cambió los botones metálicos por cuatro collares de botones plásticos, después los acomodaron y sentaron junto a cien niños aproximadamente a tomar el sol sin salir del área asignada para tal acción, cuarenta metros cuadrados aproximadamente no permitiéndoles jugar ni salir del área solo para ir al baño, todo el día se asoleaban, luego comían realizando el trueque de los botones en todo momento.

Benito explicó a Don Triste que no sabía cuándo serían liberados ya que estaban incomunicados, sin recibir respuesta a sus múltiples súplicas de comunicarse con sus familiares, eso si los tenías porque de no tenerlos tu futuro era más que incierto.

Llegada la noche eran trasladados al dormitorio y al día siguiente se repetía el mismo ciclo. Don Triste y su nuevo amigo Benito vieron transcurrir cuatro días más sin saber nada acerca de su futuro que se veía incierto. Con tal de comer bien e ir al baño cuando querían Don Triste gastó uno de los collares de botones quedándole solo tres que cuando mucho durarían ocho días más y después ¿quién sabe? La situación comenzaba a ser critica ya que Don Triste tenía infección en un ojo, ya no tenía zapatos los cuales le habían sido robados, razón por la cual decidió hacer algo para escapar. Comunicó a Benito su idea y éste lo contacto con un joven de los locos encargados para tratar el asunto de la fuga, por unos cuantos botones les permitieron ir al baño durante aquella noche, supuestamente en busca de su libertad el lugar estaba iluminado por velas y un joven les explicó que tenían que vender su alma al diablo para escapar.

El joven tomó un gis, pintó en el piso un circulo y llenándolo de símbolos danzó e invocó al diablo, volviéndose grotesca la escena ya que el joven saco de entre sus ropas un pedazo de vidrio, luego cortándose su propia mano para embarrar de sangre los símbolos y el rostro de los que pretendían fugarse, que en ese momento eran ya varios. Benito y Don Triste huyeron al dormitorio, con la idea de buscar otra forma más segura y simple de escapar olvidándose de tan fea y rara ceremonia, a la mañana siguiente, después de bañarse no encontraron por ningún lado a los otros niños que participaron en la ceremonia de venta de almas al diablo, los jóvenes aseguraban que el diablo los liberó tal y como había sucedido con anterioridad.

Don Triste fingió estar sumamente enfermo siendo trasladado a la enfermería, una vez ahí puso en práctica los buenos trucos aprendidos en el barrio, forzando puertas y escritorios al fin encontró la información que le hizo saber dónde realmente se encontraba.

DON TRISTE OTRA VEZ
LA LEY

Siendo este un hospicio para menores llamado el número dos, que era controlado por las autoridades policíacas del sector norte de la ciudad. En la enfermería estaban los infantes y menores de cuatro años de edad los cuales eran sujetos de adopción, además encontró información que conectaba este centro con hospitales, en esos hospitales realizaban operaciones de trasplantes, siendo seguro que los niños eran los donadores de órganos y no de forma voluntaria ni con beneficio para el donante. Más tarde Don Triste fue incorporado al grupo de los asoleados, pero traía consigo papel y plumas que robó de la enfermería, escribió su nombre dirección y el número de teléfono de su tío, también la referencia del lugar donde se encontraba, realizó lo mismo en otro papel con los datos de Benito.

Luego pagando con botones compró más papel y escribió cientos de pequeñas notas con unas improvisadas cerbatanas de papel lanzaban las notas transformadas en dardos dirigidos contra aviones también de papel. Creando un divertido juego que los jóvenes que los cuidaban se unieron al mismo, con la diferencia que los dardos de Don Triste salían disparados volando sobre los altos muros que resguardaban el lugar. Durante tres días lanzaron dardos con notas en busca de su libertad claro todo pagado con botones, una señora vecina del lugar encontró una de las notas llamo al tío Mario Alberti, él se encontraba angustiado.

Por la desaparición de su sobrino, llevaba varios días buscándolo en hospitales y cárceles sin resultado, cuando recibió la llamada llorando de alegría se trasladó de inmediato al hospicio número dos del sector norte de la ciudad. Ya en aquel horrendo hospicio preguntó por su sobrino haciéndole saber que ahí se encontraba, pero no podían entregárselo porque Don Mario Alberti no era el padre o el custodio oficial, además tenían el plan de enviarlo a otro centro de detención siendo más difícil y complicado el trámite de liberación.

AVENTURAS DE REFLEXION FILOSOFICA
LA LEY

Don Mario les suplicó que le entregaran a su sobrino, pero las autoridades del siniestro lugar se lo negaron, ¿porque lo tenían preso? No se supo nunca, pero estaba en calidad de detenido, el tío ofreció mil dólares que traía consigo, pero requirieron cinco mil y solo de contado, después de escuchar la arbitraria decisión y no creerle quien era él se retiró sin decir más. En casa realizó ciertas llamadas telefónicas y minutos más tarde tenía disponibles dos camiones de asalto con treinta hombres armados, así como dos de sus autos con gente de toda su confianza listos a colaborar, después entraron al hospicio y golpeando salvajemente a los guardias lograron un ataque certero sometiendo a todos por la fuerza.

Al Oficial Mayor y máxima autoridad del lugar lo arrodillaron frente a Don Mario Alberti, éste le ordenó que le entregara a su sobrino o los mataría, minutos más tarde lo trajeron estando sucio, delgado sin zapatos, con huellas de maltrato además un ojo infectado en fin era un desastre, tío y sobrino se abrazaron Don Mario besándolo con mucho amor lo cargó intentando salir del lugar, pero su sobrino le habló de su amigo Benito, así como de los bebés en la enfermería. Los militares fueron informados del asunto por lo que mandaron un comando y camiones para arrestar a todo el personal del hospicio y detenerlos en un centro militar sin posibilidades de salir libres impunemente, luego de escuchar la terrible verdad del lugar, Don Mario Alberti dio órdenes para liberar a todos los niños, recogieron a los bebés de la enfermería y los archivos de identificación de todos ellos.

Salieron del lugar incendiándolo poco después entregaron a todos los menores en el hospital más cercano junto con todos los archivos para la posible identificación y localización de parientes. Al día siguiente Don Mario Alberti les ordenó al Alcalde y al Jefe de la Policía de la ciudad, desaparecer los otros tres hospicios, de no hacerlo amenazó con destruir a todas las familias de los involucrados en el sucio negocio. En realidad, lo que hacían era vender a los bebes.

DON TRISTE OTRA VEZ
LA LEY

Con el pretexto de la adopción y los demás eran sacrificados para vender sus órganos vitales. Todo esto fue realizado con gran facilidad e impunidad, ya que los bebés por ser tan chicos no podían recordar a sus familiares, los grandes fueron sacrificados con la ventaja de no tener familiares, o después de un tiempo prudente los daban por desaparecidos, hicieron experimentos con ellos lo mismo que a los judíos durante la segunda guerra mundial, nunca se pudo saber algo de los desaparecidos en las extrañas ceremonias, de venta de almas al diablo de seguro fueron sacrificados.

Por fin en el lapso de dos semanas todo llegó a su fin, se cerraron oficialmente y para siempre los hospicios de protección al menor, las huellas físicas del sufrimiento en Don Triste desaparecieron rápidamente con estos sucesos descubrió que su tío era un alto miembro activo de la mafia con poderes ilimitados. Siendo culpable de varios crímenes, pero con un amor enorme por su familia y amigos, todo mundo lo quería y respetaban solo lo envidiaba su competencia, de esta manera supo que su tío lo amaba y recordó como ayudaba a la gente necesitada siendo el ángel protector del barrio, así como de la ciudad.

La relación entre sobrino y tío se volvió más fuerte siendo mayor el entendimiento y mutua comprensión, siendo un verdadero placer vivir bajo la protección de su querido tío Don Mario Alberti.

Pensamiento

¿Qué es bueno, qué es malo? Son preguntas difíciles de contestar acertadamente y más difíciles de entender, los buenos por poco y lo matan, lo privaron de su libertad sin razón alguna, los malos según las leyes y a la mala lo liberaron sin condición alguna integrándolo a su vida normal, llenándolo de amor y al mismo tiempo de confusión.

EL TRAPERO

Don Triste conoció a uno de ellos, un hombre de la calle dedicado a levantar de la basura, papel, trapos, botellas de vidrio, botes y latas de todo tipo, para venderlos a tanto por kilogramo. La gente decía sin razón alguna que estos hombres raptaban menores e infantes para después venderlos o esclavizarlos trabajando para ellos, pero esto nunca se comprobó. Él trapero tenía su territorio propio el que recorría día tras día con sus inseparables amigos, doce perros pulgosos y sucios como él. Al finalizar la tarde, el trapero cruzaba por el barrio donde vivía Don Triste en camino a su dormitorio, que era en las afueras de un cine abandonado. Confeccionaba una fabulosa cama de papel, trapos, y perros, en la que dormían y cenaban desperdicios, sobras de comida y ocasionalmente piezas de pan.

Él trapero protector incondicional de sus doce apóstoles (los perros) a quienes platicaba, trataba con gran respeto y amistad como si en verdad se trataré de los doce apóstoles, ya que los llamaba como a cada uno de ellos; Pedro, Pablo, etc. Provocando especial curiosidad a Don Triste, que trató, conoció y respeto a ese singular, pero fascinante personaje que careció de nombre o nunca se lo dijo a nadie. Por las tardes Don Triste lo esperaba, con comida para él y sus doce apóstoles, lo que agradecía narrándole historias extraordinarias, así como fantasías y aventuras siempre maravillosas de todo tipo asegurando que eran absolutamente ciertas. Después de 300 tardes aproximadamente, ocurrió que Don Triste gasto dinero indebidamente, ya que estaba destinado para comprar un estuche de matemáticas, solicitado para clases con fecha límite y de no tenerlo se corría el riesgo de perder la clase y el semestre, razón de su gran tristeza. Cuando más triste y desesperado estaba, apareció el trapero y sus doce apóstoles como todas las tardes.

Él le pregunto si podía ayudar en algo, Don Triste contestó que por ser pobre era imposible que lo ayudara, pero por tanta insistencia le contó el problema.

DON TRISTE OTRA VEZ
EL TRAPERO

Después de escuchar atentamente a Don Triste, el trapero sacó de entre sus papeles y trapos un hermoso estuche de matemáticas de gran calidad y alto precio, argumentando que en la basura encuentras cosas útiles y bellas como el estuche tan necesario en ese momento.

Trapero lo abrazo y contó que la vida es un basurero gigante y que, en él, encontrarás cosas hermosas si buscas sin asco y con fe, pero tendrás que buscar con tu corazón siendo feliz con tus hallazgos. Esa maravillosa tarde, el trapero beso y bendijo a Don Triste deseándole buena noche como siempre, con la diferencia de que jamás se le volvió a ver y nadie jamás supo nada de él ni de sus doce apóstoles.

Desapareció para siempre del barrio y de la vida de Don Triste, pero el estuche de matemáticas permaneció a su lado como prueba de la existencia y bondad del trapero, filósofo maravilloso con porte de personaje histórico. Su regalo más grande no fue el estuche de matemáticas, lo valioso fueron las historias que narro a Don Triste, las que guardó en su corazón y mente porque provenían de un hombre justo y sabio llamado solo trapero.

Durante miles de días y noches, Don Triste sigue preguntándose a sí mismo ¿de dónde vendría el trapero? ¿a dónde se fueron él y sus apóstoles? ¿qué clase de ser especial era? Porque tipos así, no se encuentran todos los días. Respuestas nunca recibió, pero sigue creyendo que el mundo es un basurero gigante, en el que con fe un día encontrará al trapero, o quizás a otro igual de valioso e inteligente que el primero.

Donde quiera que estén él y sus doce apóstoles, Dios los cuide y conserve, porque Don Triste fue afortunado al conocerlo, ojalá otros lo conozcan y sean tan afortunados como él.

Pensamiento

La universidad de la vida aquella escuela de las calles, que tiene por maestros a los personajes más sorprendentes, egresados de la reconocida facultad de filosofía callejera, individuos que no tienen casa en que habitar.

Aquellos que conforman el mundo de los desamparados, no son fracasados ni tontos, solo escogieron vivir de una manera diferente renunciando a sí mismos. Siendo felices narrando historias, fantasías y viviendo solo el momento. Sin el temor o la preocupación del futuro, serán ellos los que se equivocaron al elegir, o ¿somos nosotros los equivocados?

ARTISTA O LADRON

Durante aquellos fantásticos tiempos, en que el mundo moderno conoció la televisión, el transistor, la carrera espacial, la guerra fría, a Marlín Monroe, Martín Luther King, Niñita Krushov, Mao Tse-tung, John Fitzgerald Kennedy, Cassius Clay, Edson Arantes do Nascimento "Pele", The Beatles, Boby Vinton, James Dean, The Rolling Stones, Stanley Kubrick, Dean Martín, y Frank Sinatra, entre otros. Fue la época en que Don Triste conoció a un pintor llamado Ruperto, no muy famoso pero sus obras se exhibían vendiéndose en las mejores y más prestigiadas galerías de arte de la ciudad capital. Ruperto era un fervoroso enamorado de la corriente impresionista, porque sus pinturas eran del más puro estilo impresionista, pero al parecer de Don Triste carecían de calidad, pero en fin el arte es el arte.

Ruperto disfrutaba todas las tardes, pintando y escuchando música de Rey Connie, Petula Clark, Tonny Benet, Beatles, etc. etc. Ese era el motivo por el que Don Triste hacía sus tareas escolares junto a Ruperto, para escuchar tan maravillosa música, así como narraciones contemporáneas acerca de artistas, política y deportes. Los comentarios acertados de Ruperto eran amenizados por suculentas cenas que él mismo cocinaba, demostrando que era mejor cocinero que pintor, según el parecer de Don Triste que era un criticón de primera. Don Triste solo correspondía aquella generosa atención para su persona, lavando los trastes y limpiando un poco el hogar de Ruperto, éste era un acuerdo silencioso de mutua aceptación, como parte del rito llamado amistad.

Eran amigos de todas las tardes reuniéndose con una sola meta, disfrutar la mutua compañía, compartir sus experiencias, e intercambiar ideas, opiniones, y bromas, hasta las 10:30 p. m. tiempo en que Don Triste se marchaba a dormir, para estar listo al día siguiente y asistir a la escuela. Don Triste confiaba todo a su amigo Ruperto, no importándole que era un hombre de cuarenta y cinco años de edad aproximadamente, él a su vez.

AVENTURAS DE REFLEXION FILOSOFICA
ARTISTA O LADRON

Confiaba en Don Triste a pesar de ser tan solo un chiquillo de edad escolar y con ideas bastante extravagante. Fueron muchas tardes agradables de platica y música sin cambios extraordinarios, hasta que un día Don Triste confesó a Ruperto que él no compraría ninguna de sus pinturas. Decía que no les veía calidad además para él carecían de profundidad en cada uno de los temas tratados, pero respetaba su amistad y la honestidad con que se conducía en todos los aspectos de su vida. Ruperto quedó mudo por largos e interminables minutos, luego dijo que sus pinturas no eran buenas porque él no era pintor, mucho menos un hombre honesto ya que su única habilidad era la de robar, siendo la pintura una careta para ocultar su verdadera profesión de ladrón.

Para Don Triste fue sumamente difícil comprender y creer lo que había escuchado de labios de su gran amigo, pero su habilidad analítica le decía que era cierto y que Ruperto era tan solo un ladrón. Él supuesto pintor contó su triste historia, porque todo ladrón tiene una historia triste que contar; Ruperto tuvo una familia en una ciudad lejana. Eran felices, él robaba protegiéndose con la mentira de ser en apariencia un fotógrafo profesional, vendía sus fotos en galerías y museos de arte muy prestigiados. Su familia descubrió su verdadera profesión, y le preguntaron ¿por qué? Contestando que era lo único que sabía hacer y además lo hacía muy bien, brindándoles todo tipo de comodidades de la época, ya que vivían decorosamente sin angustias económicas.

Por convicciones solo religiosas intransigentes e inmutables, no quisieron saber nada más y fue arrojado a la calle con la amenaza de ser denunciado a las autoridades y sin ninguna posibilidad de arreglo entre ellos.

Ruperto les suplicó, pero ellos no se dignaron a escucharlo, solo decían avergonzarse de él y de su profesión tan baja, dando como solución única el olvido y su destierro voluntario para siempre de sus vidas.

DON TRISTE OTRA VEZ
ARTISTA O LADRON

Después de muchos intentos fallidos para ser aceptado de regreso en su casa, al fin cansado, hambriento y sin dinero en los bolsillos. Decidió robar para más tarde enviar dinero a su familia, dinero que aceptaban siempre sin ningún remordimiento, pero con la única condición de que no volviera jamás. Mucho tiempo después, cientos de robos, ciudades, penas, riesgos y falsos oficios lo llevaron como destino al barrio en que habitaba Don Triste. Fue ahí donde se conocieron e hicieron gran amistad, esa era toda su verdad, después guardó silencio esperando ansioso la respuesta de su pequeño amigo.

Don Triste sólo acertó a abrazarlo y decirle que entendía y lo quería mucho, además propuso también aprender a ser ladrón solicitándole sus enseñanzas. Porque la escuela es lo mejor, pero con demasiadas mentiras, así es que, ¿por qué no? Aprender un oficio tan interesante para no decir más al siguiente día inicio su nueva clase con el mejor de los maestros, aprendiendo que robar es el arte más fino y hermoso solo comparable al Premio Nobel. Deberás repartir siempre el botín con los necesitados, realizar buenas acciones con el dinero mal habido.

Ruperto ayudaba sin ningún interés a todos los vecinos, les prestaba dinero que en realidad nunca le regresaban, pero él era feliz porque les solucionaba problemas de momento. Pagaba los estudios a estudiantes para darles un futuro seguían los envíos de dinero a sus familiares, donaba dinero a la Cruz Roja, asilos de ancianos, orfanatos, etc. etc. Era todo un ángel protector de los desvalidos, era un héroe ante los ojos de Don Triste. Las clases incluían educación física de alta calidad, tenías que ser fuerte, veloz y ágil como campeón olímpico, mirar y caminar bien en la obscuridad incluyendo tecnología de alarmas, cerraduras, electricidad, electrónica, etc. etc. Aprendió controlar emociones propias y ajenas, usar los instintos, desarrollar el sentido común, deducción, y análisis deductivo, en fin, una educación superior en todos los aspectos.

ARTISTA O LADRON

Con el tiempo llegó la ansiada práctica, así como el también esperado examen final. Durante las madrugadas ambos caminaban por las calles demostrando gran habilidad y espectacularidad, penetraban negocios, edificios, escalando muros, burlando perros de guardia, así como sistemas de seguridad, logrando robos limpios no dejando el menor rastro. Don Triste disfrutaba al máximo su nuevo oficio ocultándolo con sus actividades escolares y ayudando a los más necesitados. Ruperto confió a Don Triste el sistema de enviar personas a las galerías para solo comprar sus pinturas y de esa manera justificar sus ingresos, creándose fama de buen pintor.

Por cierto, nunca le faltaron los ingenuos que compraron sus pinturas influenciados por los falsos compradores, otros tontos presumían de ser expertos como críticos de arte, en fin, eso pretendían, pero el resultado era bastante positivo para el buenazo de Ruperto. Ésta rara y divertida amistad duró por lo menos veinticuatro meses hasta que cierto día, Ruperto tuvo que cambiar de ciudad por motivos de seguridad, además decidió retirarse del peligroso oficio e invertir su dinero en algún negocio menos peligroso. Realizó todos los preparativos convenientes para emigrar, dando consejos y abrazos a Don Triste, ordenándole el acordado retiro inmediato. Después Ruperto desapareció para siempre de su vida, dejando en su joven mente y corazón lecciones maravillosas.

Nunca robes a alguien que conozcas, no robes a tus amistades, ni pobres, ni ricos honrados, roba a los que roban, a los deshonestos. De esa manera seguirás siendo ladrón, pero al menos con un código de honor, en fin, ser un ladrón honrado y honesto contigo mismo. Por cierto, Don Triste recordó a Ruperto como pintor y amigo más que como ladrón, honor y gloria para el excelente pintor de bondades y milagros, con magia en sus actos de verdadera camaradería y amistad, maestro de excelencias, solo conocido como Ruperto el pintor, siendo el corazón de Don Triste su mayor robo.

DON TRISTE OTRA VEZ
ARTISTA O LADRON

Pensamiento

El ser noble y bueno permite el abuso de otros sobre ti, el ser dulce y tierno les permite a otros atreverse a ultrajarte, no lo permitas, pero no cambies sigue siendo noble, bueno, dulce, tierno y comprensivo para que tarde o temprano entiendan que están equivocados, la verdadera razón de ser así será solo para ser feliz contigo mismo y con los tuyos que al fin y al cabo es lo único que cuenta.

EL SABIO PERKINS

Durante la maravillosa época del colegio, Don Triste estudiaba en la vocacional de ciencias físico matemáticas, por lo cual su colegio era considerado para sabios o locos, por cierto, Don Triste era de los locos, pero él se consideraba todo un genio. En las afueras del colegio, había una biblioteca rodeada por un inmenso parque, que servía como área de recreo, encuentros deportivos, e incontables feroces encuentros boxísticos entre los estudiantes. Así como romántico centro de reunión para enamorados, en general era el clásico conjunto escolar de esparcimiento de todo colegio de gran ciudad. Lo que convirtió en especial ese parque, fue la presencia de un extraño, especial e impresionante personaje. Nadie supo de donde vino, pero se convirtió en el centro de atención del parque, la escuela, estudiantes y de los mismos maestros catedráticos del plantel. En aquel mencionado gran colegio de físicos matemáticos y todos locos, aquel estudiante o maestro que mostraba conocimiento y sabiduría respetuosamente se le apodaba Perkins. Pero el personaje del parque fue tan especial y sorprendente que se le llamó tanto por respeto, como por admiración y cariño: El Sabio Perkins.

Como si fuese un empleo de lunes a viernes, el Sabio Perkins acostumbraba siempre llegar al parque puntualmente a las doce del mediodía, se instalaba en la misma banca colocaba varios lápices y un sacapuntas. Lo rodeaban algunos perros que lo acompañaban, a veces dos otras veces seis en fin no todos lo seguían a diario. La mayor de las veces sus clientes lo esperaban, eran muchos estudiantes ansiosos que solicitaban sus servicios de matemático, a cambio de bebida para él y algo de comida para los perros. Eran estudiantes del colegio, que necesitaban de su ayuda para resolver problemas de cálculo, los que les eran asignados diariamente por maestros como tarea. La mayor de las veces sus clientes lo esperaban, eran muchos estudiantes ansiosos que solicitaban sus servicios de matemático, a cambio de bebida para él y algo de comida para los perros. Eran estudiantes del colegio, que necesitaban de su ayuda para resolver problemas de cálculo.

DON TRISTE OTRA VEZ
EL SABIO PERKINS

los que les eran asignados diariamente por maestros como tarea. Éstos eran tan complicados que, en ocasiones, podían tardar hasta cuarenta y cinco minutos en cada uno de ellos para lograr resolverlos, y claro contando con libros y todos los recursos incluyendo calculadora científica. El Sabio Perkins usaba solo lápiz y papel, tardaba algo así como quince minutos por problema y en los más complicados entre veinte y veinticinco minutos. Afirmo que él no usaba calculadora alguna, no se equivocaba en sus respuestas era todo un maestro catedrático, cuando explicaba la manera fácil de resolver algún problema.

El Sabio Perkins tomaba entre sus manos sucias la hoja, o las hojas que contenían las preguntas, las analizaba durante unos treinta segundos, y emitía su respuesta que era algo así. Bueno estos problemas te costarán una botella de bebida de cuarto de litro, más medio kilo de carne y hueso para los perros, en esa época era el equivalente a medio dólar americano. De esta simple manera se acordaba el costo por resolver el problema, entonces el estudiante caminaba a lo largo de dos calles, hasta llegar a la tienda de ultramarinos para comprar lo solicitado por el Sabio Perkins. Después caminaba de regreso hasta el parque, por lo regular cuando llegaba ante el Sabio Perkins su tarea estaba resuelta. Durante el transcurso del día y hasta las cuatro de la tarde, era un ir y venir del parque a la tienda de ultramarinos que parecía desfile.

Los perros comían hasta hartarse por lo tanto algunos desaparecían únicamente para volver al día siguiente en busca de comida, otros se iban con el Sabio Perkins agradecidos por su bondad.

A las cuatro de la tarde cargaba sus botellas de bebida, abandonando banca y parque con rumbo desconocido, regresando como siempre al día siguiente a realizar su grata tarea de ayudar a los estudiantes.

AVENTURAS DE REFLEXION FILOSOFICA
EL SABIO PERKINS

Al paso del tiempo la curiosidad de Don Triste lo llevó a observar al Sabio Perkins, comprobando que el mote de sabio le quedaba pequeño, era un hombre sumamente hábil e inteligente. Se podía decir que tanta inteligencia solo se podía comparar con la de un sabio, pero su apariencia era la de un pordiosero o un simple trapero. Lleno de curiosidad, así como de respeto, empezó acercándose al Sabio Perkins con la idea de conversar, descubriendo que eso no era de su agrado. El solo platicaba y resolvía problemas matemáticos dando cátedras y mini conferencias acerca de esta ciencia maravillosa.

Perkins no aceptaba ninguna amistad, no platicaba de asuntos personales, diariamente Don Triste lo observaba, inclusive trato de investigar acerca del personaje tan especial, pero en realidad nadie sabía más de lo que él sabía, es decir nada. Intento varias veces entablar platica con él, pero evadiéndolo una y mil veces, además rehusó darle su nombre respondiendo que él era Perkins y nada más. El Sabio Perkins bebía demasiado como cualquier alcohólico. Durante las cuatro horas diarias de trabajo no probaba alimento alguno. Por supuesto que si comía porque de no ser así hubiese muerto hace mucho tiempo, así es que Don Triste se preguntó así mismo que era lo que Perkins comía y que le gustaba comer.

A partir de ese momento les obsequiaba alimentos tanto al Sabio Perkins como a los perros, pero él guardaba los alimentos entre sus ropas o los compartía con los perros. Siempre agradecía el alimento, pero seguía sin entablar plática alguna con Don Triste. Así transcurrieron bastantes días y Don Triste no lograba hacer amistad con Perkins. Un día Don Triste preparó los mejores emparedados que puedas imaginar, utilizando varios tipos de carnes frías y quesos, con la mejor habilidad culinaria logrando hacer unos emparedados deliciosos. Don Triste se los llevó al Sabio Perkins, y éste le agradeció como era su costumbre, Don Triste mencionó que él mismo los preparo para él.

DON TRISTE OTRA VEZ
EL SABIO PERKINS

Sucedió que Don Triste se enfermó, no fue grave, pero requirió de reposo en cama, por lo tanto, no asistió a clases durante una semana, la cual le pareció eterno a Don Triste. Sus amistades lo frecuentaron en casa durante su reposo y le dijeron que todo mundo lo había extrañado tanto, que inclusive el Sabio Perkins había preguntado por él. Esa fue la mejor noticia que había escuchado y solo esperaba el siguiente día escolar para ir en busca del Sabio Perkins. Al terminar la clase de las doce del mediodía Don Triste corrió hasta la banca del parque iba en busca del Sabio Perkins, encontró solo estudiantes que también lo esperaban.

Todos estaban confundidos porque en realidad Perkins era siempre puntual. Más tarde Don Triste cansado de esperar regresó a clases. Finalmente, al término del día escolar, a las dos de la tarde Don Triste corrió de nuevo hacia el parque, pero en la banca solo estaban tres tristes perros porque ese día no comerían. Así que Don Triste corrió hasta la tienda de ultramarinos compró carne y huesos para los perros, regresó al parque y distribuyó la comida entre los perros tal y como lo hubiese hecho el Sabio Perkins.

Permaneció en el parque jugando a la pelota con amigos como todos los días, pero siempre con la vista atento a la banca del Sabio Perkins que permaneció vacía. Para las cuatro de la tarde él y sus amigos decidieron partir cada quien para su hogar. Don Triste se mostraba preocupado porque si Perkins estuviera enfermo, nadie podría ayudarlo además no tenía ni siquiera idea de dónde podía buscarlo, se dirigió hacia el hogar, pasando por la tienda de ultramarinos como último recurso.

Entro a la tienda y preguntó a los que atendían si acaso habían visto al Sabio Perkins, dijeron que escucharon de él, pero que nunca lo habían visto en persona. Don Triste agradeció la información proporcionada y reanudó el camino a casa sintiéndose realmente hambriento.

Apresuraba el paso cuando sintió una mano en el hombro, al mismo tiempo escuchó una clara voz conocida diciendo,- ¡hola que tal! veo que estás mejor y eso me da gusto-. Volteó y se encontró de frente al Sabio Perkins, el cual mostraba una sonrisa amable nunca antes vista en su serio rostro. Don Triste reaccionó preguntando si acaso él estaba enfermo, porque no había asistido al parque y tanto perros como estudiantes se mostraron tristes. Perkins mostró satisfacción por las palabras de Don Triste, pero sólo dijo que estaba cansado y también necesitaba vacaciones como cualquier trabajador y ese día fue su descanso.

Se despidieron casi al instante tan sólo diciéndose mutuamente que pases buena tarde y nos vemos mañana en el parque como de costumbre sin más se encaminaron por rumbos opuestos, pero muy adentro con el pensamiento y el sentimiento de la naciente amistad el siguiente día escolar no fue distinto ya que Don Triste esperaba las doce del mediodía para reunirse con el que él consideraba su amigo. Ya frente al Sabio Perkins éste sonrío y lo convidó a sentarse invitándolo a cotizar lo que él consideraba su trabajo. Don Triste mencionó que él no era sabio, pero Perkins mostrándole la misma sonrisa del día anterior le dijo. El secreto de saber cobrar por el trabajo es: Primero saber hacerlo bien para que te resulte fácil. Segundo observa al cliente y nunca le cobres más de lo que pueda pagar, de esa manera se sentirá agradecido contigo y tu estarás contento con tu trabajo.

Aunque eso no parecía difícil Don Triste prefería observar para aprender y con el tiempo ayudar, sonriendo ambos acordaron que así sería. Por lo tanto, Perkins continuó solo resolviendo problemas, pero en voz alta para aprendizaje de Don Triste. Por cierto, tú no has sido cliente mío ¿por qué? Preguntó Perkins, ¿acaso eres muy inteligente? Don Triste sólo sonrío, contestando que no era malo para el estudio además tenía sus trucos y no le gustaba eso de ir y venir de compras a la tienda de ultramarinos.

DON TRISTE OTRA VEZ
EL SABIO PERKINS

DON TRISTE pasaba el tiempo con Perkins haciendo su tarea, al terminar ambos con sus respectivas obligaciones se ocupaban de platicar y sobre todo de las innumerables aventuras diarias de Don Triste, por cierto, que Perkins reía mucho con sus ocurrencias porque era divertido. Perkins mostraba facilidad y una gran habilidad para resolver los problemas además ellos dos jugaban con acertijos adivinanzas, y demás, a veces en esa cuestión Don Triste derrotaba al Sabio Perkins, bueno lo más seguro es que le permitía ganar. Se divertían a lo grande pero puntualmente a las cuatro de la tarde se despedían sin preguntarse nada, solo prometiéndose verse al día siguiente así transcurrieron tres semestres escolares durante los cuales su amistad se acrecentó.

Perkins seguía bebiendo a diario, compartían algunos emparedados, en ocasiones Don Triste los llevaba desde su casa. En otras Perkins los mandaba comprar, de la cafetería de la escuela o de algún otro lugar cercano que Don Triste recomendaba. En fin, eran grandes amigos y estaban satisfechos de su amistad, ésta no implicaba ningún compromiso para ninguno de los dos, porque no platicaban de asuntos personales que pudiesen herir la buena relación entre los dos. Don Triste tenía curiosidad de saber el porqué, un hombre tan inteligente era borracho y sucio sin preocuparse por nada, pero por temor a perder la amistad se concretaba solo a disfrutar el momento.

En verdad era sorprendente ver como Perkins, disfrutaba viendo jugar soccer a Don Triste, ya que era un jugadorazo, además jugaba con un gusto tan solo comparable a su habilidad, era el mejor jugador de la escuela y en el parque era todo un ídolo. Su más grande y nuevo admirador era Perkins y éste se lo hacía saber diciéndole; que, así como él resolvía fácilmente los complicados problemas de estudiantes de matemáticas, Don Triste resolvía hábilmente los partidos de soccer.

AVENTURAS DE REFLEXION FILOSOFICA
EL SABIO PERKINS

Para Don Triste el contar con la amistad del Sabio Perkins, era algo especial y apreciaba la suerte de ser el único alumno que se sentaba a su lado tan solo a platicar, él nunca acudió por ayuda matemática tampoco tenía que hacer los viajes de ida y vuelta a la tienda de ultramarinos. Por desgracia no todo lo que marcha bien dura eternamente, así que el distanciamiento entre los dos amigos empezaba su proceso. Alguien dijo que cuando tienes un buen amigo esclavizas algo de ti en él. Es muy cierto porque te duele lo que le afecta a él y aquello que lo lastima te lastima a ti también.

Perkins un día preguntó a Don Triste que ¿cuál era su nacionalidad? Porque actuaba distinto, por cierto, sus emparedados eran tipo europeo. Don Triste palideció y dijo que quizás era distinto por que viajaba mucho de pequeño a distintas escuelas en Europa y que un tío le enseñó a hacer esa clase de emparedados. Perkins mirándolo mencionó, que aquella primera ocasión en que Don Triste preparó aquellos ricos emparedados para él, vinieron a su mente recuerdos agradables de su vida familiar.

Recordo haber comido ese tipo de emparedado en Italia en su viaje de luna de miel, al lado de su adorada y desaparecida esposa. El especial sabor de la mostaza y de los quesos lo hicieron remontarse a esos tiempos hermosos de su vida, Perkins tuvo la intención de preguntar a Don Triste el porqué de aquel detalle tan sencillo de los emparedados, pero no pudo hacerlo porque Don Triste permaneció ausente toda una semana por enfermedad.

Luego al siguiente día Perkins lejos del parque, prefirió aguardar hasta el término de clases y esperando en aquel viejo portón de un edificio abandonado cercano a la tan popular tienda de ultramarinos. Observó como Don Triste compró comida para los perros, regresando más tarde a la tienda para preguntar acerca del ausente sabio Perkins.

DON TRISTE OTRA VEZ
EL SABIO PERKINS

Fue cuando decidió ser amigo de aquel joven loco, que tenía un cierto encanto, creador de emparedados con sabor a gratos recuerdos. Así fue como Perkins le abrió las puertas de su corazón a Don Triste, con el tiempo llegó a estimarlo y admirarlo por su juego habilidoso. Después de un silencio con sabor a melancolía Perkins preguntó a Don Triste ¿bien y tu cuándo decidiste ser mi amigo?

Don Triste sonriendo contestó que en otro país y en otro tiempo tuvo un amigo maravilloso, al que llamaba "trapero". Era un vago, alcohólico, con perros, un gran filósofo, apareció y desapareció sin advertencia alguna, pero Don Triste supo que así había más personajes. La primera vez que vio al Sabio Perkins, renació su curiosidad por saber si era todo un personaje de novela como aquel trapero. Descubrió que era especial y repleto de sabiduría ¿pero ¿cuál sería su secreto o desgracia que lo hacía vivir una vida llena de penas y soledad? En ese momento decidió ser su amigo.

Perkins con voz clara contó la triste historia que lo convirtió en el Sabio Perkins, dijo ser un estudiante pobre sostenido y apoyado por el amor de su madre, quien le proporcionó los medios para tener una buena educación universitaria. No conoció padre alguno, pero aun así se gradúo y como el mejor de su generación, muy joven logró alcanzar ser uno de los más brillantes matemáticos en la nación. Conoció a una mujer hermosa con quien se casó, teniendo dos hijas haciendo junto a su querida madre una familia feliz. Él daba conferencias viajando alrededor del mundo, siendo catedrático en varias universidades y de esa manera ganaba bastante dinero para poder brindarle a su familia una vida muy diferente a la que él tuvo durante su infancia. En fin, la felicidad era su amiga y lo acompañaba a diario. Cuando él era entrevistado por los medios de comunicación decía que el secreto de su éxito eran las cuatro mujeres que completaban su familia. Tenían una grande y hermosa casa en la que juntos disfrutaban el mayor tiempo posible.

AVENTURAS DE REFLEXION FILOSOFICA
EL SABIO PERKINS

Ya que su tiempo lo ocupaba trabajando dando todo tipo de cátedras matemáticas, seminarios y conferencias alrededor del mundo. Grande era su éxito que la N.A.S.A. se interesó en obtener los servicios del afamado Sabio Perkins ofreciéndole trabajo en el nuevo centro espacial localizado en la ciudad de Houston, Texas en la Unión Americana. Éste había sido uno de sus sueños por años, así que sin pérdida de tiempo compró boletos de avión para toda su familia. Su intención era firmar el contrato mientras su familia paseaba y buscaban una casa para establecerse en dicha ciudad de, o quizás en los alrededores.

Faltando dos días para el viaje, un catedrático amigo se enfermó no pudiendo reemplazarlo para brindar una conferencia como ellos lo habían acordado por lo tanto él tendría que viajar un día después de la fecha acordada lo más sensato para no cancelar todos los pasajes, fue que la familia viajaría a Houston, TX y él lo haría al día siguiente después de la conferencia, de esa manera solo cancelarían un boleto.

La feliz familia abordo el avión, viajaban con rumbo a Houston, TX mientras que Perkins participaba en la conferencia que no pudo cancelar. Después al término iría a casa. Para al día siguiente muy temprano viajar y reunirse con ellas. Después de participar en la larga conferencia se trasladó feliz a su hogar, al llegar esperaba encontrar algún mensaje de su familia, pero no había nada. Más tarde ya cansado de esperar por alguna llamada telefónica el decidió llamar al hotel donde se hospedaría su familia.

Pero su familia aún no había arribado al hotel, llamó a la línea aérea para preguntar si el vuelo estaba retrasado pero el vuelo no se retrasó, ¡el avión sufrió un terrible accidente!, se trasladó al aeropuerto recibiendo confirmación de que los pasajeros y tripulantes murieron en el trágico accidente, y sin esperanza alguna de encontrar sobrevivientes. Después de llorar por horas y varios días sin saber cuántos.

DON TRISTE OTRA VEZ
EL SABIO PERKINS

Caminó sin rumbo fijo además no probó alimento alguno sólo un poco de agua que encontró casualmente. En alguna de tantas fuentes y vertederos públicos, vagó sin rumbo por días, ingiriendo bebidas alcohólicas tratando de ahogar la pena. Después el dinero en los bolsillos se le acabó, pero aun así no volvió a su casa. ¿Quién se quedó con su casa? ¿Sus autos? ¿Y su fortuna? No lo supo ni le interesó decidió vivir en el olvido. Con su habilidad para las matemáticas se instaló en la banca afuera de lo que un día también fue su colegio. Dedicándose a resolver problemas matemáticos, a cambio de bebida y un poco de comida para los perros que lo rodeaban siendo simplemente sus amigos ocasionales, dormía donde pudiese sólo a beber alcohol y comer un poco para no morir.

Descubrió que fácilmente ganaba suficiente para beber, por lo tanto, se retiraba temprano para erróneamente en la soledad emborracharse olvidando su pena. No recuerda cuántos años transcurrieron así, ¿tal vez tres o cuatro? No lo recordaba, pero tampoco quería saberlo. Decía que durante su infancia lo único que valía era su madre, más tarde su esposa para completar su mundo con dos lindas niñas para un total de cuatro mujeres que completaban su mundo de felicidad.

Perkins no culpó a nadie, no molestaba a nadie, lo único que hacía era minar su propia resistencia física, para algún día no muy lejano morir en algún callejón y de esa manera reunirse con su familia, durante todo ese tiempo nunca pidió ayuda, condenándose a vivir o a medio morir de esa manera, pero fue su elección. Don Triste escuchó atentamente, sin interrumpir en algún momento la historia desgarradora del Sabio Perkins. Sólo acertó a limpiarse las lágrimas y súbitamente abrazarlo diciendo que contaría siempre con él ya que eran amigos. Pero Perkins dijo que no quería involucrarse con nadie más, así que era tiempo de desaparecer y dejar la banca para algún otro personaje que llegase al parque. Se despidieron y caminaron por rumbos opuestos Don Triste iba llorando porque intuía que no volvería a ver jamás al Sabio Perkins.

AVENTURAS DE REFLEXION FILOSOFICA
EL SABIO PERKINS

Sabía que era el adiós, súbitamente corrió hacia Perkins y le dijo que andaba mal en matemáticas y necesitaría de su valiosa ayuda. Así que no podía abandonarlo en un momento tan difícil. Perkins sonrío tal y como le sonrío la primera vez diciendo que ya sabía el truco de Don Triste para salir adelante en matemáticas y otras materias escolares. -Un futbolista de tu categoría es aprobado en las materias.

Sin importar si estudia o no, sólo por el hecho de jugar con la selección del colegio para tratar de ganar los más campeonatos posibles para el plantel-. Así como el reconocimiento de tener el mejor equipo de futbol en la nación que era el sueño de todo entrenador y de todo director escolar, así que tu no me necesitas, pero agradezco el intento.

Sin decir más ambos emprendieron sus caminos, pero Don Triste continuó llorando sin parar hasta llegar a su hogar. Luego tomó un libro de matemáticas y empezó a estudiar en honor al Sabio Perkins. Sabía que Perkins no volvería tal y como le pasó con el trapero sabía que era afortunado por conocer tipos como ellos y pensó que quizás algún día escribiría sus experiencias, eso lo hacía sentirse mejor por la pérdida del Sabio Perkins.

Nunca imaginó Don Triste que otra persona contaría y escribiría sus experiencias, pero lo importante es que no quedaron en el olvido, a partir del siguiente día, no se volvió a ver ni a saber nada del Sabio Perkins. Todos lo extrañaron, todos lo querían y por algún tiempo lo buscaron en los callejones cercanos a la escuela también en varias tiendas de ultramarinos al pasar el tiempo los estudiantes volvieron a sus cotidianas actividades en el parque, y hasta los perros dejaron de ir en busca de Perkins.

Don Triste nunca buscó al Sabio Perkins, tampoco volvió a jugar futbol en el parque, sólo se limitó a estudiar matemáticas para no hacer truco futbolero en honor de su amigo.

DON TRISTE OTRA VEZ
EL SABIO PERKINS

Don Triste se gradúo en aquel colegio y no volvió. El parque perdió para siempre al sabio y al futbolista siendo ambos su mayor atracción, hoy quizás nadie los recuerde, pero yo sí.

Pensamiento
Cuando tienes amigos verdaderos esclavizas algo de ti en ellos y ellos en ti, fue Gibran Jalil Gibran quien lo dijo es cierto, pero también es cierto que un amigo te regala su tiempo su comprensión y cuando lo necesitas ahí está contigo.

Pero por más amistad que exista siempre hay quien prefiere sanar su dolor en completa soledad siendo difícil respetar esa soledad porque suena como abandono, o por temor a que se convierta en ausencia. El amor, la amistad y la lealtad son sólo cuestión de decisión no de sentimiento, tú quieres a alguien, o alguien te quiere solo cuando así lo deciden. Pero esta es una elección digna de respeto.

EL BOXEADOR

Don Triste y todos sus primos trabajaban en el restaurante tan sólo los fines de semana, siendo la escuela su principal actividad. Cierta tarde un cliente extranjero, insultó y calificó de tonto a uno de los meseros del restaurante sin razón alguna, teniendo que intervenir Don Triste.

Pero el cliente fuera de si le tiró golpes a lo salvaje, obteniendo por respuesta una lección de boxeo inolvidable por parte de Don Triste, que sin saberlo empezaba su nueva profesión que le causaría glorias, satisfacciones y muchas amarguras.

Él cliente quedó tendido en el suelo, bañado en su propia sangre, como si lo hubiese atropellado un camión y Don Triste no tenía ni siquiera un rasguño. Don Mario Alberti había observado de principio a fin sin intervenir, luego llamó a su sobrino conduciéndolo al interior de su oficina preguntándole cómo había sido posible lo que sucedió.

Don Triste quiso explicar su inocencia, pero el tío volvió a preguntar cómo había sido posible, pero refiriéndose a la facilidad y habilidad de su boxeo que calificó de fino, elegante y efectivo.

Esa misma noche tío y sobrino salieron juntos, a mirar boxeadores profesionales, peleando clandestinamente por cantidades enormes de dinero. Don Triste por vez primera se encontró en un centro de peleas clandestinas, sintió miedo, pero el respeto que todos mostraban a su tío le devolvió la confianza.

Él lugar era un estacionamiento subterráneo amplio, donde encontrabas gente de todos los niveles socio-económicos, políticos, sacerdotes, artistas famosos, profesionistas y mafiosos. Todos ellos acompañados de mujeres guapísimas, pero obsesionados todos ellos con apostar todo el dinero al boxeador de su preferencia.

DON TRISTE OTRA VEZ
EL BOXEADOR

Las reglas eran profesionales y con un árbitro controlando las acciones, cuando la pelea rebasaba el tercer round, el tiempo ya no se detenía ni existían los descansos, la contienda continuaba sin cesar hasta ganar o perder uno de los boxeadores. En pocas palabras a partir del tercer round la pelea se convertía en pelea mortal sin cabida para el empate, con sus contadas excepciones.

Por razones de seguridad las peleas se realizaban en distintos lugares, los cuales eran confirmados por teléfono el mismo día de la pelea y con un hermetismo digno del sistema creado por la organización llamada o conocida como "mafia" la que controlaba todo el evento de principio a fin. Los buenos boxeadores ganaban hasta dos mil dólares por pelea, pero ese dinero era repartido entre el patrocinador, el entrenador, un preparador físico, un doctor. Dos peleadores que conformaban el equipo que preparaba al boxeador antes y después de cada pelea.

Don Mario propuso a Don Triste convertirse en peleador profesional, la idea no le agradó, pero aceptó por obediencia, más tarde fue instalado un gimnasio en una de las salas de la casa. Contrataron un entrenador, dos preparadores físicos, un doctor y dos boxeadores. Una semana después, empezaron los duros entrenamientos para Don Triste que seguía estudiando, ya que el trato fue de no abandonar la escuela.

Tres meses después fue su gran debut, ganando fácilmente su pelea obteniendo en pocos meses fama y renombre permaneciendo invicto, el fino y elegante boxeo impresionaba por su efectividad. La admiración que él sentía por Cassius Clay (Mohamed Ali) lo motivaba a pelear, imitándolo a la perfección realizando el mismo estilo de boxeo. Solo que en diferente peso y tamaño además contaba con una velocidad de manos. Que rallaba en el límite de lo increíble, siendo éstas su mejor arma, así como su inmejorable defensiva.

EL BOXEADOR

Don Triste no recibía dinero directamente por sus peleas, pero disponía de todos los lujos a su alcance y capricho, ya que Don Mario Alberti lo mimaba y no reparaba en gastos con tal de complacerlo. De cualquier manera, sus gustos eran por lo regular simplemente viajes a conocer lugares lejanos para olvidar su profesión de peleador y convertirse tan sólo en un viajero. Fueron algo así como veintiséis meses peleando, Don Triste se consolidó como uno de los mejores, su record fueron ciento cinco peleas. Cien ganadas, dos empates y tres derrotas, de sus victorias setenta fueron resultado de su enorme suerte que lo acompañó en cada una de sus peleas.

Lo característico de sus peleas fue que siempre perdió el primer round, ya que nunca pudo odiar a sus contrincantes dedicándose sólo a defenderse sin atacar, su equipo de esquina pasaba con gran angustia horribles momentos desesperados, nunca entendieron su proceder siendo su reacción sólo después de recibir golpes, cambiando su táctica utilizando su ofensiva de velocidad.

Finalizó ganando con cierta facilidad, pero otras peleas las ganó milagrosamente, ya que al final era conducido a hospitales clandestinos, para recuperarse del terrible castigo recibido durante las contiendas. Don Mario Alberti y el equipo de esquina ganaron mucho dinero y pensaban como ganar más. Don Triste sólo pensaba como retirarse ya que algunas de sus peleas se tornaron salvajes y brutales como si se tratase de peleas mortales. En realidad, nunca le agradó la idea de pelear, a lo largo de todo ese tiempo él continuó sus estudios, deportes y aventuras como cualquier estudiante, nunca hubo cambio notorio en su comportamiento ya que en realidad mantenía su vida de peleador muy separada de la de estudiante. Ocultó hasta donde pudo su terrible actividad de peleador callejero profesional, no le agradaba la idea de pelear por más tiempo, pensando siempre en como retirarse a tiempo antes de terminar sumamente golpeado.

DON TRISTE OTRA VEZ
EL BOXEADOR

Él mismo no sabía cómo parar, hasta que llegó a su vida lo inesperado y el resultado fue que cambio su vida de forma drástica y se convirtió en Don Triste tal y como se le conoce en esta historia.

Pensamiento

Pelear se ha dicho que es un arte y lo es, aparte muy complicado pero el placer más grande de este arte es, la fina habilidad de la defensa, que puede lograr tu integridad física y mental salvándote de agresiones sin tener que ser agresivo.

Pero la única defensa posible en una pelea es la razón, para ganar siempre deberás tener la razón de lo que haces o mejor no lo hagas, el aprendizaje es claro, la razón te conduce a no pelear sólo a defenderte.

UNA LUZ EN LOS OJOS

En cierta ocasión llegó al barrio una linda jovencita llamada Inía, estaba asustada, golpeada y pedía protección. Don Triste preguntó ¿por qué? Y ¿contra quién? Inía le contó que su madre murió hacía tan solo dos días antes. Su padrastro atacó sexualmente a su hermana golpeándola primero, e intentó hacer lo mismo con ella, pero Inía era excelente para pelear y se defendió atacándolo con una botella de licor. Las consecuencias no se hicieron esperar, así que Inía fue amenazada de muerte porque el padrastro era un trabajador del protector. La protección de que gozaba era a causa de que era distribuidor de drogas ilícitas con grandes dividendos para el protector del sector donde vivían.

La situación se volvió critica para Inía, ya que había individuos armados buscándola con órdenes estrictas de matarla, razón por demás valedera para huir a otro sector y solicitar protección. Sabía que Don Triste era peleador callejero, ya que ella había estado presente en algunas de sus contiendas y sabía que él era sobrino de Don Mario Alberti.

La situación era crítica y simple al mismo tiempo, ya que si él no la ayudaba nadie más lo haría y todo por temor a las represalias del protector, Don Triste rápidamente explicó la situación a su querido tío solicitando su ayuda.

Don Mario Alberti habló con el protector de aquel sector y todo quedó solucionado con la condición de que Inía no pusiera un pie jamás en aquel sector.

Inia, aunque bella tenía un pasado sucio, pero conservaba buenos sentimientos, ya que aprendió raterías y trucos sucios desde temprana edad por necesidad, empleándolos para sobrevivir en un mundo sucio que le fue asignado sólo por haber nacido entre drogas, rateros y asesinos como compañeros. En fin, ella no fue culpable de ser como era, nació entre lo peor y luchaba ferozmente por ser buena y dulce.

DON TRISTE OTRA VEZ
UNA LUZ EN LOS OJOS

Inia pidió a Don Triste no pelear más, ya que cada pelea se convertía en un calvario para ella, ya que era difícil soportar su famoso primer round que siempre perdía. Ella sentía en carne propia cada uno de los golpes que él recibía, además no tendría que entrenar, teniendo más tiempo para disfrutar de su mutua compañía, ya que a los pocos días se habían enamorado y lo que buscaban era más tiempo para estar juntos. Inia habitaba en un cuarto de hotel y Don Triste se quedaba con ella, pero a escondidas ya que él era hijo de familia, además Don Mario Alberti no quería del todo a Inía.

Un tanto por su pasado y otro tanto por ser la causa del retiro repentino de Don Triste de la salvaje actividad de peleador callejero. Don Mario Alberti no festejaba el noviazgo de la pareja, ya que consideraba sucia y perdida la relación entre ellos, por lo tanto, redujo al mínimo la mesada de su sobrino para que no tuviera manera de ir con Inía, pero sucedió lo contrario ya que se les veía juntos a todas horas disfrutando de su amor al máximo.

Inia y Don Triste asaltaban a borrachos en las afueras de bares, y cantinas una vez que tenían suficiente dinero, se iban a cenar y después a dormir al hotel. Temprano Don Triste regresaba a casa, entrando secretamente pretendiendo haber dormido en su cuarto, desayunaba y se trasladaba a la escuela, mientras tanto Inía desayunaba y comía en un restaurante, buscando en que entretenerse mientras llegaba la tarde, para ir en busca de su enamorado ya que solamente vivía para él.

Por más que intentaron no pudieron separarlos, ya que su relación se convirtió en algo especial, nunca hablaron de formalidades, porque su relación era sólida y permanente, con dinero o sin éste gozaban al máximo sólo con estar juntos compartiéndolo todo. Así transcurrieron siete meses entre aventuras y romance, los robos nocturnos empezaron a ser más peligrosos y ellos a tener fama de rateros y demás. Una noche Inía obsequió a Don Triste una pistola.

La cual el rechazo argumentando que por nada en el mundo el usaría o portaría un arma. Le regresó el arma a Inía, diciéndole que sería mejor que ella la conservara como instrumento para su protección, ya que por algunas noches ella permanecía sola mientras él estudiaba para los exámenes escolares.

Una noche Inía contó una historia tan extraña e increíble que Don Triste no supo que decir, Inía y Don Triste tenían un brillo en los ojos demasiado intenso como especial, había ocasiones en que a gran distancia por eso se reconocían y en la obscuridad se manifestaba como un destello de gran resplandor que era visto solo por ellos. Ella platicó que su mamá, antes de morir le platicó que el destello en los ojos, era el símbolo de una generación diferente con habilidades especiales. Se reconocían entre ellos, por los destellos en los ojos y que los comunes de la gente no percibían tal destello, sólo los que lo poseían.

Las personas con el destello, tienen la cualidad de hacer tanto el bien como el mal, pero en grandes proporciones, cuando encuentras a alguien con el resplandor en los ojos, ese alguien puede ser tu felicidad o tu desgracia. Don Triste e Inía eran felices en esos momentos, tal y como la mamá de Inía lo decía. Don Triste no supo que decir simplemente sonrío y quedó pensativo. Pero entendió que eran felices y gustaban de mirarse a los ojos, ya que el brillo los motivaba a continuar amándose tal y como lo hacían en ese momento.

Inia decía que el brillo era el símbolo de que estaban predestinados para algo grande y único, pero entenderlo y encontrar el camino a seguir era difícil, ya que requería sabiduría y habilidad mental, así como tiempo para entenderlo. Era una historia extraordinaria e interesante, pero nada más, o al menos así pensó Don Triste. Inía decía amarlo como nunca creyó poder amar a alguien, prometiendo que, si ella moría.

DON TRISTE OTRA VEZ
UNA LUZ EN LOS OJOS

Volvería con él para ayudarlo porque ellos serían inseparables. Don Triste dijo no creer que los muertos regresen, pero Inía dijo creerlo al grado de prometerle con lágrimas en sus brillantes ojos, que regresaría con él a ayudarlo después de morir. Don Triste se despidió de ella y se fue a su casa, a estudiar para los exámenes escolares, dejando a Inía en el hotel de siempre, pero con la pistola para su protección y seguridad.

A la mañana siguiente, Don Triste fue despertado bruscamente por Villi, su mejor amigo, quien se notaba triste y alarmado, preguntando a Don Triste si había pasado la noche con Inia, Don Triste contestó que no y que la dejó en el hotel alrededor de las 10:00 de la noche regresando a casa para estudiar. Villi dijo que en el hotel habían encontrado muerta a Inia, y supuestamente asesinada de tres balazos, Don Triste quedó mudo sin poder creer lo que había escuchado, pero la tristeza en el rostro de Villi confirmaba lo dicho.

Se encaminaban rápidamente al hotel, cuando la policía detuvo y arrestó a Don Triste, como sospechoso de la muerte de Inia, considerando que era un caso de asesinato pasional. Fueron tres días largos y espantosos, durante los cuales Don Triste permaneció detenido en la cárcel con motivo de las investigaciones del caso. Después lo liberaron por no encontrar sus huellas digitales en el arma homicida, más el testimonio de Don Mario, de que su sobrino permaneció esa noche estudiando en casa como siempre.

Velaron y enterraron dignamente a Inia, Don Mario Alberti se encargó de todos los gastos del funeral, permitiendo su entierro en el cementerio familiar, demostrando arrepentimiento por haber juzgado mal a Inia, que resultó ser buena, dulce y queriendo a Don Triste lealmente. Durante los últimos tres días Villi contó a Don Mario Alberti, como Inia amaba limpiamente a Don Triste y que el pasado sucio de ella era circunstancial, ya que ella no escogió ese tipo de vida, ni ese barrio, fue el cruel destino quien se lo otorgó.

Don Triste se encerró en su cuarto, muy dolido porque ni siquiera vio a Inia para el último adiós, ahora sólo tenía una fría tumba como único recuerdo de aquella hermosa mujer que amó y que lo amó. A partir de ese momento se convertiría en Don Triste, tal y como se le conoce en esta historia, recordando la promesa de Inia de volver de la tumba para estar con él. Día tras día buscaba entre los ojos de la gente, aquel destello tan maravilloso que había sido su felicidad y que ahora era su desdicha.

La policía no esclareció el crimen, archivándolo como otro caso más sin darle importancia, Villi por su lado había realizado averiguaciones e inclusive estuvo en la escena del crimen. Encontrando una plumilla Fender triangular, de las que se utilizan para tocar guitarra, sin que nadie la notara, minimizando su importancia como clave del asesinato. Villi y Don Triste se trasladaron al sector donde vivió y creció Inia, en busca de alguna pista para resolver el crimen, durante días y días no encontraron nada. Pero una noche mientras cenaban en un café cantante vieron un cartel con la imagen de Francis, era un guitarrista muy popular por interpretar bien las canciones de los Beatles, además de ser; gigoló, drogadicto, pandillero y criminal.

Averiguaron que Francis había sido encarcelado, por ahorcar con una cuerda de guitarra a su amante en un cuarto de hotel!, sin consideración ni remordimiento. Además, tocaba guitarra usando una plumilla triangular Fender, que decía era su preferida y que era el mismo tipo de la encontrada en la escena del crimen. Más tarde Villi y Don Triste, localizaron la casa musical, donde Francis compraba cuerdas y plumillas para su guitarra.

Averiguaron que plumillas Fender triangulares eran sólo de tres clases; delgada, mediana y gruesa y que Francis usaba Fender delgada.

DON TRISTE OTRA VEZ
UNA LUZ EN LOS OJOS

Para ellos esto significó la primera clave para resolver el crimen, ya que la plumilla encontrada por Villi era triangular Fender delgada, así que ya contaban con un sospechoso, ahora solo bastaría encontrarlo y probar que él cometió el crimen, cosa nada fácil, pero lo intentarían todo. Iniciaron la búsqueda de Francis, pero éste había emigrado a otra ciudad turística, donde le era fácil encontrar trabajo como músico, ya que era el mejor guitarrista del sector en lo que se refería a interpretar Beatles.

Buscando saber los verdaderos motivos del crimen, regresaron al sector donde vivió Inia, sobornando amigos y conocidos de Francis se enteraron de que él amaba a Inia con locura, pero fue rechazado por ella. Él insistió, pero no logró nada, así que motivaba al padrastro de ella a darle malos tratos, para que ella huyera de casa, refugiándose en sus brazos, pero eso nunca sucedió. Francis y el padrastro de Inia, se drogaban y enloquecían, para buscar ambos los favores sexuales de Inia, la que aparte de bella, era escurridiza y escapó siempre de sus pretensiones. Ella finalmente huyó al sector de Don Triste, recibiendo la protección de Don Mario Alberti, no habiendo posibilidades para Francis, por lo que dejó de molestarla, pero al parecer solo en apariencia.

Después se enteraron que el arma que tenía Inia era la misma con que la asesinaron y ésta a su vez había sido un regalo de Francis, para su protección y como una mera disculpa por todo lo anteriormente ocurrido entre ellos. Don Triste no contaba con los medios para ir en busca de Francis, ya que serían grandes los gastos y por otro lado no sabía cuántos días, semanas, o meses le llevaría está desesperada búsqueda. Villi su inseparable amigo le recordó que también se puede vivir de la música, ¿por qué no aprender a tocar bien un instrumento? Y así poder sufragar los gastos durante la búsqueda de Francis. Más tarde Don Triste y Villi, se robaron una guitarra comenzando a escondidas, el arduo y bello trabajo de aprender a tocar guitarra.

Don Triste practicaba, atando las cuerdas con una servilleta de tela, para no hacer ruido y practicar por horas durante la noche, realizaba ejercicios con los dedos, escuchaba música día a día hasta que su vida se llenó de música. En esa época el mundo entero estaba loco por la música de los Beatles, a Don Triste le agradaban, pero no lo alocaban, su gusto era más universal. Trató de interpretarlos lo más original al disco, tratando de imitar su sonido y sonar igual en un 100%

Cuatro meses más tarde, Don Triste interpretaba exitosamente al cuarteto de Liverpool aceptablemente, y lo consideraban un buen guitarrista, redobló sus prácticas día y noche realizando presentaciones dos meses más tarde.

Pensamiento
Nunca le temas a la felicidad, no la esquives por temor a que no sea real o definitiva, solo tómala y lucha por mantenerla a tu lado. Pase lo que pase no te rindas ni dejes que pase de largo, porque de no hacerlo al tiempo sabrás que te equivocaste, pero será tarde la felicidad es la respuesta, a todas las preguntas y acertijos creados por la desdicha.

LA BUSQUEDA

Juntó algún dinero y se embarcó en el ferry, iniciando la búsqueda de Francis, Villi demostrándole su hermosa y valiosa amistad, lo despidió recordándole lo peligroso del sujeto. Más la desventaja de estar solo en todo momento, lejos de la casa sin tío protector y para colmo con poco dinero. Después del viaje en ferry abordó un tren, que lo trasladó rápidamente a la ciudad más importante a nivel turístico. Buscando en bares, cafés cantantes, y todo lugar relacionado con la música de rock and roll, le decían que Francis se había presentado en varios lugares, pero partió a otra ciudad.

Don Triste hizo presentaciones en varios cafés cantantes, juntó algún dinero y viajó tras Francis, pero la historia se repitió por varios meses y otras tantas ciudades. Tanta practica lo transformó en un excelente guitarrista, con estilo muy personal y cosas de la vida, al tocar utilizaba una plumilla Fender triangular delgada como Francis, conservando aún la encontrada por Villi, en el hotel donde murió Inia.

Por correo y ocasionalmente por teléfono, Don Triste siguió en contacto con su mamá, su tío y Villi que le continuaba proporcionando valiosa información y apoyo incondicional digno del mejor amigo del mundo. En un café de tantos que recorrió, después de escuchar su música, el propietario comentó que tenía otro guitarrista que interpretaba Beatles, y que no sería mala idea que tocaran juntos en una misma presentación. Mencionó que el nombre del guitarrista era Francis, provocando en Don Triste una sensación de triunfo, por fin lo había encontrado, le preguntó la dirección diciendo que ambos venían del mismo sector de la isla, y que eran amigos de la infancia.

Él propietario recomendó a Don Triste tener precaución por aquel barrio feo, difícil y peligroso de transitar para propios y extraños. En efecto el lugar era feo, sumamente sucio y se podía oler el peligro, pero no distaba mucho de ser como los barrios de Don Triste, así que no le preocupó.

AVENTURAS DE REFLEXION FILOSOFICA
LA BUSQUEDA

Se detuvo frente al edificio, Francis supuestamente rentaba un cuarto en el segundo piso de la sección en ruinas, Francis abrió la puerta y cortésmente le pidió a Don Triste entrar, ofreciéndole asiento en un sofá viejo y mal oliente. Francis tomó la palabra diciendo que estaba al tanto de su búsqueda y que antes de cualquier ridícula revancha, tenían asuntos en común muy importantes que resolver de una vez, y para siempre. Francis le preguntó, si sabía de la historia de la luz en los ojos, después de recordar un poco respondió que escuchó algo ¿pero eso qué tenía que ver en ese momento?

Francis contestó que era más importante de lo que hubiese imaginado, porque era una historia tan fascinante como real. El resplandor de los ojos era algo más que eso, los que tienen el brillo pueden cambiar el destino de las gentes, pudiendo brindar tranquilidad, felicidad, e inclusive hacer milagros. No muy grandes, pero al fin y al cabo milagros, con la condición de que sean en beneficio de otros y no en el propio. Como saber quiénes son de esta clase es fácil se identifican por el brillo en los ojos, ya que el común de las personas, no pueden ver ni sentir nada especial, acerca de este raro y sencillo resplandor. Don Triste miró por vez primera a los ojos de Francis, descubriendo el mismo resplandor a la par de los ojos de Inia.

Cuando Francis conoció a la bella Inia, descubrió el brillo especial en sus ojos enamorándose de ella perdidamente. Descubriendo que si no la conquistaba sería infeliz para siempre, trató y buscó por todos los medios de conquistarla sin lograrlo, siendo mayor su sufrimiento, por tal motivo decidió matarla, al mismo tiempo no permitiría la felicidad de ellos, porque él si sabía que ambos tenían el brillo en los ojos.

Esa era su única y verdadera razón por la cual llegó hasta el crimen, lo que para él no era nada nuevo, y ahora lo que deseaba era matar a Don Triste.

DON TRISTE OTRA VEZ
LA BUSQUEDA

Porque según su versión acerca de la historia de la luz en los ojos, decía que cuando hubiese sólo un sobreviviente con la luz en los ojos. Éste contaría con poderes inimaginables por lo tanto él quería ser el único sobreviviente. Dejó la plumilla con toda intención sabiendo que sería una pista para Don Triste, así después matarlo lejos del barrio y sobre todo sin protección alguna de Don Mario Alberti.

Don Triste no podía creer esa historia ya que sonaba más a fantasía que a verdad, absurda en absoluto, pero Francis aseveró que era la única y verdadera razón durante toda su existencia. Contó que han existido hombres y mujeres con las mismas facultades y que las han utilizado tanto para bien como para mal.

Grandes héroes personajes de la historia que tenían en común el destello en los ojos, pero aun así ellos no eran sus héroes, porque al final sacrificaron sus vidas en beneficio de otros, y él no pensaba hacer lo mismo mencionó criminales como Hitler el dictador, el asesino intelectual del presidente Kennedy, Jack el destripador, y otros tantos criminales a los cuales él admiraba. Según él porque mataron sin ninguna compasión y trataron de mantenerse vivos, para lograr ser los únicos en el mundo con el resplandor en los ojos.

Francis sacó de entre sus ropas una pistola, preparándose para matar a Don Triste, pero una luz muy intensa con silueta de mujer iluminó la habitación deslumbrando a Francis. Ese momento fue aprovechado por Don Triste para arrojarse encima de Francis, cayendo ambos al vacío a través de una ventana.

Por un instante Don Triste no supo nada de sí, ni tampoco se percató de la caída que fue a lo largo de dos pisos. Lanzó su brillante mirada hacia la ventana y para su sorpresa no descubrió ventana alguna, sólo se miraban sucios muros por lo que se sintió confundido.

LA BUSQUEDA

Sintió en su mano derecha dolor y al mirar se percató de que un dedo estaba atravesado por una delgada varilla metálica. Como pudo y no sin dolor liberó su dedo que sangraba escandalosamente, al mismo tiempo que descubrió cuan afortunado fue, ya que cayó encima del cuerpo de Francis y de esa manera se protegió de otras cuatro varillas, que atravesaron de lado a lado el cuerpo de Francis muriendo instantáneamente. En fin, las cosas se complicaban porque nadie sería capaz de creer que había sido accidente y mucho menos en defensa propia, razón por la cual huyó a toda prisa del lugar. Después de vendarse el dedo comenzó el retorno a casa, iba en busca de la protección de su tío Mario Alberti, viajó en varios trenes y en ferry de regreso a la isla. Recordó los errores que cometió durante la búsqueda de Francis, dio su verdadero nombre y datos del hotel donde se hospedó. El propietario del café, podía informar como localizar y arrestar a Don Triste así que era de nuevo el sospechoso número uno.

Después de narrarles su aventura a Villi y a su tío, confesó su temor de ser apresado, pero su tío movió todos sus contactos y fue enterado, que habían girado una orden de arresto contra su sobrino. Por tratarse de Don Mario Alberti, concedieron diez horas tiempo suficiente para que pusiera a su sobrino lejos y a salvo del arresto. Después de abastecerlo de abrazos, dinero y contactos, así como un cúmulo de lágrimas, Don Mario y Villi lo despidieron. Le vieron partir a bordo de un barco pesquero en ruta a Barcelona, España. Ya que la policía custodiaba los ferris en ruta que partían a Italia.

La despedida fue triste como era de esperarse, pero Don Triste se fue contento, ya que descubrió que su tío lo amaba más de lo que él se imaginó. Con Villi comprobó que tenía amigo para toda la vida, siendo estos regalos muy preciados para él. Con el dinero proporcionado por su tío, Don Triste huyó hacia América no sin antes atravesar parte de Europa, tal y como se planeó la fuga.

DON TRISTE OTRA VEZ
LA BUSQUEDA

Varios meses después ya en América, se dedicó a tocar música de rock and roll con un grupo, que viajaban por la frontera del país vecino. Aprendiendo el acento, y cultura como un escudo para que no fuera descubierta su verdadera nacionalidad y personalidad no necesito aprender el idioma, sólo aprendió el acento, modismos y costumbres de la cultura que en ese momento le permitían respirar como hombre libre.

Don Triste siguió esperando el retorno de su querida Inia, buscando en toda mujer aquel hermoso brillo en los ojos. También tenía pesadillas acerca de Francis, la eterna tristeza de perder a sus familiares y preparar el retorno a casa de su madre, en la capital del país donde murió su padre, que desde ese día sería su país, para ocultar su pasado y comenzar una nueva vida. Don Triste recordó a todos sus asombrosos amigos, personajes maravillosos que conoció y afirmó que ellos tenían el destello en los ojos. Ahora entendía, y sabía cuál era la razón de su actitud tan rara pero extraordinaria. La historia era cierta y se le presentaba la oportunidad de ser bueno, útil al mundo y a sus semejantes.

Entendiendo que no sería en beneficio personal, pero era una misión hermosa, la cual solo tendría que seguir acatando. Además, la hermosa Inía volvería con él, como parte de esa historia tal y como ella lo prometió, Don Triste entendió y aceptó su nuevo destino. Siguió fielmente creyendo en la promesa que Inia le hizo de, algún día volver con él y bueno así fue como se convirtió en Don Triste, tal y como se le conoce en esta historia.

De aquí en adelante su vida y su carácter serían tan especiales e increíbles, que lo único que se puede decir es que la historia de la luz es real, ya que su vida lo comprueba. Sus historias y aventuras fueron reales, pero fascinantes como un libro de aventuras imaginarias, reales como su espíritu y su fe que nunca se quebrantaron, ni cambio su manera de ser, así como tampoco dejó de buscar a su querida Inia.

Pensamiento

La venganza tiene dos lados, unos la ven como justicia, otros la condenan como un sentimiento negativo, que sólo acarrea más desdicha y problemas interminables para quien la pretende llevar a cabo, alguien dijo que la venganza es como un bosque en el que te puedes perder.

Otro dijo que es un placer sumamente dulce Don Triste nunca pensó en la venganza sólo buscaba saber una verdad, cuando se encontró frente a la verdad, no realizó ninguna venganza y se vio envuelto en problemas interminables, quiere decir que bajo ninguna circunstancia la venganza es correcta, sólo te hará daño a ti mismo.

EL MURO Y LA FE

Durante el año 1975 Don Triste fue enviado a trabajar a una turística bella ciudad portuaria, en la que el gobierno federal construía una gigantesca planta termoeléctrica para generar electricidad mejorando el servicio tanto a la industria como a los ciudadanos. El proyecto era gigantesco ocupaba a quince mil trabajadores distribuidos en tres turnos. En su primer día de trabajo, fue asignado al almacén de importación por su facilidad para el idioma inglés. Al finalizar el día laboral se dedicó a buscar casa para rentar, ya que esperaba radicar en el puerto por lo menos doce meses.

Encontró una casa cómoda y económica en un barrio bonito cerca de la playa, por las tardes disfrutaba dedicándose a correr por varias horas a lo largo de la rivera, que presumía de bella por lo que él se sumaba aseverando que era un lugar hermoso. Cierto día despertó soñando que nadaba en el azul del mar, pero para su sorpresa si estaba casi nadando, ya que la casa se inundó a causa de la torrencial lluvia que se dejó sentir durante toda la noche. Llamó al trabajo argumentando que no trabajaría ese día, ya que tenía problemas que resolver.

Los vecinos limpiaban y sacaban el agua con cierta naturalidad provocando su curiosidad preguntándoles que tan frecuente ocurrían ese tipo de inundaciones, respondiéndole que en tiempos de lluvia sucedían todos los días ya que el barrio estaba ubicado en una cuneta.

Inmediatamente abordó un taxi, solicitando lo llevara al barrio más alto a nivel del mar, con la intención de rentar una casa alejada de las inundaciones. Por fortuna encontró una colina y en lo más alto una bella casa que dominaba toda la ciudad, gozando de una maravillosa vista en fin era el lugar que cubría su necesidad de no ser inundado por segunda ocasión, después de contratar un servicio de mudanzas y muchas horas de esfuerzo logró por fin dormir esa noche en su flamante, nueva, segura e inundable locación.

Al día siguiente tuvo que caminar a lo largo de tres calles empedradas, hasta llegar a la avenida principal por la que transitaba en ruta hacia la planta termoeléctrica y de regreso el camión que a diario transportaba gratuitamente a todos los trabajadores de la planta. Llamó su atención un gran muro de piedra a lo largo de toda una manzana, a decir verdad, eran cuatro altos muros, Don Triste preguntó que había dentro de aquellos muros y fue enterado que presos, era una cárcel.

Un sentimiento de repudio hizo que tomase entre sus manos una piedra, que arrojó contra el muro con el deseo de terminar con dos mundos divididos. Gente buena y mala por ambos lados, pero condenados sólo los que estaban dentro. Para él eso no era justo ni representaba lo que llaman justicia, después de arrojar otra piedra continuó su camino en busca del camión que lo llevaría hasta el trabajo.

Después al finalizar su día laboral, abordó el camión que lo llevaría de regreso a casa, al ver el muro de la prisión ni tardo ni perezoso le arrojo una piedra con todas sus fuerzas, con el profundo deseo de derribarlo. Más tarde salió por su acostumbrada carrera hacia la playa, así que tanto de ida como de regreso arrojó piedras contra el muro.

Comenzando así sin saber un rito diario de protesta contra el muro, solo en favor de los inocentes que habitaban en el interior del penal.

El diario ir al trabajo, la carrera a la playa y alguna otra salida nocturna, daban como resultado entre cuatro y seis caminatas frente al muro, las cuales eran acompañadas por el mismo número de piedras lanzadas contra el mismo.

Más tarde en el trabajo, conoció a Gabriel un ex-comunista, ex-preso político y loco proveniente de la ciudad capital asignado al mismo departamento de trabajo.

DON TRISTE OTRA VEZ
EL MURO Y LA FE

Iniciaron inmediatamente una amistad que duró por mucho tiempo, algo así como más de lo que imaginaron compartieron la vivienda, aventuras y amistades ya que eran populares y divertidos, tanto en el trabajo como en la ciudad todos los días caminaban hasta el trabajo y de regreso, pero el rito de la piedra a su amigo le parecía absurdo y en ocasiones le molestaba, sobre todo porque lo creía demente.

Cierta mañana en que caminaban tarde en busca del camión, Don Triste se regresó como siempre a lanzar la piedra contra el muro, pero Gabriel lo miró con enojo ya que era tarde. Cuando llegaron a la avenida vieron cómo se alejaba el camión sin poder darle alcance. Sin decir nada por el momento Gabriel miro a Don Triste y señaló un restaurante con el deseo de ir al interior. Don triste protestó porque debían ir al trabajo, pero Gabriel sin atender sus protestas literalmente lo arrastró hasta el interior del mencionado lugar. Luego ordenaron algo de tomar sentándose a la mesa uno frente al otro, Gabriel argumentó que estaba cansado de la estúpida actitud diaria respecto al muro Decía que ambos llegaban tarde porque siempre tenía que esperarlo a que arrojara la famosa piedra, así que sin importar nada solicitaba una explicación.

Después de beber un trago de jugo de naranja, Don Triste relató la historia que le inspiraba el famoso muro, y que la gota de agua continua quiebra la roca y que eso pasaría si insistía todos los días lanzando piedras contra el muro. Al finalizar la explicación Gabriel se burló diciendo que eso era lo más ridículo que había escuchado en toda su vida, aseverando que primero morirían y que el muro no caería. Y que nunca más llegaría tarde, porque jamás lo esperaría a que arrojase la estúpida piedra. A partir de ese día Gabriel no esperaba por Don Triste, e inclusive cuando tenían visitas les contaba su fantasía, como él la llamaba y se burlaban, pero no logró su enojo, ya que Don Triste continuó arrojando piedras contra el muro.

Así transcurrieron varios meses durante los cuales su amistad creció sin importar las burlas ni las piedras. Gabriel logró solucionar problemas con su esposa y por fin la hizo venir a radicar con él, ella era una mujer con carácter de ángel que todo perdonaba y entendía con sonrisas llenas de profunda ternura. Ambos se convirtieron para Don Triste como hermanos mayores que cuidaban de él, por saber que estaba solo en ese lugar contando sólo con ellos, además porque creían que estaba loco por seguir arrojando piedras contra el muro de la prisión. Por fin llegó el día en que Don Triste decidió regresar a la ciudad capital y continuar sus estudios, además especiales circunstancias lo ameritaban, pero no doy detalles por ahora ya que esa es otra maravillosa historia que contaré más tarde. Por lo pronto empacó sus pertenencias, se despidió de todo mundo y regresó al lado de su madre, quien le recibió contenta y orgullosa como siempre.

Ya estando en la ciudad capital semanas después, los noticieros hablaban del hermoso puerto con alarmantes noticias acerca de tragedia y destrucción, causadas por un huracán, así como varios tornados, quedando el bello puerto sin comunicación por varios días. Don Triste se volvía loco por no saber nada de Gabriel y esposa, porque la casa era segura para inundaciones, pero, para huracanes era insegura por estar ubicada en una colina y para mala suerte la más alta de todo el puerto.

Ya se imaginarán su angustia durante todo el tiempo que no supo nada de ellos fueron doce largos días. Las horas transcurrían sin saber nada de ellos, hasta que se le ocurrió ir a las oficinas centrales del gobierno federal y solicitar comunicación con la planta termoeléctrica, por medio de la radio, después de varias horas se enteró que gozaban de salud y sin problemas tanto Gabriel como la esposa. Fue un gran alivio saber que estaban bien, además mencionaron que habían enviado una carta y varios recortes de periódico con las noticias de todo lo ocurrido a causa del huracán.

DON TRISTE OTRA VEZ
EL MURO Y LA FE

Más tarde Don Triste recibió la carta enterándose de lo siguiente: -Querido amigo, tuvimos suerte ya que la casa resistió bien los embates de la tormenta. Sólo se quebraron algunos vidrios mojándose los muebles de la casa, pero no pasó a mayores, mi esposa y yo estamos bien, pero el muro se cayó y me refiero al muro al que le arrojabas piedras, quedando en pie solo los otros tres muros a los que nunca les arrojaste piedras.

Ambos hemos llorado, porque no nos perdonamos el error de no haber comprendido el alcance de tu fe y lo grande de tu espíritu, escribimos esta carta con lágrimas, deseando abrazarte y pedirte perdón por las estúpidas burlas. Queremos decirte que te queremos con toda el alma, tienes nuestro respeto eterno por la fe tan grande que tienes, la que deseamos conserves para ejemplo de incrédulos como nosotros. Con amor para ti de tus hermanos.

P.D. volvieron a levantar el muro, ahora mi esposa y yo lo apedreamos a diario en tu honor. Los fines de semana nos visitan viejos amigos los cuales también arrojan piedras contra el muro. Nos duele saber que no caerá porque sólo tú puedes tirarlo, así que te necesitamos para tirar éste y otros muros más.

Inmediatamente Don Triste tomó uno de los recortes leyendo lo siguiente; el huracán derribó uno de los muros de la prisión, lo cual fue aprovechado rápidamente por diez prisioneros que se dieron a la fuga, tomando ventaja de la confusión y el caos causado por el fenómeno de la naturaleza.

Otro recorte mencionaba que seis de los reos habían sido recapturados, y que otros tres habían sido acribillados por las autoridades por resistirse al arresto, además de que los fugitivos contaban con armas, no habiendo otra salida más que el enfrentamiento. Un prisionero no fue encontrado por ningún lado, por lo que se cree ya debía encontrarse muy lejos del lugar, y quizás hasta en otro país siendo difícil su captura.

EL MURO Y LA FE

Leyó la carta, así como los recortes alrededor de treinta veces. Y después concluyó que no supo en que se podía basar el beneficio de su fe. Ojalá y el único prófugo libre haya sido inocente, para que se justifique toda la fe que tuvo para derribar el muro de la prisión, porque de no ser así todo habría sido inútil. Al paso del tiempo cuando Gabriel y Don Triste volvieron a reunirse en la ciudad capital, platicaron poéticamente del asunto y así lo siguen recordando.

Como una simple poesía dedicada a la actividad inútil de apedrear un muro gigantesco, por un pequeño ser dotado de fe y un arsenal ilimitado de piedras las cuales siempre encontró sin problema alguno.

Ojalá algún día Don Triste pueda derribar los muros de la incomprensión que separan a los hombres justos de los no tan justos, a los ricos de los pobres, a los sabios de los no sabios y sobre todo a los filósofos de los políticos para vivir en un mundo sin muros.

AL tiempo se enteró, que cayó el muro de Berlín en Alemania, el que separaba una nación de hermanos. Quisiera decirles que también Don Triste anduvo por allá arrojando piedras al muro, pero eso no es cierto, pero como le hubiese gustado arrojarle una piedra al famoso muro de Berlín.

Pensamiento
La libertad es el regalo más preciado para todo ser viviente, cuando pierdes la libertad dejas de vivir y solo sueñas con ella, es mejor tenerla y soñar con lo que harás con tu libertad, recuerda es tuya no la arriesgues, sólo gózala día a día.

LAS BOTAS AMARILLAS

Durante la época en que Don Triste trabajó en la construcción de la planta termoeléctrica en aquel bello puerto donde radicó alrededor 10 meses, sucedió un día en que él revisaba la entrega de varias órdenes con pedidos de pares de botas de trabajo para los peones, y se percató de un error en una de las entregas.

200 pares de botas destinados para los peones del almacén habían sido entregados a varios ingenieros de otros departamentos, pero los pares de botas pertenecían a los peones del almacén. Don Triste revisó los números de requisición y los comparó con los números y fechas de las entregas y comprobó que se trataba de una equivocación.

De inmediato se presentó ante el Sr. Palacios jefe de almacenes y mostrándoles las órdenes de requisición y las órdenes de entrega haciéndole saber que los pares de botas habían sido entregados al departamento equivocado y que las órdenes de los ingenieros tardarían en llegar al almacén aproximadamente 60 días o más.

Él Sr. Palacios revisaba los papeles, al tiempo en que Don Triste sonreía satisfecho por su descubrimiento, pero para su sorpresa el Sr. Palacios le explicó que intercambiar la entrega había sido un movimiento ordenado por él mismo y que era correcto.

Y que cuando se recibieran los pares de botas para el departamento de ingeniería éstos serían entregados a los peones del almacén, por lo tanto, era algo de lo que no debiera preocuparse ya que era algo sin interés, y por supuesto que los peones podían esperar.

Don Triste al salir de la oficina del jefe de almacenes, fue directamente a todos los almacenes para revisar todas las ordenes entregadas durante los últimos 10 meses.

AVENTURAS DE REFLEXION FILOSOFICA
LAS BOTAS AMARILLAS

Él resultado después de revisar las ordenes fue el siguiente; las órdenes de requisición por pares de botas eran las de los peones del almacén, que por ser el departamento más grande contaba con aproximadamente 3000 empleados, de los cuales eran 2800 peones con salario mínimo como sueldo por lo tanto eran los que necesitaban los pares de botas con urgencia.

Durante los últimos 10 meses sólo les habían entregado 200 pares de botas y el resto de las órdenes habían sido entregadas a otros departamentos y los peones del almacén y otros de otras áreas tenían que esperar hasta que se entregaran las órdenes de otros departamentos. Al instante Don Triste recorrió la planta haciendo un inventario de quiénes tenían ya botas y quiénes no, resultando que el total de peones de la planta no tenían sus botas ya que los 200 pares de botas entregados al almacén fueron para el personal técnico y de oficina por lo tanto ningún peón de salario mínimo tenía un par de botas.

Los peones usaban zapatos viejos desgastados, tenis rotos, y huaraches en su mayoría por lo tanto estaban expuestos a lesiones al faltarles protección en los pies por carecer de botas, eso fue indignante y vergonzoso. Al día siguiente Don Triste continuó revisando todas las órdenes y entregas de botas, descubriendo que en su totalidad habían sido entregadas a varios departamentos como ingeniería, contabilidad, administración, transporte y soldadores en fin a los empleados que recibían entre 8 y 15 salarios mínimos de sueldo y los peones que ganaban un salario mínimo no podían participar del beneficio de tener un par de botas gratuito.

La conclusión era simple y fácil de entender, se trataba de un abuso por parte del Sr. Palacios jefe de almacenes hacia los peones de la planta y peor aún de su propio departamento, favorecía a otros departamentos para tener buenas relaciones.

DON TRISTE OTRA VEZ
LAS BOTAS AMARILLAS

Con altos jefes y no le molestaba dejar casi descalzos a los peones. Don Triste enfrentó al Sr. Palacios preguntando directamente ¿el porqué de ese favoritismo? ¿Por qué dejar a los peones sin pares de botas y sin protección para sus pies? El Sr. Palacios argumento que él era el jefe de almacenes y podía disponer de los pares de botas como él quisiera, Don Triste observó los pies del Sr. Palacios y éste calzaba un flamante par de botas gratuitas. Durante los siguientes 3 días Don Triste estuvo hablando con el departamento de compras, explicándoles la situación les pidió que lo ayudaran apurando a los fabricantes de las botas para que elaboraran y entregaran 4000 pares de botas en un lapso no mayor de 3 semanas.

Más tarde los fabricantes explicaron lo difícil que sería cumplir los pedidos en tan sólo 3 semanas, cuando esta respuesta llegó al conocimiento de Don Triste él le hizo saber al departamento de compras que podían adquirir los pares de botas en otras fábricas sin importar que se buscaran en otras ciudades. Ya imaginarán lo que ocurrió con el dueño de la fábrica, se esmeró y preparando a su personal a trabajar horas extras comunicó que cumpliría con la entrega en el lapso de 3 semanas. Haciendo profundas investigaciones en todos los almacenes, preguntando a peones y oficinistas, Don Triste fue enterado que la situación de abuso era algo común, además era ya de varios años atrás.

Y nadie hacía nada para cambiar la triste situación, era de conformidad de todos porque a quién le podía importar los peones de salario mínimo.

Los pares de botas por su valor económico, requerían para su entrega la firma del que los recibía en un vale para comprobar la entrega, además se debían de regresar al almacén al ser despedidos, al renunciar o simplemente al recibir un reemplazo, estos vales eran firmados por el almacenista o por el asistente del almacén.

AVENTURAS DE REFLEXION FILOSOFICA
LAS BOTAS AMARILLAS

Durante las 3 semanas en que se fabricaron los 4000 pares de botas Don Triste preparo los vales a nombre de cada uno de los peones siendo 3950 aproximadamente, además se les comunicó a todos para que estuviesen listos y presentes el día de la entrega. Esas semanas fueron de esperanza para los peones ya que por fin tendrían acceso a los soñados pares de botas que nunca habían tenido y todo por injusticias ya que legalmente tenían derecho a obtener esas botas para su protección, eso era algo obligatorio por parte de la compañía y en este caso por parte del Sr. Palacios jefe de almacenes.

Los días pasaban y había comentarios encontrados, unos decían que en el último instante los pares de botas irían a parar a otros departamentos como había ocurrido durante los últimos 3 años. Otros mantenían la confianza en Don Triste diciendo que él no permitiría más injusticias y que los pares de botas les serían entregados. Otros permanecían callados, sin decir opinión a favor o en contra, pero con la esperanza de que Don Triste no se doblegara ante las circunstancias, que podían ser adversas.

Durante todo ese tiempo Don Triste continuó su vida cotidiana y tanto de ida como de regreso a casa continuaba apedreando el muro de la prisión, su inseparable amigo Gabriel y la esposa lo apoyaban en su proyecto de favorecer a los peones con la entrega de pares de botas. Por supuesto Gabriel siendo todo un comunista alababa la idea de Don Triste y decía que los pares de botas eran del pueblo, para el pueblo y el derecho de todo trabajador pobre que cumplía con una labor para el país, por supuesto que el gobierno comunista o no sería el responsable de proteger a sus trabajadores y con mayor razón si eran peones de salario mínimo.

En fin, Gabriel hacía elocuentes discursos acerca del tema, por supuesto se decía involucrado tanto como si hubiese sido su idea, haciéndose de un crédito que no le correspondía.

DON TRISTE OTRA VEZ
LAS BOTAS AMARILLAS

A Don Triste eso no le preocupaba ni le quitaba el sueño ya que él decidió hacerlo con o sin ayuda de nadie. La verdad es que el departamento de compras apoyó a Don Triste porque odiaban al Sr. Palacios y otro tanto porque Don Triste era amigo de todos en la compañía.

Don Triste trataba bien tanto a los peones como a directores, inclusive turnaba sus horas de comida por lo tanto en ocasiones comía con los peones y en otras ocasiones con los directores, razón que le permitía hacer muy buen trabajo y comunicarse a todos los niveles comprobando que el puesto de coordinador general de almacenes era un puesto que se ganó por su esfuerzo y habilidad, además de ser un trabajador incansable.

Todas las cosas tienen un sentido y razón de ser, aún aquellas que parecen incomprensibles así fue la situación de los pares de botas amarillas como se mencionan en esta historia. El desenlace fue algo inesperado, no pensado por nadie excepto por Don Triste que supo bien lo que sucedería, pero no le importó ni quiso cambiar su decisión ni su manera de ser porque así era él, un simple ser dotado de luz interna basada en la justicia y de ser necesario siempre listo al sacrificio en beneficio de los necesitados.

Todos los plazos se cumplen y por fin los pares de botas fueron entregados al almacén por el departamento de compras, por supuesto con todo hermetismo y casi en secreto. Don Triste había pedido a los peones que hicieran fila en el almacén de consumo diario por ser el más lejano de la oficina del Sr. Palacios por lo cual no se daría cuenta de la entrega de las mencionadas botas o lo haría demasiado tarde sin que tuviera oportunidad de impedirlo.

Al entregar el primer par de botas el jefe de aquel almacén de consumo diario se negó a firmar el vale de entrega lo mismo que su asistente.

LAS BOTAS AMARILLAS

Para Don Triste eso no fue impedimento ya que el entendía lo que significaba firmar, podía ser comprometedor y salir tan afectado como perder el empleo o algo por el estilo. Ya se imaginarán Don Triste en su calidad de coordinador general de almacenes contaba con la autoridad suficiente para firmar y aceptar la responsabilidad de la entrega de pares de botas para los peones.

La entrega comenzó aproximadamente a las 7:30 de la mañana y se prolongó hasta cerca de las 4:00 de la tarde, tiempo en que Don Triste no fue a comer para no desperdiciar tiempo. Ya que entregar 4000 pares de botas dando la medida correcta, firmar quien las recibía y firmar Don Triste, así como guardar el vale en orden alfabético era algo que consumía demasiado tiempo.

Lo cual era agotador Don Triste aseguraba que le dolían los dedos y la mano tan solo de firmar, uso 4 bolígrafos repito fue agotador, pero la sonrisa de agradecimiento de cada uno de los peones era la mayor recompensa para Don Triste, eso le dio ánimo para terminar su larga tarea.

Al término de la entrega Don Triste solo menciono "justicia divina" realizada por un ser con voluntad de servir a los demás.

Los empleados que estuvieron presentes de principio hasta el final de la entrega de todos los pares de botas, lo miraron con respeto y admiración porque sabían que se atrevió a hacer lo justo y lo que ellos nunca hubiesen hecho.

Afortunadamente el Sr. Palacios no se enteró de la entrega ese día, pero al siguiente día fue enterado porque el departamento de contabilidad requería de 100 pares de botas y no había ningún par en el almacén, por lo tanto, reclamaron al Sr. Palacios porque estaban enterados de que el día anterior el almacén había recibido 4000 pares de botas.

DON TRISTE OTRA VEZ
LAS BOTAS AMARILLAS

Así que el Sr. Palacios preguntó ¿qué había pasado con aquellos pares de botas? Fue enterado que Don Triste los había entregado en una sesión maratónica. Ya se imaginarán mandó llamar a Don Triste y ya en el interior de su oficina lo reprendió diciéndole que hizo mal al entregar los pares de botas sin siquiera consultarlo.

Don Triste solo respondió "hice lo correcto" no había razón de comunicárselo ya que todos los días se entregaba una innumerable cantidad de productos y herramientas en todos los almacenes y no se requería de su conocimiento o autorización.

Solo eran necesarios ambos cuando se entregaban los productos como reemplazo a otros departamentos y en esa ocasión no fue así, por lo tanto, correctamente no se requirió de su autorización. El Sr. Palacios explotó fuera de sí, le dijo a Don Triste que estaba despedido, que fuera al departamento de contabilidad para recibir el cheque de su liquidación.

Mientras tanto el Sr. Palacios elaboraría un memorando explicando las faltas cometidas por Don Triste y las razones por las cuales lo despedía. Don Triste se trasladó a las oficinas del sindicato de trabajadores comunicándole al secretario general de la penosa situación.

Él Sr. Fong jefe sindical le pregunto si sabía que había cometido una grave falta al entregar los pares de botas equivocadamente y sin autorización del Sr. Palacios Don Triste comentó que la entrega había sido correcta, por lo tanto, no había cometido ninguna falta o error alguno.

Al mismo tiempo el Sr. Palacios hacía entrega del memorando al departamento de contabilidad, argumentando lo mal que hizo Don Triste, sin ocultar su enojo solicitando la destitución de Don Triste.

AVENTURAS DE REFLEXION FILOSOFICA
LAS BOTAS AMARILLAS

Todos los trabajadores de las oficinas de almacenes apoyaban a Don Triste y corrieron la voz por toda la planta termoeléctrica de lo que estaba sucediendo y solicitaban su ayuda para ir en auxilio de Don Triste. Minutos más tarde fue de gran sorpresa para el Sr. Palacios y para el jefe del departamento de contabilidad ver fuera de sus oficinas más de 4500 personas, es decir casi la totalidad de los empleados de ese turno, peones y no peones, todos gritando que Don Triste hizo un acto de bondad y justicia.

Los peones pedían que no lo despidieran y que no se moverían de ahí hasta que Don Triste fuera re instalado como coordinador general de los almacenes al momento corrieron a las oficinas del sindicato de trabajadores comunicándole al Sr. Fong de la crítica situación, por lo tanto, el Sr. Fong y Don Triste se presentaron ante el contador, el Sr. Palacios y la multitud de trabajadores.

Él Sr. Fong le pidió a Don Triste que pidiera a la multitud regresar a sus ocupaciones, Don Triste accedió y agradeciéndoles su apoyo, pidió que regresasen a sus labores cotidianas y que todo estaría bien para él, después de escucharlo empezaron a quitarse las botas para que dejasen en paz a Don Triste.

Apenas empezaban a quitarse los pares de botas cuando Don Triste les gritó con autoridad que no lo hicieran porque sería en vano todo lo que él hizo además él tenía los papeles para comprobar que hizo lo correcto y que no se preocuparan ya que todo saldría bien y que los vería unas horas más tarde como siempre, como el coordinador general de almacenes así que era mejor regresar a sus labores.

Uno a uno empezaron a reintegrarse a sus actividades cotidianas con la esperanza de que Don Triste no perdería su trabajo. Después se reunieron, el jefe de contabilidad, el enojado Sr. Palacios, el Sr. Toledo jefe de compras, el ingeniero Fabre director general de la planta, el Sr. Fong y Don Triste.

DON TRISTE OTRA VEZ
LAS BOTAS AMARILLAS

En la reunión Don Triste mostró a todos las órdenes de requisición por los pares de botas de los almacenes y las órdenes de compra por las mismas. Cotejadas con las órdenes de entrega, así como con las fechas de requisiciones siendo las más antiguas las órdenes de los almacenes.

Por lo tanto, eran las órdenes que debían entregarse tal y como Don Triste lo había realizado en su maratónica entrega, así que Don Triste no había cometido ni error ni falta alguna de respeto o pasar sobre la autoridad del Sr. Palacios, jefe de almacenes.

Él Sr. Toledo jefe de compras tenía copias de requisiciones y compras que estaban exactamente como las de Don Triste así que indicaban que la entrega de pares de botas del día anterior había sido una entrega correcta y que la acusación en contra de Don Triste era incorrecta pidiendo que se le diera una disculpa por el mal momento.

El Sr. Fong jefe sindical exhortó al Sr. Palacios a regresarle su posición de coordinador general de almacenes a Don Triste, así como la correspondiente disculpa. El jefe de contabilidad y el director general miraron al Sr. Palacios en espera de corregir su error, el Sr. Palacios ofreció disculpas a Don Triste y mencionó que le restituía la posición de su trabajo claro que no podía ocultar su disgusto, así que de inmediato se retiró. El jefe de contabilidad rompió el memorando de la acusación y se retiró junto con el director general de la planta.

El jefe de compras abrazo a Don Triste y lo felicitó porque ambos habían triunfado haciendo lo correcto y muy en el fondo eran cómplices de aquella hazaña sin haber alterado documentos, pero repitos cómplices porque el jefe de compras odiaba al Sr. Palacios por abusar de los peones que eran nobles trabajadores.

Él Sr. Fong jefe del sindicato que había sido el que recomendó y ayudó a Don Triste para trabajar en la planta termoeléctrica estrechó su mano.

LAS BOTAS AMARILLAS

Le agradeció el no haber cometido nada malo porque así quedarían bien los dos y se sentía orgulloso de haberlo recomendado para trabajar, y que no se preocupara del Sr. Palacios ya que él hablaría más tarde con él.

Don Triste le agradeció y comentó que la decisión de irse la había tomado desde tiempo antes y eso sólo le dio fuerzas para hacerlo ya que él tenía planes de regresar a casa de su mamá y terminar la universidad la cual ahora era su meta, así que se despidieron y Don Triste le pidió al Sr. Fong que se encargara de que le dieran su cheque de liquidación para cuanto antes marcharse a casa.

Sonriendo el Sr. Fong pidió a Don Triste que regresara por la tarde al día siguiente y que todo estaría listo, además si cambiaba de opinión no sería problema inclusive podía cambiarlo a otro departamento y no trabajaría más en los almacenes.

Don Triste sonrío y se alejó, momentos más tarde a la salida de la planta termoeléctrica todos los empleados de la obra mostraban agradecimiento a Don Triste abrazándolo, estrechándole las manos, dándole suaves palmadas en la espalda, un sin fin de muestras de aprecio, después como todos los días abordó el camión junto a Gabriel y emprendieron el regreso a casa.

Ya se imaginarán Don Triste mencionó que todo se arregló, pero no mencionó que se iría de la ciudad. Bajaron del camión y después de arrojarle piedras al muro de la prisión, Don Triste platicó a Gabriel y esposa sus planes para el día siguiente.

Ir tan sólo a recoger su cheque, despedirse de todos en la planta tomarse 3 días de vacaciones y después partir a la ciudad capital para incorporarse a la universidad y radicar en casa de su mamá.

DON TRISTE OTRA VEZ
LAS BOTAS AMARILLAS

Al siguiente día, en la planta termoeléctrica se despidió de todos haciéndoles saber que se iba a estudiar, después paso 3 días de descanso paseando y por las noches yendo a bailar en las diferentes discotecas de la ciudad.

Por cierto, que durante esos 3 días se le vio acompañado de una chica bonita que nadie supo de dónde salió o no tuvieron tiempo de averiguar. Merecidamente se divirtió de lo lindo después del esfuerzo para que todos los peones calzaran un par de botas amarillas.

Gabriel estuvo platicando en la planta termoeléctrica, haciéndoles saber a todos los días en que Don Triste partiría y que lo haría viajando desde la estación de autobuses de oriente, porque viajaría de noche para dormir y en la mañana llegar a su destino. Por fin se llegó el día de la partida de Don Triste, así que Gabriel con su esposa y varios amigos fueron a la estación de oriente para despedirlo.

Don Triste después de obtener su boleto para abordar al autobús se sorprendió que había peones con botas amarillas por todos lados y otros más llegando, todos ellos calzaban las botas amarillas. 15 minutos más tarde la estación se llenó de personas calzando botas amarillas, los había en los andenes, dentro y fuera de la estación porque resultó insuficiente para recibir tal cantidad de personas, ya que era una estación pequeña.

Todos traían familiares, hijos, amigos, un aproximado de 9000 personas, resaltando las botas amarillas que se veían por miles, cargaban pollos, guajolotes, canastas con frutas, verduras y flores, bebés corderos y bebés puerquitos. Los empleados de la estación y el equipo de seguridad, así como policías que se presentaron de inmediato porque creían que se trataba de un político distinguido, un artista de cine o alguien sumamente importante porque nunca habían visto tantas personas en aquella estación.

AVENTURAS DE REFLEXION FILOSOFICA
LAS BOTAS AMARILLAS

Eran peones agradecidos que decidieron darle una despedida de héroe porque así lo consideraron y así lo recordarían, como "el héroe de las botas amarillas"

Cuando estuvo listo para abordar el autobús lo abrazaron Gabriel y esposa deseándole lo mejor, los peones empezaron a despedirlo tratando de regalarle los bebés puerquitos, flores, canastas de frutas y verduras, etc. Don Triste menciono que siendo tan pobres él no podía aceptar esos regalos, les dijo la mejor excusa de que no podía llevar todo en el autobús y para no ofender a los que no tomara su obsequio decidió no tomar ninguno, pero sí quiso estrechar la mano de cada uno de los peones presentes.

Ya se imaginarán el estrechar las manos de tantas personas que lloraban y sonreían como cuando despides a tu mejor amigo o a un hermano querido tomó más de una hora y sin terminar el chofer y los miembros de seguridad pidieron a Don Triste que abordara el autobús porque ya se habían atrasado en salir y todo a causa de él, por cierto, que no entendían aún que era lo que estaba pasando, mucho menos entender quién era él.

Así que sin más ni más abordo el autobús y siguió despidiéndose por la ventanilla pudiendo observar la gran línea de botas amarillas que escoltaban el autobús en su partida, vio manos agitándose deseándole lo mejor, fue algo inimaginable era una despedida más que especial. Por fin el autobús salió de la estación.

Don Triste lloró viendo cómo se alejaba de las botas amarillas que inundaron aquella estación en su honor, no recuerda cuanto tiempo lloró y después un profundo sueño lo cobijó por todo el trayecto hasta llegar a la gran ciudad, para despertar con una sonrisa que marcaba el final de sus aventuras en aquel bello puerto.

DON TRISTE OTRA VEZ
LAS BOTAS AMARILLAS

Pensamiento

Al través de la historia universal y religiosa, encontramos capítulos donde se relatan actos heroicos y otros milagrosos, historias que se recuerdan como únicas y especiales, ¿pero ¿qué sucede con los actos heroicos y milagrosos que suceden a diario? Hay madres que, sin familia, sin esposo sin nadie que las apoyen, alimentan a sus hijos día a día, dándoles cariño y protección sufriendo todo tipo de calamidades, pero felices de cumplir con su hermosa tarea de ser madres. ¿Qué hay de los padres que proveen todo a su familia durante toda su vida sin esperar nada a cambio?, haciendo todo tipo de sacrificios brindándoles; educación, alimentos, diversiones y un mundo de cosas más, ¡para mi esos son milagros y esos son los héroes que luchan a diario.

Recuerdo la historia de las botas amarillas, en la que un simple individuo calzó a cerca de 4000 personas, haciendo lo justo sin temor a perder su empleo, porque le fue más satisfactorio ayudar a la gente humilde, dio lecciones de justicia a los que tienen el poder, Don Triste usó el poder en beneficio de otros, hoy pocos lo recuerdan, otros no, pero que importa la historia, sucedió, afortunadamente yo fui testigo y la recuerdo como "el milagro de las botas amarillas"

EL FENOMENO DEL UKA PUKA

Don Triste platicó esta historia que a su vez le fue platicada por el trapero. El fenómeno del Uka Puka es tan antiguo como moderno, ya que sigue vigente hasta nuestros días y sumamente desarrollado entre los países que componen las llamadas sociedades económicas.

Hace 1,650,000 A.C. la humanidad se encontraba en la llamada época de las cavernas, todos los individuos nacían libres y propietarios de todo lo que les rodeaba, sólo les bastaba tomarlo para poseerlo. Los cavernícolas eran los dueños de todo lo imaginable como: agua, ríos, árboles, animales, insectos, etc. etc. Cuando les gustaba algún lugar por ser seguro, con agua, caza y pesca se convertía en el lugar apropiado para habitar.

Se establecían un tiempo en ciertos lugares hasta que las circunstancias cambiaran en ocasiones la curiosidad de ver que había más allá del horizonte, los hacía emprender el viaje buscando otro lugar seguro, con buena caza y pesca que garantizara la seguridad y bienestar de toda la comunidad. Estas sociedades antiguas que se convirtieron al agruparse en villas, tribus, aldeas, serían el inicio de las sociedades y comunidades actuales. Algunas raramente se regían por matriarcado otras por patriarcado, pero el resultado era el mismo se constituyan en pequeñas comunidades que se guiaban por sus propias reglas.

Tenían gente encargada de la seguridad de la tribu, algo así como el ejército, tenían gente que se encargaba de cazar y pescar para alimentar a la tribu. Ellos eran cazadores y pescadores quienes eran no sólo respetados, sino admirados por sus habilidades y astucia, porque descubrían nuevas maneras de caza y pesca.

Las mujeres en su mayoría cuidaban de los niños y se encargaban de todo proceso alimenticio, que consistía en quitarles la piel y el pellejo a los animales y pescados.

DON TRISTE OTRA VEZ
EL FENOMENO DEL UKA PUKA

Para después cortarlos en pedazos pequeños, los que se repartían entre los miembros de la tribu. Dando porciones dobles a los cazadores y pescadores y al o a los patriarcas. En fin, eran comunidades que se reorganizaban debido a sus descubrimientos. Tenían dificultades para expresar sus ideas, ya que carecían de idioma, usaban señas, gestos y gritos guturales que eran el principio de lo que después llamamos voz y más tarde lenguaje. Era tan difícil comunicarse que en ocasiones terminaban en peleas, tan cruentas y sangrientas que se mataban unos a otros tan solo por un simple malentendido, tal y como sucede en nuestros días, ahora por causa del idioma y antes por falta del mismo.

En el año 1,521,327 A. C. Al mediodía hora central Don AG hizo uno de los grandes descubrimientos de la historia antigua. Su descubrimiento consistió en plantar raíces y obtenía algo similar a la soya actual, sólo que con más proteínas y sin los problemas tóxicos creados por los fertilizantes artificiales modernos.

Don AG plantaba tantas raíces como podía y cada vez cosechaba más hierbas de soya, razón por la cual poco a poco iba ocupando más terreno para sembrar la soya. Después de varios meses algo así como un sábado por la tarde Don AG descubrió el efecto del agua sobre los sembradíos así que decidió establecerse en esa área,

Creando el sistema de riego para no viajar más en busca de alimentos, la agricultura fomentó el arraigo a la tierra por lo tanto se estableció el sistema de vida sedentaria.

Los nómadas acarreaban todo tipo de raíces para luego plantarlas en otras tierras sin tener que interrumpir sus largos viajes a causa de la agricultura este descubrimiento fue en su inicio benéfico para la comunidad, porque brindo la oportunidad de alimentarse aun cuando no hubiese buena pesca o caza, pero no todo descubrimiento viene acompañado de beneficios.

También trae efectos negativos. Fue algo así como el año 1,521,326 A. C. A las 6:30 de la mañana hora central, Don AG empezó a colocar varias piedras, todas de tamaño similar alrededor de lo que se podía considerar más o menos una parcela.

Le llevó varias horas porque la parcela era algo así como una hectárea después de terminada su tarea consiguió un garrote de tamaño similar a un palo de baseball, pero el señor AG no pretendía jugar baseball, lo que quería era proteger la parcela delimitada por las piedras que había colocado durante todo el día.

Más tarde a las 5:00 de la tarde hora central, un vecino entró a la parcela cruzando por las piedras, no hubo caminado mucho cuando el Sr. AG les cayó encima a palazos hasta hacerlo salir de la parcela. Una vez afuera el señor AG señalaba las piedras y le gruñía Uka Puka, dándole a entender que la parcela le pertenecía solo a él y que ningún individuo podía entrar sin su permiso. El vecino espantado corrió y buscó ayuda de otros miembros de la tribu los cuales fueron a la parcela del Sr. AG, solo para recibir palazos y la letanía del Uka Puka.

Los días pasaron y la gente se acostumbró a no pasar por el área del Uka Puka para evitar la tanda de golpes. Al paso del tiempo, otros cavernícolas siguieron su ejemplo, otros escogieron una parcela más grande, la rodearon de piedras y con un garrote gritaban Uka Puka como símbolo de propiedad, así fue como nació la propiedad privada. Algunos más ambiciosos escogían propiedades tan grandes que nunca terminaban de rodearla con piedras.

Luego eran familias enteras que con sendos garrotes según protegían su adquisición gritando Uka Puka y golpeando a todo aquel individuo que se acercara a su propiedad. El grave daño causado por el descubrimiento de la propiedad privada.

DON TRISTE OTRA VEZ
EL FENOMENO DEL UKA PUKA

Sigue siendo motivo de pleitos y guerras para obtener propiedades como medio de riqueza. El Uka Puka se estableció como algo normal con la idea de proteger la propiedad privada, pero provocó la pérdida de lo que en realidad le pertenece a todo ser humano.

Todo lo que nos rodea nos pertenece a todos por igual, pero hombres con ambiciones desmedidas han tomado o robado las propiedades naturales comunitarias convirtiéndolas en terrenos y áreas de propiedad individual. Comercializando lo que en realidad nos pertenece a todos. Sabemos de gente adinerada que poseen cientos y miles de hectáreas, edificios, así como propiedades comerciales.

Otros todo lo contrario, no poseen ni siquiera un pequeño terreno para fincar una casa, familias que sólo pueden rentar un apartamento. Sólo para enriquecer a los propietarios y nunca pueden comprar una casa, porque todo el dinero que ganan lo emplean en pagar renta. Es injusto, pero lo llaman negocio, así que si eres hábil tendrás que pagar y luchar para solo ser propietario de un terreno, pudiendo enriquecerte si compras más terrenos, fincas viviendas y las rentas.

Eso es hoy en día negocio siendo legal, válido y protegido por la ley, garantizando la propiedad privada como exclusividad reconocida por un título de propiedad. El error fue aceptar esta situación porque como seres humanos todo nos pertenece por igual pero no es así, hay quienes son dueños del agua. Otros son dueños de los árboles, en fin, todas esas cosas son propiedad de todos los seres humanos sin distinción de raza. Hoy son sólo sueños de seductor, porque hoy en día la propiedad con dinero se compra y se vende bajo reglas de comercialización. Sin importar que hay seres humanos que carecen de un lugar donde habitar y todo por el famoso descubrimiento de la propiedad privada llamada en sus inicios Uka Puka.

EL FENOMENO DEL UKA PUKA

Cuando el feo señor AG descubrió el Uka Puka o propiedad privada tuvo suerte de que no lo mataran los miembros de la tribu, tuvo suerte que otros tan ambiciosos y feos como él siguieran su ejemplo. por eso es que existe la propiedad privada, éste es un error en que todos los seres humanos hemos caído alguna vez.

Inclusive Jesucristo cometió el mismo error de considerarse propietario de algo que en realidad nos pertenece a todos. Si no me creen explicare su error al respecto con la propiedad privada o el fenómeno del Uka Puka. Jesucristo caminaba por Jerusalén y encontró un templo dedicado a la adoración del Dios Padre, el gran templo estaba convertido en un tianguis comercial con mucha gente haciendo todo tipo de trueques, pollos, camellos, comida, esencias, joyas, en fin, todo lo normal que encontrarías en un mercado de esa época. Jesucristo vio y se enfadó comenzando a ofender a todos los comerciantes, diciendo que el templo de su padre era sólo para oración y no para comercio.

Jesucristo cometió el grave error de golpear a los comerciantes con un látigo y manifestando su cólera los ahuyento a todos del templo. Quizás éste fue uno de los motivos por lo que el pueblo judío no quiso a Jesucristo y más tarde lo condenó a morir crucificado, el pueblo se sintió ofendido, porque ese templo no era propiedad de él, él no ayudó durante su edificación ni aporto dinero para los materiales.

El pueblo era gente pobre, pero habían contribuido realizando todo tipo de sacrificios porque eran creyentes que realmente amaban su religión. Los comerciantes eran gente trabajadora y lo que hacían era trabajar para ganarse el pan de cada día, tal y como Dios Padre mandaba. Jesucristo se equivocó al creerse dueño absoluto del templo o que su padre lo era, siendo que el templo era propiedad del pueblo judío, se equivocó al igual que el señor AG, actuando como propietario de lo que en realidad no le pertenecía.

DON TRISTE OTRA VEZ
EL FENOMENO DEL UKA PUKA

El Uka Puka convertido ya en aspecto legal y sus miles de modificaciones, afectaron el curso normal de la humanidad todos poseían el todo sin deberle nada a nadie, pero la propiedad privada sólo cayó en manos de unos pocos, para miseria de muchos. Fue así como se inició la lucha por obtener más que otros, sin importar que nos pertenece a todos por igual. No pretendas ser dueño de algo que no es tuyo, porque en realidad lo que posees no está de ninguna manera garantizado que honradamente sea tuyo.

Piensa en cuántos seres humanos, no tienen ni donde morir porque hasta los cementerios están comercializados por el fenómeno del Uka Puka. No tenemos nada ni somos nada, la prueba es que cuando finalmente morimos no nos llevamos ninguna propiedad con nosotros. Jesucristo cometió el mismo error que el Sr. AG que golpeó a sus coterráneos, todo en nombre de una propiedad que pertenecía a todos. El error de ambos fue grande porque mientras el Sr. AG descubrió la propiedad privada.

Jesucristo descubrió según él que los templos son propiedad de Dios Padre, sin importar que son construidos con el dinero y esfuerzo de los más pobres de este mundo, los cuales sueñan con un mundo mejor y vida después de la muerte como premio a su sacrificio.

Pensamiento
Compartir por igual, como iguales, sin distinción hubiese sido el real y mejor descubrimiento de la humanidad, su real existencia y actualidad hubiese garantizado la verdadera igualdad entre todos los seres humanos, sin importar color, raza o religión.

Algo similar al sueño de un mundo sin fronteras, por cierto, estoy enterado que la superficie lunar está siendo comercializada, así que el Uka Puka rebasa la frontera planetaria como un error infinito.

LA VERDAD Y SOLO LA VERDAD

Confieso la manera en que fui involucrado en esta historia, de todo lo relacionado con Don Triste y su mundo maravilloso. Tuve la fortuna de vivir y convivir cerca de él, desde su infancia hasta su retiro viajé cerca de él, pero justo al margen, fui su sombra, su protector anónimo y en ocasiones casi fui su ángel guardián.

Tuve la gran fortuna de conocer a todos los personajes de sus maravillosas historias, conocí a su maravilloso amigo Villi, pero impresionante fue conocer a Inia. Era no solamente hermosa, era un ser con tantos valores humanos, que podías enamorarte de ella al instante de verla. A mí me ocurrió, pero nunca me afectó el no ser quien que gozara de su amor, confieso que me hubiese gustado, aunque el dolor de perderla me hubiese convertido en Don Triste como a él.

Fui uno más de los tantos niños, que después de ser rescatados de aquellos centros de detención, llamados falsamente hospicios infantiles, encontramos un mundo con oportunidades de ser lo que tu deseases o simplemente pudieses. Después de que Don Mario Alberti y sus amigos nos rescataron.

Fuimos entregados al hospital más cercano con los archivos para lograr nuestra identificación. Algunos de ellos fueron entregados con sus padres, otros con tíos, primos, abuelos, hermanos mayores, en fin, los que tuvieron familia fueron re-localizados. Los que no tuvimos familiares fuimos enviados a escuelas tipo internado donde tuvimos educación, hospedaje y alimentos, pero con la libertad de salir al exterior los fines de semana.

Todo fue a causa de la intervención de Don Mario Alberti con las autoridades, las cuales se hicieron responsables de nosotros hasta nuestra mayoría de edad (18 años). En el hospital al que fuimos entregados por Don Mario Alberti, no quedamos desamparados a nuestra suerte.

DON TRISTE OTRA VEZ
LA VERDAD Y SOLO LA VERDAD

A partir del día siguiente llegaban buenas personas enviadas por Don Mario Alberti para velar por nuestra seguridad. Al paso de una semana más Don Mario Alberti inicio sus visitas en el hospital, dando muestras de cariño hacia todos los que quedamos sin familiares. Fue siempre muy amable, en sus visitas nos llevaba dulces, chocolates, juguetes sencillos como yoyos, canicas, juegos de mesa, y por supuesto pelotas.

Preguntaba ¿cómo estábamos? ¿Si nos trataban bien? Sabíamos que se preocupaba por nosotros y platicaba con todos. En especial conmigo porque le platicaba de todas las peripecias de su sobrino, porque yo sentía un afecto especial por Don Triste, porque lo vi compartir sus botones con Benito y otros que nos acercamos a él.

Explique a Don Mario Alberti como fue que Don Triste involucró a todos con el famoso juego de los dardos, mismos que llevaban mensajes de esperanza para nuestra libertad, y decía nuestra libertad porque pensó en todos los que estábamos ahí recluidos. Confesé que me di cuenta del truco de los mensajes, pero traté de cubrirlo porque sabía que buscaba el bien de todos.

Cuando fuimos rescatados supimos que él nunca nos abandonó, porque el rescate era sólo para él, pero convenció a su tío para salvarnos a todos, Don Mario Alberti no lo llevó a visitarnos porque quería que él no recordará esa triste aventura, pero Don Mario nos platicaba historias de su adorado sobrino como él lo llamaba.

Don Mario Alberti dijo que, si me portaba bien en la escuela, él me daría trabajo en su restaurante los fines de semana, con la condición que no dijera que estuve en el hospicio. Que tan solo mencionara mi nueva escuela y no dijera que conocí a Don Triste, mucho menos en el horrible hospicio, el primer sábado cuando por fin me presente en el restaurante fue algo como cuatro meses después de estar en la nueva escuela.

Mi trabajo ese fin de semana fue lavar platos y cubiertos a manera de entrenamiento, en la noche fui hospedado en una de las tantas recámaras de aquella gran casa, al día siguiente volví a la tarea de lavaplatos quedándome a dormir en la misma recámara.

Temprano por la mañana del lunes siguiente Don Mario Alberti me llevó a uno de los comedores de la casa donde desayunamos y me entregó dinero a manera de pago por mi trabajo, invitándome a volver todos los fines de semana, pero siempre y cuando siguiese estudiando.

Transcurrieron tres o cuatro meses sin cambios, hasta que un sábado por la tarde Don Triste entró a la cocina y saludándome cortésmente preguntó quién era yo a lo que contesté soy el 'lavaplatos' aprendiz de 'cocinero', se sonrío dándome la bienvenida sin saber que tenía varios meses trabajando.

Él no sabía de mi existencia porque cuando él trabajaba en el restaurante junto a su primo Plinio, lo hacían en la caja registradora o en la recepción, dando la bienvenida a los clientes tomando sacos y abrigos para colocarlos en el guardarropa por lo tanto ambos muy rara vez entraban a la cocina otras veces andaban de compras en el mercado para surtir la despensa del restaurante y la de la casa.

Así pasaron varios años, mientras en la escuela yo obtenía calificaciones altas, por lo tanto, recibí el beneficio de salir de la escuela por las tardes y regresar a las diez de la noche sin falta ni excusas.

Siempre iba a "Benito barrio de la amistad" porque tenía amigos y como sabían que trabajaba con Don Mario Alberti gozaba de respeto y podía estar cerca de Don Triste.

DON TRISTE OTRA VEZ
LA VERDAD Y SOLO LA VERDAD

Mis amigos no eran tan amigos de los de Don Triste pero esa situación era benéfica para mí, porque estaba cerca de Don Triste al mismo tiempo estaba lejos además siempre desapercibido. Así me sentí bien porque estaba y no estaba, algo así como un fantasma, pero con alegría y diversión a diario, porque ese barrio era especial al igual que todos sus personajes.

Ahí encontrabas artistas, boxeadores, mecánicos, deportistas, escritores, profesores, prostitutas, rateros, músicos, doctores, políticos, estudiantes, sacerdotes, sastres, etc. etc. Un mundo de gente con una variedad infinita de actividades y creencias, que convertían al barrio en cosmopolita y único en su género.

En el barrio sucedían todo tipo de locas aventuras que sólo suceden en películas o libros, pero ahí se veían en vivo y a todo color todos los días.

Los partidos de futbol eran algo así como la gran final de la copa del mundo, jugaban con gran pasión, el peor de los participantes podía ser jugador profesional en equipos profesionales de primera categoría.

Los mejores jugadores eran tan especiales que ya habían recibido varias ofertas para convertirse en profesionales. Pero nunca aceptaban por dedicarse a estudiar soñando ser profesionistas académicos algún día, los feos encuentros boxísticos también eran fantásticos como de película.

Este barrio era conformado por amigos, que se agrupaban en ciertos sectores del barrio, siendo cada uno de estos grupos casi enemigos de los otros, pero al mismo tiempo eran un sólo grupo contra algún agresor de barrios vecinos. Competían entre sí por ser los mejores del barrio en todos los aspectos, incluyendo lo romántico, considerándose algunos de ellos los caritas del barrio.

En fin, te divertías de lo lindo participando en cualquier grupo que te aceptase o simplemente siendo neutral pero la emoción y diversión eran garantizadas los grupos se denominaban por su cercanía al número de la calle donde se reunían o habitaban, los del 28, los del 25, los del 21, y los del 12. Había grupos sin número que se mencionaba sólo por el nombre del líder de ellos como adjetivo descriptivo, tales como: el Villi el Francis el Oso: etc. etc. Todos ellos conformaban los chicos de "Benito barrio de la amistad"

Cuando estos grupos jugaban entre si futbol americano, eran tan habilidosos, que la calle se convertía en un divertido campo de juego, donde también mostraban su inteligencia, librando los obstáculos mismos de la calle, así como también al contrincante.

Jugaban tan bien, que los transeúntes se quedaban parados convirtiéndose en espectadores y lo hacían con placer porque disfrutaban cada una de las jugadas tanto ofensivas como defensivas donde mostraban alegría infinita por el juego. Sus juegos eran tan competitivos que por lo regular se decidían por la diferencia de una anotación y llegaban a prolongarse por 4 horas o más.

Durante las cuales entraban y salían jugadores de refresco, quedando solamente unos cuantos, que siempre soportaban el juego en su totalidad mostrando el porqué de su liderazgo.

Así que se mostraban fuertes, siempre competitivos, para hacerse notar sin tener que hacerlo por medios salvajes como pelear u ofender a los demás, se trataba de ser el mejor en cada uno de los juegos. Los veía jugar convirtiéndome en uno más de sus fervientes admiradores, pero nunca participé por temor a no mostrar tanta habilidad y si por el contrario la hubiese tenido sería popular y eso no era para mí, ya que yo quería pasar desapercibido.

DON TRISTE OTRA VEZ
LA VERDAD Y SOLO LA VERDAD

Don Mario Alberti, sólo quería que Don Triste no recordara su mala experiencia en el hospicio. Quizás yo mal entendí y traté siempre de ser nadie para no hacerme notar eso no fue lo que el tío me ordenó repito que yo lo mal interpreté, pero al paso del tiempo fue lo mejor que pude haber decidido ya que de esa manera me fue fácil cumplir lo que más tarde se convertiría en mi misión.

Les diré que estos juegos se convertían en algo increíble cuando se enfrentaban a otros barrios, la competencia incluía; orgullo y honor de batir "al otro barrio" eran como la guerra fría, sin armas de por medio, pero al fin y al cabo igual que la guerra.

Don Triste y sus amigos por ser de los medianos, participaban en el juego, pero la carga la llevaban los grandes, que eran los verdaderos líderes del barrio. El líder absoluto respetado y querido era Allo, el mejor jugador, el mejor peleador, estudiante de universidad e hijo de un militar retirado, el cual le brindaba todo su apoyo para que fuese lo que él quisiera sin imponerle condiciones.

Ese era el líder de todos y en especial de Don Triste, todos querían ser el tipo de líder justo, que enseñaba a todos a jugar mejor, con estrategias nuevas inventadas por él mismo. Allo era un líder más que ejemplar porque, aunque era un peleador callejero, peleaba como último recurso y sólo por causas justas, proteger a los desvalidos contra los abusivos que eran muchos, pero cobardes que nunca pudieron vencerlo.

Mantenía el barrio tranquilo dedicándonos al deporte y juegos como meta de todo joven. Con él platicábamos de la NFL, la copa mundial de soccer, grupos musicales, programas de televisión, etc. etc. Por cierto, algo divertido es que todos los sábados después de jugar platicábamos con él, pero al punto de las 7:00 de la noche.

Todos los jóvenes, medianos y chicos corríamos para ver dos programas uno eran los "Monkees" y el otro "Perdidos en el espacio". Por varias semanas ocurrió lo mismo, hasta que un sábado por curiosidad se unió a los medianos y chicos para ver los programas mencionados al término de ambos programas dijo que no nos entendía, ya que eran programas demasiado infantiles pero que respetaba nuestro mal gusto.

Por cierto, él era feliz viendo el salvaje salvaje oeste en lo que todos coincidíamos era en ver los partidos de la NFL, de la copa del mundo FIFA, de la serie mundial de baseball, y los increíbles combates de Cassius Clay. Creo que el boxeo era el deporte favorito por televisión de todos en el barrio. En verdad fue una época divertida donde íbamos a la escuela, pero en las tardes jugábamos toda clase de deportes.

Por las noches platicas, música con guitarras, y por supuesto aquellos momentos de coquetería y conquista con las muchachas bonitas del barrio y también con las de otros barrios. Esto nos acarreaba problemas con los jóvenes de los barrios vecinos porque se encelaban de nuestra suerte y popularidad entre las jóvenes de esa época.

Voy a retomar la historia de nuevo con relación a Don Triste, ya que las emociones de recordar esos tiempos me vuelven nostálgico, porque fue la época de oro de Benito barrio de la amistad. Mi vida transcurrió entre la escuela, el restaurante, el barrio y mi fantasmal presencia de no hacerme notar, pero estar al tanto de todo así transcurrieron varios años, al tiempo nos alcanzó la adolescencia, acercándonos donde nos considerábamos los más grandes del barrio, teniendo por ley substituir y tomar el liderazgo absoluto con todas sus responsabilidades. Cuando el padre de Allo murió, su familia se mudó a otra ciudad para dedicarse todos a estudiar y trabajar para económicamente y ayudar a su madre.

DON TRISTE OTRA VEZ
LA VERDAD Y SOLO LA VERDAD

Nunca lo volvimos a ver, sabemos que le fue muy bien y que se gradúo de la universidad. Repito tristemente nunca, nunca lo volvimos a ver. Reemplazarlo se convirtió en algo sumamente difícil, había varios candidatos unos que no lo merecían, otros sí, pero la comparación con él siempre los hacía verse como no listos para la misión. Entre los candidatos se encontraba Don Triste, pero él estaba muy ocupado con su casi secreta tarea de peleador callejero, además recién conoció a Inia motivo por lo que el liderazgo no estaba en sus planes.

Pero si estaba al tanto de quién sería el líder, él propuso a Villi, Villi propuso a Alessandro, Plinio a Beticus, en fin, todos proponían. Decidieron que el liderazgo sería compartido por el grupo que había permanecido con Allo. Todo se decidiría por votación como un grupo democrático para evitar equivocaciones por corto tiempo así fue, pero Don Triste fue quien tomó el lugar de Allo por voluntad de todos.

Conocí a Inia en un juego de futbol, donde el equipo deportivo de "Benito barrio de la amistad" enfrentaban al equipo del sector donde ella habitaba.
Cuando la vi entre las chicas del grupo de amigas que apoyaban a su equipo resaltaba su figura esbelta, pero bien formada, de cabello largo sedoso, con ojos claros color café, con rasgos muy finos, vestida sencillamente a la moda, pero parecía modelo de revista, o más bien modelo de ensueño.

Observando me di cuenta que el juego pasaba a segundo término, ya que todos los jóvenes que estábamos ahí mirábamos atentos aquel grupo de bellas jovencitas, pero muy en especial todas las miradas estaban dirigidas hacia Inia. Ella sólo tenía ojos para el juego, se daba cuenta de la atracción que ejercía en todos, parecía no importarle ya que su atención era sólo para el juego. Aunque era partidaria del equipo contrario, le atraía el juego caballeroso y habilidoso de Don Triste.

Durante el descanso del medio tiempo me dirigí a ella preguntándole su nombre y mencioné que la vi disfrutar del partido, mirándome a los ojos dijo llamarse Inia y claro que le encantaba el deporte, sobre todo viendo participar a Don Triste.

Porque era tan buen jugador como buen boxeador. Mi sorpresa fue grande que pregunté ¿boxeador? él es sobrino de Don Mario Alberti ¿cómo podría ser boxeador? Mirándome a los ojos sonrío y dijo, ¿no lo sabias? Él es peleador callejero y lo hace por dinero-, respondí que no sabía pero que no podía creerle.

Como dicen para no discutir mucho me invitó a la próxima pelea que sería al día siguiente, pero por seguridad se sabría el lugar, sólo unas cuantas horas antes de comenzar las peleas.

Así que, si quería ver pelear a Don Triste, ella me llamaría al día siguiente para ir juntos, le hice saber que trabajaba los fines de semana con Don Mario Alberti, creo que sólo por eso ella me tuvo confianza.

Al siguiente día en la escuela recibí su llamada telefónica, citándome cerca del muelle de los pescadores, para de ahí irnos juntos al encuentro boxístico, mi emoción era grande ya que Inia era muy bonita y me sentí afortunado por saber que esa tarde sería su acompañante.

Nos reunimos a la hora convenida y por supuesto venía con un vestido rojo que le quedaba de lo lindo realzando su belleza. Caminamos con rumbo al mercado de mariscos y en el estacionamiento subterráneo que era grande, nos introducimos y fue como conocí el mundo de las apuestas y sus incontables participantes. Se dio cuenta de mi nerviosismo y comento que me controlara, porque sólo bastaba que dijera que trabajaba con Don Mario Alberti y me respetarían. Le mencioné que yo trabajaba en el restaurante y que no mentía.

DON TRISTE OTRA VEZ
LA VERDAD Y SOLO LA VERDAD

Dijo que ella decía lo mismo pero que ella si mentía porque en realidad nunca había cruzado una palabra con aquel gran señor, pero eso no importaba, lo bueno es que todos lo creían y la respetaban. Confesó que le gustaban las peleas pero que Don Triste peleaba tan diferente a todos que le atraía de manera especial al igual que cuando jugaba futbol.

Fue cuando supe que su gusto era Don Triste y que me había escogido sólo como informante, por trabajar en el restaurante del tío de Don Triste. Antes de proseguir debo aclarar que en esa época de mi narración a Don Triste lo llamábamos por su nombre y que fue hasta después de la muerte de Inia cuando cambiaría y se le conocería como Don Triste.

Soy yo el que escribe esta historia, escogiendo conservar su real nombre para mí y los que lo conocimos, como un recuerdo que no deseamos compartir con nadie, porque nos pertenece sólo a los afortunados que lo conocimos. Durante esa pelea de Don Triste sucedió lo de siempre, perdió el primer asalto, pero en el segundo asalto emparejó las cosas ganando en el tercer asalto con facilidad.

Bueno así se veía a lo lejos, porque se le veía agotado, después del gran esfuerzo de venir de atrás hasta conseguir el triunfo. Era una victoria que Inia celebraba con gran júbilo y con ganancia ya que había apostado dinero en favor de Don Triste.

Salimos del estacionamiento, me sentí deprimido porque vi en ella todo el interés del mundo por Don Triste, eso me condenaba a obtener sólo su amistad y siendo tan bella no sería suficiente, así que me preparaba para ser sólo su confidente. Como era natural preguntó cómo conocí a Don Mario Alberti y a su sobrino, así que sin dudarlo le platiqué la historia. Pero cuando estábamos en lo interesante tuve que despedirme, porque se llegaba la hora en que tendría que volver al internado.

Prometimos vernos al día siguiente en el muelle de los pescadores, salí prácticamente volando para no llegar tarde al internado tuve suerte porque llegué exacto al tiempo convenido así que fui a cenar a la cocina, yendo después al dormitorio solo para soñar con Inia, la cual sería mía sólo en sueños.

Al día siguiente después de mis clases, corrí hasta el muelle para encontrarme con Inia quien ya me esperaba. Vestía y lucía bien, con un toque de distinción comparado sólo a su gran belleza. Después de saludarnos nos fuimos a una cafetería cercana solicitándome que continuara aquella historia del hospicio.

Después de varias tazas de café con leche como ella lo acostumbraba, la historia llegó a su fin narrándole hasta el momento en que la conocí a ella durante aquel juego de pelota tomó mis manos y dijo que yo carecía de un brillo en los ojos por lo que no sentía quererme, pero me estimaría mucho y que seriamos amigos por siempre.

Confesó que sentía amor por Don Triste, además de que él tenía un destello en los ojos el que indicaba que él era su destino, ese fin de semana fue maravilloso, porque durante el día trabajaba con Don Mario Alberti y por la tarde salía a platicar con la hermosa Inia. Claro siempre me preguntaba por Don Triste y sus actividades, pero descubrí en sus ojos y en sus palabras que realmente lo amaba por lo que le pregunté, que si tanto lo quería por qué no acercarse y decírselo.

Ella dijo que su situación, no era como la de Don Triste y que de seguro Don Mario Alberti nunca la aceptaría como enamorada de su sobrino. Contesté que eso sonaba como historia de amor antigua y que Don Mario Alberti no era quien para aceptarla o rechazarla.

DON TRISTE OTRA VEZ
LA VERDAD Y SOLO LA VERDAD

En fin, cambiamos el tema de la plática y me hizo saber lo cruel que era su padrastro con su madre, con su hermana y con ella misma. Inia decía no poder cambiar las circunstancias, pero si podía vivir arriba de ellas, y era lo que hacía tanto para sobrevivir como para sentirse mejor.

Pasado algún tiempo recordarán aquella ocasión en que Inia huía de sus perseguidores y alcanzó refugio en los brazos de Don Triste, siendo éste siempre su enamorado casi en secreto, logrando enamorarlo instantáneamente al conocerse. Su romance era de película, se amaban realmente y sin lugar a dudas.

Mientras Don Triste estaba por las tardes en la escuela, me reunía con Inia convirtiéndome en su confidente y amigo, siendo testigo del amor que los unía. Ella era tan sencilla y al mismo tiempo con tanta clase que nunca podías imaginar que viniera de un barrio tan sucio, con gente tan mala que no tenía nada que ver con su maravillosa manera de ser.

Cuando más se amaban sucedió la trágica muerte de Inia, envolviendo en un manto de tristeza toda la vida de "Benito barrio de la amistad". Propios y extraños se vieron afectados por el suceso, Don Mario Alberti comprendió su error a través de las pláticas con Villi.

Supo que se equivocó al mal juzgar a Inia y que ella era tan bonita como tan noble de corazón. Fui golpeado por la tristeza ya que ella era mi única amiga con la cual compartíamos secretos. Y a partir de su muerte yo sería una persona sumamente solitaria creo que tanto como Don Triste.

Después Villi y Don Triste comenzaron la ardua investigación del terrible crimen para encontrar al culpable, yo sabía de las visitas de Francis al barrio para saludar a Inia, supe lo del regalo de la pistola, así que informe de todo a Villi, de esa manera tenían pistas para continuar su búsqueda del criminal.

AVENTURAS DE REFLEXION FILOSOFICA
LA VERDAD Y SOLO LA VERDAD

Al término de sus investigaciones descubrieron que el asesino de Inia fue Francis, Don Triste sólo pensaba en buscarlo y hacerle pagar su crimen.

Francis era un enemigo más grande que Don Triste con muchas mañas y amigos criminales, en fin, se veía como una misión difícil de cumplir.

Con la idea de aprender a tocar guitarra para sustentar el viaje en búsqueda de Francis, todo se volvió música en la vida de Don Triste, con los Beatles como sus mejores aliados. Todos los días practicaba, con la idea de lo más rápido posible, estar listo para salir en busca del criminal.

Como saben por capítulos anteriores Don Triste lo encontró y por suerte, o como lo quieran llamar Francis encontró su trágico final, pagando por su crimen.

Mientras que Don Triste después de regresar a casa tuvo que partir en un barco mercante, con rumbo a España la que sería su base para viajar por Europa y tiempo más tarde trasladarse hasta América, que siempre fue su sueño, aunque no de esa manera.

Cuando Don Triste partió hacia España como fugitivo, la preocupación de Don Mario Alberti no tenía límite y se sentía impotente para ayudar a su sobrino. Así que sólo tuvo un pensamiento, enviar a alguien en ayuda y auxilio de Don Triste por lo que pudiera suceder.

Su primera opción fue pedirle a Villi que siguiera a Don Triste por mar y tierra para asegurarse que estuviese bien. Villi no pudo aceptar la oferta por motivo de sus clases escolares más por tener que estar con su madre que lo necesitaba porque hacía sólo un año que su padre había fallecido, no pudiendo aceptar la oferta de Don Mario Alberti.

DON TRISTE OTRA VEZ
LA VERDAD Y SOLO LA VERDAD

Poco después la oferta me la hizo a mí y muy tentadora, por cierto, ofreció un sueldo mensual bastante cómodo, para que me instalara en América siendo la sombra de Don Triste, pero sin que él lo supiera para que no se sintiera mal o por si no estuviese de acuerdo.

Sin pensarlo mucho acepté, estando en contacto siempre con Villi y Don Mario Alberti comencé la persecución de Don Triste. Don Mario Alberti me consiguió los papeles legales tanto para Europa como para América mi primera escala fue Barcelona, Don Triste estaba viviendo en una vieja pensión para estudiantes africanos, de esa manera pasaba desapercibido y no conocido como siciliano.

Cuando llegué a la pensión él había ya partido hacia Francia y en especial a París en la pensión dejó la mayor parte de su equipaje, dejó pagado un mes de renta por lo que sólo tendría que esperar su retorno.

Durante ese tiempo me dedique sólo a conocer y disfrutar la ciudad, que por cierto era hermosa y muy moderna. Un mes después Don Triste regresó a la pensión estuvo solamente unos días, porque preparaba su viaje con destino a Hamburgo, Alemania. Mientras tanto me hice amigo de la dueña de la pensión y aunque pagaba renta le ayudaba en los quehaceres menores de la pensión y ella me daba propinas.

Para que Don Triste no supiera de mi desde que llegué caminaba cojeando diciéndole que de chico me enfermé de poliomielitis y mi pierna quedó corta con la consiguiente cojera. Además, durante ese mes me hice muy amigo de los encargados de una tienda de magia y trucos, los cuales me ensañaron a disimular mi nariz, mi pelo chino, y un color de piel distinto al mío. Ya se imaginarán cuando me presenté ante Don Triste y le dije que yo estaba a su servicio como mandadero no me reconoció.

AVENTURAS DE REFLEXION FILOSOFICA
LA VERDAD Y SOLO LA VERDAD

Me gané su confianza hablando español feo por parte mía y un buen español por parte de él, por lo tanto, me corregía y ayudaba, mientras que yo le traía y le llevaba cartas al correo, a una caja privada a nombre de un consejero escolar para no dar su nombre.

Tenía yo la ventaja de leer sus cartas y luego cambiarlas de sobre para re enviarlas, así como otras cartas a Villi y a Don Mario Alberti. Después Don Triste fue a Hamburgo como lo planeo, pero regresaría un mes más tarde así que volví a quedar en la pensión mientras aprendía magia, trucos y español.

Don Triste preparaba el viaje hacia América, meses después decidió viajar a Nueva York por ser la entrada normal hacia América, partió en barco, mientras tanto yo viaje en avión hacia América para prepararme y esperar a Don Triste. Me instalé en un hotel, como sabía el barco y la fecha en que partió conseguí fácilmente el itinerario, así como la exacta fecha de su llegada.

Mientras se acercaba el día en que llegaría Don Triste a Nueva York, aproveché para escribirle cartas a Don Mario Alberti relatándole todas sus peripecias en Europa de su sobrino. Tuve que contar todo sin ocultar detalles porque ese era mi trabajo, los meses en España los utilizó para reunirse con grupos secretos de resistencia al gobierno en el poder como la ETA conocidos por su peligrosidad terrorista.

Sus viajes eran sólo para ocultar su verdadera identidad desconozco como se relacionó con ellos, pero pasaba días en campamentos secretos a los cuales no tuve acceso. Sabía su ubicación aproximada ya que mi nueva habilidad de disfrazarme y ocultarme era casi magistral, además súper útil porque facilitaba mi seguimiento de Don Triste hasta donde pude.

DON TRISTE OTRA VEZ
LA VERDAD Y SOLO LA VERDAD

Algunas veces nos cruzamos en el camino, pero no me reconoció porque era el viejo trapero, el barrendero, el doctor, el peluquero el cartero, en fin, una serie de personajes, él fue entrenado durante todo ese tiempo, no sé cuál fue su exacto entrenamiento, pero nunca jamás lo vi envuelto en actividades de terrorismo.

Al paso del tiempo descubrí que su aprendizaje fue musical aprendió música de protesta la música revolucionaria. Música de los pueblos oprimidos que manifiestan su pacifica protesta con profunda huella difícil de borrar al paso del tiempo. Eso fue lo que a Don Triste le gustó de aquel grupo que se inició como protesta pacífica, terminando al tiempo como un grupo terrible de terrorismo.

Ya en Nueva York se instaló en un barrio cerca del Bronx, porque disfrutaba los juegos de baseball de sus queridos Yankees confieso que, al seguir a Don Triste a los juegos, me convertí en fanático de los Yankees.

Además, me disfrazaba de todo lo que quisiera sin ser descubierto por él. Recuerdo un día fui de hot dog gigantesco y todo el juego estuve sentado al lado de Don Triste y nunca supo que era yo su fiel guardián.

Transcurrieron varios meses en Nueva York con viajes a los alrededores durante los fines de semana, inclusive dos viajes en tren a Canadá. Visitas a todos los cafés cantantes de la ciudad neoyorquina, en los cuales participaba como aficionado interpretando siempre la música de los Beatles.

La que lo acompañaría siempre como su refugio interno para soportar la pérdida de su amada Inia. Lo vi y escuché interpretar con una melancolía que dolía y gustaba al mismo tiempo, pero a mí me hacía derramar lágrimas al escucharlo porque yo también extrañaba a Inia y compartía el dolor de Don Triste.

Finalmente viajamos hasta la frontera sur de los Estados Unidos nos establecimos en San Diego, California. Lugar donde perfeccionamos nuestro español aprendimos costumbres mexicanas malas y no tan malas.

Cruzábamos a Tijuana, México donde escuchábamos música de rock and roll de gran calidad, interpretada por grupos de mexicanos y norteamericanos que juntos sonaban como los mismos discos y en ocasiones superaban las versiones originales de músicos famosos.

Debo aclararles que cuando yo dije viajamos y visitábamos Tijuana, México Don Triste y yo lo hacíamos en plan de grandes amigos, pero ya se imaginaran. Yo era nacido en América hijo de padre guatemalteco y madre española. Así que se justificaba mi acento de tonto, más mi disfraz de existencialista con melena, anteojos negros, encajaba a la perfección en un mundo de músicos, rocanroleros, poetas, escritores, vagos, viciosos, hippies que se confundían entre si conformando la juventud de la época.

Por varios meses disfrute por fin de la amistad de Don Triste, sin que sospechara que yo cobraba un sueldo por protegerlo e informar a Don Mario Alberti de todos sus pasos. Proporcionaba detalles de sus actividades diarias, en ocasiones sentí que tenía el mejor trabajo del mundo y que era muy afortunado. Pensaba que, si esto se terminaba en ese momento que sería de mí, por lo tanto, comprendí que yo estaba atado a la suerte de Don Triste y que quizás esto sería de por vida.

Durante esa época nuestra real amistad se afirmó y teniendo confianza me platicó historias que me dejaron pensando para siempre. Dijo que tuvo buena amistad con algunos miembros de la ETA en España. Su relación no era como terrorista, los miembros de la ETA eran en sus inicios, miembros de sectas secretas tan antiguas las cuales provenían de los caballeros templarios.

DON TRISTE OTRA VEZ
LA VERDAD Y SOLO LA VERDAD

Aquellos caballeros que durante los años 1200 D.C. a 1300 D.C. fueron los guerreros más hábiles, ricos y místicos de la historia de la humanidad eran alquimistas, inventaron el sistema bancario, construyeron las catedrales góticas en Europa.

Su real éxito y su mayor secreto, es que guardaban el arca de la alianza que trajeron del bello templo de Salomón, también mantuvieron en secreto y bajo su protección la descendencia de Cristo hasta nuestros días. Don Triste me decía que Jesucristo fue un hombre sumamente inteligente, pero el genio de toda la estructura cristiana en sus inicios y después de la falsa muerte de Jesucristo fue Judas. Judas planeo la ejecución de todos los milagros y actos de Cristo.

Además, reemplazó a Jesucristo al momento justo antes de su arresto el que murió en la cruz fue un doble, más tarde ahorcó y sacrificó a su propio hermano al que todos confundieron con el mismísimo Judas y la falsa historia se encargó de decir que se suicidó arrepentido de su traición. Después ambos se presentaron ante los grandes personajes del gobierno romano, quienes al verlos creyeron en la resurrección, por lo tanto, cedieron bienes y poder a los resucitados. Razón que ayudó políticamente y fortaleció al cristianismo.

Al grado que Jesús fue proclamado hijo de Dios y el cristianismo se oficializo como religión única establecida en Roma. Sucedió 300 años después de la supuesta muerte de Cristo, pero todo esto fue planeado por Judas que en realidad era el genio que creo la religión que rige hasta nuestros días.

Los historiadores dicen que María Magdalena escapó al sur de Francia, donde se estableció y murió, pero no fue así ya que Cristo y Judas la alcanzaron varios años después de la supuesta crucifixión de Cristo. Por supuesto con una gran fortuna se establecieron en España, por cierto, Judas se casó de nuevo en Francia y tuvo otra mujer en España, pero esa es otra historia.

Don Triste platicaba estas historias, con detalles fechas y nombres no recuerdo todo al cien por ciento, pero en general esa fue la historia. Además, mencionaba las tantas organizaciones creadas por los verdaderos y únicos guardianes de la descendencia de Cristo.

Los templarios fueron también guardianes de la descendencia de Cristo y la de Judas, asegurando que hasta nuestros días siguen protegiendo a dos mujeres y un hombre. Que por cierto están lejos de las verdaderas enseñanzas de Cristo. Don Triste admiraba a Cristo como hombre, pero no como hijo de Dios. Sus historias se basaban en experiencias que tuvo en sus viajes a Francia, Alemania y España, tuvo contacto con gente que participaba en las sectas secretas que se mueven en un mundo casi invisible, sólo abierto para miembros o gente tan especial como Don Triste.

Nunca me dijo como se relacionó con esa gente, pero sé que todo fue cierto, porque en ocasiones difíciles siempre aparecía alguien con influencias que facilitaba las cosas para Don Triste. Más de las veces sin explicación alguna, permaneciendo como unos de sus tantos trucos y secretos que lo acompañaron durante toda su vida.

Algo sorprendente fue el hecho de que Judas era más inteligente que Cristo y que por debajo de la mesa fue el verdadero creador del cristianismo, pero sólo como instrumento para terminar con el imperio romano. Los romanos fueron el ejército más grande y poderoso de esa época, eran el gobierno más extenso del planeta y por supuesto el más rico.

Judas supo que los oprimidos por el imperio serían fácil de convertirse en sus fieles seguidores, con ofrecerles algo que el gran imperio no ofrecía. Fue un ofrecimiento inteligente que sigue vigente hasta nuestros días, les ofreció vida después de la muerte, vida eterna de felicidad fácil de obtener con solamente seguir sus reglas y sus mandamientos.

DON TRISTE OTRA VEZ
LA VERDAD Y SOLO LA VERDAD

Convirtiéndolos en fieles seguidores fervientes y tributarios para sus iglesias creando el imperio más grande de todos los tiempos y establecido también en Roma el Vaticano es un imperio distribuido por todo el planeta recibiendo tributo de todas partes del mundo llamado limosna.

Cuando alguien se ha opuesto a sus mandamientos los han asesinado con la mentira de que "en nombre de Dios" y para ejemplo les recordaremos la Santa Inquisición que eliminó a millones de personas inocentes. Y sobre todo científicos, pero todo "en Nombre de Dios" Lo increíble es que las mujeres son sus fervientes y fieles seguidoras siendo que la Iglesia Católica discriminó siempre a las mujeres, atacándolas y destruyéndolas como en la época de la quema de brujas. Como el odio de Pedro el apóstol hacia María Magdalena.

Como las leyes eclesiásticas de que las mujeres no pueden jamás ser sacerdotes, obispos, cardenales, mucho menos una mujer como Papa, pero ellas ciegas siguen entregándose a esa religión que las repudia, las discrimina, pero las utiliza.

Don Triste decía que el nacimiento de Jesús en Belén es sólo una mentira, inventada por Judas el que si nació en Belén por lo cual tenía conocimiento de la importancia de su falsa historia. Como a Jesús lo querían hacer divino empezaron con el cuento de Belén para relacionarlo con el Rey David que nació en Belén, así sería respetado y adorado por todos los judíos que seguían las enseñanzas de David.

Por el otro lado existe la verdadera identidad de su nacimiento, en el mismo nombre de Jesús de Nazaret, Jesús el Nazareno, por supuesto que nació en Nazaret y aquella historia de su juventud donde nadie sabe dónde estuvo también es falsa. Aquellos años fueron aprovechados por Judas para entrenarlo y redactar las bases de la nueva gran filosofía que se convertirían más tarde en milagros.

Fue en Belén donde ellos permanecieron haciendo planes y donde se escogieron los que más tarde serían los apóstoles. Cada encuentro cada milagro, fue una cadena de sucesos planeados por Judas, lo que nunca estuvo en sus planes fue el odio y envidia que Pedro tenía a María Magdalena.

Él plan original la pondría a ella como la única fundadora de la Santa Iglesia siendo que era la mensajera de Jesús después de la resurrección. Ese odio de Pedro y su usurpación de apóstol sucesor de Jesús fue lo que condenó el plan a un retraso de 300 años.

A Jesús le concedieron la divinidad y la inmediata oficialización de la iglesia, durante un congreso celebrado por órdenes del imperio romano. Este acto fue realizado con retraso de tanto tiempo provocado por el deseo y ambición del apóstol Pedro. Judas movió todos sus contactos y desde la clandestinidad ejecutó el sacrificio de Pedro.

Fue para elevarlo a niveles altos a los cuales en vida nunca hubiese llegado porque era ambicioso, pero no inteligente, mucho menos honesto claro tampoco seguidor de los principios de Jesucristo.

La historia fue escrita de manera muy distinta ya que Magdalena quedó como prostituta y la iglesia fundada en honor del traidor apóstol Pedro.

La religión Católica Cristiana creció al amparo y protección de la iglesia por medio de crímenes y artimañas. La iglesia ha establecido el imperio más extenso y duradero de toda la historia antigua y moderna.

Aquellos a los que ha atacado sin razón, o por saber sus muchos secretos, o por tener sabiduría han tenido que vivir en la clandestinidad. Pero por suerte también y por siglos transfiriendo conocimientos a fin de proteger a la humanidad.

DON TRISTE OTRA VEZ
LA VERDAD Y SOLO LA VERDAD

De ahí las historias unas ciertas, otras no acerca de grupos como los miembros del priorato de Sion, templarios, rosacruces, masones, y muchos grupos esotéricos divididos en buenos y malos.

Es un mundo subterráneo que inclusive protegen el Santo Cáliz y que éste no es un objeto porque la sangre de Cristo no es otra cosa más que la descendencia de Cristo y Magdalena, así como la de Judas unos grupos dicen tener las pruebas que hacen tambalear a la Santa Iglesia. Pero sólo tambalea para después fortalecerse sin saberse en realidad cuándo terminará.

Esta es una de las tantas historias que Don Triste me contó, pero cuando lo hacía brindaba datos, fechas, inclusive nombres actuales de guardianes distribuidos en todo el globo terráqueo.

Sectas que protegen la conservación de pruebas de estos secretos que día a día están dejando de ser tan secretos por lo menos algunos de ellos, como la verdad de Magdalena que nunca fue prostituta.

Ella era de familia noble y adinerada que, junto a otras mujeres, patrocinaron las peregrinaciones de Jesucristo. Fue su mujer no su amante, era el verdadero apóstol a fundar la Iglesia de Cristo, y de seguro tenía una filosofía muy distinta a la Iglesia Papal.

La iglesia actual es manejada por economistas exitosos, que sólo procuran crecer su poderío tanto económico como político. Provocando la ignorancia y miseria de sus fieles seguidores y claro que atacando criminalmente a los que no son seguidores o fieles a ellos.

Don Triste hablaba entre otras cosas del porque la historia escrita ha engañado a la humanidad y nos ha mentido diciendo cosas que no fueron ciertas, y ocultando las verdaderas, pero eso es algo que no podemos cambiar.

Don Triste platicaba cosas tan bellas como el acto de caminar, decía que caminar no es sólo un ejercicio, es todo un complejo semblante del ser humano. Nuestros primeros pasos los damos con nuestros padres y en un principio no podemos caminar al ritmo de ellos ni ellos al nuestro, pero conforme avanza nuestro entendimiento caminamos mejor al lado de ellos. Por desgracia muchos dejamos de hacerlo antes de alcanzar la plenitud y orgullo de caminar al mismo ritmo de nuestros padres.

Cuando observas como una madre y sus hijos caminan a un mismo ritmo sabes que su vida es armoniosa, por supuesto si no caminan juntos al mismo ritmo su vida no es armoniosa y mucho menos de comprensión.

La segunda enseñanza es caminar a ritmo con tu pareja, son dos seres distintos, pero armonizan sus pasos juntos al igual que armonizan su mente y su corazón, es posible que ella camine rápido y él lento o viceversa.

Pero juntos caminan a un mismo ritmo eso se llama armonía y les causa un gran placer. Decía con gran orgullo que Inia caminaba muy, pero muy especial y tan diferente a cualquier otra persona, pero ellos cuando caminaban juntos lo hacían con un ritmo, el del verdadero amor, el de la comprensión y los sueños por alcanzar. El ritmo de su caminar mostraba el hermoso ritmo de sus corazones.

Recuerdo muy bien cuando los vi juntos caminar por "Benito barrio de la amistad", en verdad que caminaban con un ritmo que causaba envidia y al mismo tiempo alegría de verlos tan felices.

Todos sabíamos que se amaban verdaderamente y mostraban su felicidad contagiando a todos de su gran amor del uno hacia el otro hermoso era su caminar.

DON TRISTE OTRA VEZ
LA VERDAD Y SOLO LA VERDAD

Es cierto creo que caminar es todo un arte, todo un derroche de armonía que debemos aprender y practicar. Ahora sé por qué los sicólogos recomiendan caminar y platicar con tu pareja sobre todo cuando hay problemas, sé que hay algo bueno en caminar, pero nunca lo vi de la manera que Don Triste lo vio.

Su soledad era notoria cuando caminaba solo ya que no había ritmo, no había sentido, ni mucho menos dirección. Caminar a ritmo con tus seres queridos, es el regalo más grande que tu mente y piernas puedan alcanzar con sólo intentarlo. Por lo tanto, trata lo que Don Triste descubrió, camina con quien tú quieras, pero intenta el ritmo que después será el ritmo que tendrá tu vida con esa persona. Caminar al lado de los que quieres, o los que te quieren, caminar con ellos al ritmo del amor, del entendimiento. De la amistad, de la comprensión y si no lo crees sólo inténtalo. Caminarás bien con los tuyos, pero nunca podrás caminar a ritmo con tus enemigos.

Caminar te prepara desde tu tierna infancia, para después cuando no puedas caminar más y sólo observaras a los demás caminar, que también tiene su encanto, lo creo porque era un deleite ver caminar a Inia y a Don Triste con sus manos entrelazadas con aquellas sonrisas de aventura y promesas de amor. Don Triste hablaba de cosas increíbles, algunas sumamente maravillosas, era un gran platicador. Movía las manos al ritmo de su voz, endulzaba con sonrisas su charla con amenos comentarios terminaba un tema para empezar otro entendí porque tanto Villi y muchos amigos de "Benito barrio de la amistad" extrañaron a Don Triste por faltarles aquellas charlas nocturnas que se extendían hasta la madrugada. Sé que así fue porque en el tiempo que conviví con él, platicábamos hasta amanecer y al acostarnos teníamos pensamientos positivos alimentados con pláticas llenas de conocimientos y no sólo de aventuras.

Después de tantos años sigo extrañando aquellas pláticas nocturnas que nos hicieron palidecer hasta parecer vampiros por las desveladas, pero aun así me gustaría estar platicando con Don Triste, en vez de estar narrando sus historias. Sé que tengo limitaciones para expresar todo lo que él me relató, no sé decir las cosas como él lo hacía, pero estoy tratando de relatarles lo especial que fue Don Triste.

Tiempo después viajamos hacia la ciudad de México, Don Triste fue a visitar un viejo amigo de su padre, él era un ex presidente de la República dedicado al turismo, era el presidente del Consejo Nacional de Turismo y el verdadero creador del turismo en ese país. Fue ese personaje el que le brindó a su padre una nueva nacionalidad y lo hizo también con Don Triste para que no fuera descubierta su verdadera personalidad.

Con verdadero agradecimiento al padre de Don Triste, este gran personaje le proporcionó educación universitaria al través de una beca escolar, que más tarde el mismo Don Triste se encargó de aumentarle los beneficios a su beca a cambio de jugar soccer mostrando su habilidad para ese deporte.

Don Triste se dedicó a estudiar, trabajando solo durante los veranos para el honorable Consejo Nacional de Turismo, relacionándose con gente importante que al tiempo influirían en su vida. Su benefactor era miembro de un grupo como los masones, secretamente participaba como miembro activo de alto rango.

Él se reunía con personajes sumamente hábiles, inteligentes y preparados para procurar el bien de la nación y la protección de los hombres de ciencia. Por supuesto contaba con enemigos poderosos a los cuales no les agradaban las actividades altruistas, ese hombre fue su maestro y protector, brindándole apoyo y cariño comparable al de su tío Mario Alberti, así que Don Triste quedó seguro y tranquilo para formar su propio destino.

DON TRISTE OTRA VEZ
LA VERDAD Y SOLO LA VERDAD

Por medio de aquel Consejo Nacional de Turismo, Don Triste viajaba durante los veranos ya que trabajaba con su protector, así que durante uno de sus viajes me presente ante el Presidente del Consejo de Turismo haciéndole saber de mi misión.

Era un hombre demasiado inteligente, con tantos contactos alrededor del mundo ya que estaba enterado de mi actividad, razón por la cual también me protegió dándome la oportunidad de trabajar y estudiar al igual que Don Triste. Mantuvo el secreto de mi misión para que siguiera cuidando a Don Triste, informando a Don Mario Alberti. Don Triste se ganó la amistad, respeto y cariño de este personaje y de ahí en adelante ganó más amigos. Por cierto, Villi alcanzó a Don Triste con todo y su familia para comenzar una nueva vida a su lado, continuando las aventuras y desveladas a causa de platicar por las noches hasta la madrugada como placer interminable de grandes amigos.

Pensamiento

Si tienes amigos que juntos caminan con ritmo, más platican de manera agradable y divertida, cuídalos porque son realmente tus amigos. Los amigos platican para hacerte amena la vida y te escuchan para sentir que comparten el tiempo contigo. Te hacen charlas tan divertidas como interesantes siempre llenas de algo que se llama entendimiento.

Caminar tan sólo con tus hijos charlando de las actividades cotidianas, se puede convertir en el rito más placentero. Los padres recordarán esas caminatas cuando los hijos un día caminen lejos de ellos. Los hijos recordarán a sus padres siempre que den pasos lejos del hogar. Llegará el día en que también camines solo pero lleno de recuerdos que serán tu ritmo. El ritmo de los recuerdos, el ritmo del amor, el ritmo de Don Triste.

HISTORIA TRISTE DE UN SUEÑO IMPOSIBLE

Difícil será narrarles la historia de un individuo, que involucro su vida al mismo tiempo con la felicidad y con el infortunio siendo su destino conservar solo el infortunio, llamarlo a él por su nombre sería injusto condenándolo a burlas o sentimientos de lástima que no serían de su agrado, así que lo conocerán como "el hombre del espejo"

La ciudad de Houston, en el estado tejano de la unión americana que se encontraba con temperaturas de 45 grados Fahrenheit mostraba el encanto invernal de sus calles y sus habitantes, que vestían atuendos acordes al frio y cubriéndose de las ventiscas caminaban por las calles de la ciudad.

Algunas personas mostraban opulencia y buen gusto combinando elegantemente la ropa guardada en los roperos por 10 largos meses, otras personas vestían de buen gusto sin la opulencia de los primeros y los más humildes con vestimentas sencillas mezclándose todos ellos, conformando un colorido desfile de modas callejero en donde las prendas caras y las baratas competían rabiosamente por ser las prendas más atractivas o confortables del improvisado desfile invernal.

Al hombre del espejo lo conocí en el 2015, nuestro grato encuentro fue en una tarde invernal con ventiscas de hasta 20 millas por hora que te obligaban a caminar por las calles citadinas como si fuéramos individuos en una embarcación a la deriva, mi cuerpo clamaba por una bebida caliente y un refugio que brindara confort, mis ojos enrojecidos por el viento callejero vislumbraron una de las entradas a los túneles subterráneos del centro de la ciudad, así que moviendo mi frio cuerpo me introduje a lo largo de unas escaleras hasta el interior del túnel e inmediatamente mi cuerpo mostro la alegría de disfrutar temperaturas de 80 grados Fahrenheit y la ventaja de no tener que torear las ráfagas del viento que ululaban en la superficie.

DON TRISTE OTRA VEZ
HISTORIA TRISTE DE UN SUEÑO IMPOSIBLE

La red de túneles del centro de la ciudad es la más extensa del mundo, en su interior encuentras todo tipo de negocios, como cafeterías, restaurantes, papelerías, librerías, zapaterías, inclusive un centro comercial, la gente camina de un lugar a otro usando las entradas y salidas correctamente para evitar el tráfico y las inclemencias del tiempo como calor excesivo en verano y frio en invierno, además los túneles cuentan con aire acondicionado, calefacción así como excelente servicio de limpieza y mantenimiento que le dan un aspecto grato y seguro.

Observe una cafetería en la cual se notaba el ambiente cálido, así que me introduje y me acomode lo mejor que pude, de inmediato una mesera acudió a darme servicio, le solicite un café capuchino y un rollo de pan con queso, coloque mi abrigo en el respaldo de la silla no sin antes haberme quitado los guantes, olvidándome del frio disfrutaba mirando a mi alrededor.

En el interior de los túneles y en la cafetería continuaba el desfile de moda invernal, además entre los transeúntes había mujeres jóvenes, maduras que llamaban mi atención por su belleza y atractivo, ya que algunas parecían modelos profesionales, también había viejitos, viejitas que se veían confortables y alegres con su vestuario, todo a mi alrededor era bonito.

Después de paladear el pan ordene una segunda taza de café y observando a un personaje cercano a mi mesa, que vestía de manera elegante, con zapatos lustrados dando la impresión de ser un caballero, su cabello era blanco, su mirada vaga como si su mente estuviese lejos de la cafetería, su figura erguida y esbelta de aspecto europeo, parecía ser un buen tipo y anticipe que quizás un buen conversador. Me acerque diciendo hola como está usted tratando de entablar conversación, el con una sonrisa respondió a mi saludo ofreciéndome una silla e invitándome a sentarme a su lado.

Le dije mi nombre y el respondió sonriendo que ojalá yo no fuera un tipo peligroso, porque él era alérgico a la violencia. ¿Le pregunte cuál era su ocupación? contesto que estaba retirado disfrutando del tiempo libre que en su juventud fue limitado.

Sonriendo que parecía ser lo usual en él, pregunto por mi profesión le conteste que era escritor de historias cortas en inglés y castellano al mismo tiempo, siendo libros didácticos, no solo divertidos o interesantes porque ofrecían la oportunidad de aprender uno de los dos idiomas.

Mencionando que sonaba interesante, que cual era mi fuente de inspiración, le conteste que todas mis historias eran reales, vividas por los personajes y algunas por mí mismo, de esa manera disfrutaba poder expresar mis sentimientos o los sentimientos de mis personajes, viviendo en carne propia cada una de las historias.

Redactar para mi es más que interesante por el tiempo dedicado a cada historia, encontrar y conocer al narrador. entenderlo y ganar su confianza para entenderlo y ganar su confianza para posteriormente escribir la historia sin perder la esencia que se convierte en todo un reto, para finalmente producir algo que valga la pena de leer. Dijo que por estar retirado, viejo y solitario podría narrarme la historia más triste jamás contada, lo único que tendría que hacer seria escucharlo y después decidir si valía la pena o no. Claro que yo estaba interesado y quise saber su historia así que de inmediato acordamos una cita en el mismo lugar, a la misma hora al día siguiente, sonriendo ambos y con un apretón de manos quedamos de acuerdo. Esa fría noche pensé que el hombre del espejo tendría una historia interesante pero cuando menciono "la historia más triste jamás contada" me hacía pensar miles de cosas y al mismo tiempo ninguna, al siguiente día se aclararían mis dudas y tendría conocimiento de su relato, que de antemano supe que era más que interesante.

DON TRISTE OTRA VEZ
HISTORIA TRISTE DE UN SUEÑO IMPOSIBLE

Los ruidos citadinos y la tenue luz invernal de un nuevo día me despertaron de buen humor, después de alistarme a tomar un desayuno ligero, trace una ruta de viaje hacia el centro de la ciudad siendo más fácil abordar un autobús público que me transportaría hasta la calle de Luisiana, así no tendría que buscar ni pagar por el estacionamiento que era caro y escaso.

Después caminaría hasta un lujoso hotel que en su interior tenia al través de unas escaleras eléctricas un acceso a los túneles, caminaría una milla o más hasta llegar al frente de la cafetería a encontrarme con mi nuevo amigo. Él ya estaba cómodamente instalado en la misma mesa del día anterior, lucía una camisa blanca con corbata tejida al igual que su boina de color guinda que combinaban perfectamente con su pantalón gris Oxford y con una capa británica tipo abrigo, en pocas palabras parecía personaje de película clásica del pasado mostrando su garbo y distinción.

Sonriendo extendió su mano calurosamente e invitándome a sentarme a su lado, correspondiendo a su amable saludo me instale cómodamente a su lado, le hizo saber que estaba emocionado por conocer su historia, porque la curiosidad aguijoneaba mi mente la cual siempre ha sido el mejor instrumento para redactar las historias que después de escucharlas atentamente tendría que entenderla, motivo por lo cual tomaría notas contando con su autorización.

Solicite dos tazas de café capuchino y le sugerí que probase el rollo de pan con queso ordenando dos también, me aliste a escuchar el inicio de su narración. El carraspeo aclarando su garganta dando comienzo a la historia diciendo así: mi infancia transcurrió en un barrio de clase media humilde, en la cual carecí de padre, confieso que me hizo falta tanto que hoy en mi vejez sigo necesitando de su presencia, mi madre trabajaba alrededor de 12 horas diarias para poder tener una economía aceptable, brindándome un nivel económico mejor que el promedio del barrio.

AVENTURAS DE REFLEXION FILOSOFICA
HISTORIA TRISTE DE UN SUEÑO IMPOSIBLE

Tuve acceso a educación, ropa, libros, juguetes, diversión, paseos y todas aquellas cosas materiales requeridas en la infancia y adolescencia. A finales de la década de los 50's era popular ir a donde exhibían películas antiguas mudas de blanco y negro sumamente divertidas, de Charlie Chaplin, Oliver & Stanley (el gordo y el flaco) The three Stoges (los tres chiflados) y muchos más que de momento no recordaría a todos. Varios cines eran realmente especiales como uno que proyectaba todos los días de la semana caricaturas de Tom y Jerry, el Súper Ratón, La Zorra y El Cuervo, sin faltar los clásicos personajes de Walt Disney como el pato Donald y sus sobrinos, el ratón miguelito que no era otro más que el famoso "Mickey Mouse" con Pluto, Tribilin, Ciro Pera loca, con su pequeño ayudante en fin podría mencionar muchos más.

Las proyecciones cinematográficas eran en compañía de los clásicos vendedores de golosinas, palomitas de maíz, paletas, refrescos y muchas cosas más, transitaban por los pasillos entre las butacas durante todas las películas pregonando sus productos como merolicos, nadie se molestaba y todos tratábamos de comprarles alguno de sus productos evitándonos el viaje al mostrador de golosinas, de esa manera no perdíamos detalle de las películas.

Durante el intermedio entre película y película era un griterío, corretear de niños por todos los pasillos del cine, que instantáneamente se detenían cuando se apagaban las luces corriendo hacia nuestros asientos dando comienzo la función. Disfrute esos días infantiles porque al principio mi Mami me llevaba a ver las películas. En cuanto cumplí 9 abriles gocé de la libertad y confianza para gastar mi dinero en el cine, golosinas, acudiendo a las llamadas matinés desde las 9:00 de la mañana hasta las 2:00 de la tarde, salíamos del cine como vampiros todos deslumbrados después de estar en penumbras por tantas horas gozando de caricaturas o películas de blanco y negro que incluían noticieros y caricaturas cortas al comienzo de las funciones.

DON TRISTE OTRA VEZ
HISTORIA TRISTE DE UN SUEÑO IMPOSIBLE

En otros cines las matinés eran de 3 películas de aventuras como Simbad el Marino, Sherlock Holmes, El Zorro, otras veces de terror como Drácula, el Hombre Lobo, eran fantásticas aquellas funciones donde no importaba en lo más mínimo que eran blanco y negro, no nos molestaba que carecían de color porque así era nuestro mundo inocente, dulce, realmente los seres humanos nos podíamos llamar humanos ya que nos respetábamos, nos protegíamos unos a otros. La vida en los barrios era bonita porque conocíamos a cada uno de las personas que vivían o deambulaban alrededor de nuestro vecindario, lo cual facilitaba la diaria convivencia, claro no faltaban los problemas y los busca pleitos, pero eran los menos y la mayoría que eran los mejores siempre se imponían, así que los barrios eran lugares divertidos y tranquilos donde valía la pena vivir.

La época decembrina era hermosa con sus posadas que se celebraban del 16 al 24 de diciembre, en las posadas había piñatas llenas de dulces y frutas, que los niños disfrutábamos a mas no poder. Se cantaban las letanías por todos los participantes con velitas en las manos y luces de bengala que hacían un ambiente acogedor y que algunos utilizábamos para quemarle el cabello a las chicas o chicos con la única excusa de divertirnos cuidando por supuesto que no se convirtiese en tragedia.

Los adultos se divertían con su famoso ponche de frutas que le agregaban una bebida alcohólica dándole vuelo al baile, jovencitas y mujeres hermosas eran el atractivo de las posadas, claro los niños jugábamos a conquistar a las chicas de nuestra edad haciéndonos de aventuras románticas. Si tenías suerte te conseguías novia en cada posada, pero durante los días siguientes andábamos con la angustia de que se enterasen todas ellas y te mandasen a volar no sin antes insultarte y propinarte un trompón en la nariz, eso no nos detenía de disfrutar ese maravilloso tiempo de posadas que terminaba en la víspera del día de Navidad.

AVENTURAS DE REFLEXION FILOSOFICA
HISTORIA TRISTE DE UN SUEÑO IMPOSIBLE

Él I Nuevo Año nos provocaba el prometer un sin número de cosas que pasadas unas cuantas semanas pasaban al olvido y prometer lo mismo el año siguiente, esa era la hermosa vida de blanco y negro que yo viví y disfruté tanto que con solo recordar esos tiempos sonrió con labios y corazón.

También fue la época de oro de la radio, las familias enteras se reunían alrededor de un receptor y escuchaban con atención durante varias horas los programas musicales, aventuras, romances, etc. todos los actores eran personas que se multiplicaban para con sus voces interpretar un sin número de personajes haciendo creer al público que los programas eran realizados por un numeroso elenco pero en realidad eran unos pocos actores de los cuales varios eran actores improvisados por la creciente demanda de la audiencia.

Los efectos especiales se realizaban con simples cubetas, campanas, serruchos, botellas de vidrio, etc. en fin era la época de la radio que deleitaba los oídos de los radioescuchas. que decir de la incipiente industria televisiva que transmitía en blanco y negro, existían solo dos canales televisivos transmitiendo de las 6:00 de la tarde hasta las 11:00 de la noche. un canal transmitía programas infantiles y juveniles como caricaturas, comediantes como Charles Chaplin, el Gordo y el Flaco, también algunos comediantes locales, todos ellos eran el deleite de los menores que veíamos la televisión.

El otro canal que transmitía series policiacas, películas, novelas de capítulos diarios, programas locales de variedades, entrevistas y noticieros que los adultos veían. Recuerdo con agrado el rápido crecimiento de la industria de la televisión que incluía más canales, horarios más extensos de transmisión, lo increíble y fantástico las primeras transmisiones en color, que de momento muchos no entendíamos porque para poder disfrutar de los programas a color se necesitaba otro tipo de televisor que fuera especialmente hecho para verse en color.

DON TRISTE OTRA VEZ
HISTORIA TRISTE DE UN SUEÑO IMPOSIBLE

De la noche a la mañana nuestros transmisores se convirtieron en viejos y pasados de moda no pudiendo disfrutar de la programación en color, todos los canales empezaron a transmitir en color, los divertidos programas viejos de blanco y negro desaparecieron para dar paso al modernismo. fue el final de los tiempos de blanco y negro avanzando a la época que el color nos traía nuevas desgracias y cosas inevitables en nombre del progreso como las guerras que eran de gran distracción según los noticiarios donde nos embobaban con programas tontos y noticias falsas mientras que el gobierno hacia cosas no correctas para el país.

Estábamos en la década de los 60's donde el mundo cambiaba con cada uno de sus giros dándonos a diario sorpresas buenas y malas, las faldas subieron de la rodilla entre 5 y 7 pulgadas convirtiéndose en todo un escándalo, se pusieron de moda los "hot pants" que eran lindos shorts entallados muy cortos como minifaldas, se usaban con pantimedias otro nuevo descubrimiento, zapatos altos o botas largas hasta las rodillas, los pantalones cortos femeninos dejaban de ser de uso deportivo.

La moda de los hombres también cambio como los "jeans" que eran los pantalones de mezclilla que les dábamos un tratamiento especial que hoy ni lo van a creer así que se los explicare con lujo de detalles. Primero comprabas tus pantalones de mezclilla de color azul marino.

En esos tiempos era el único color disponible, después de quitarles etiquetas de papel, grapas, etc. los sumergíamos dentro de una cubeta llena de Coca Cola eran necesarios algo así como dos galones dejándolos sumergidos por lo menos 24 horas, usabas piedras previamente lavadas para mantenerlos sumergidos y que no tuvieran manchas, después los dejabas secar tendiéndolos al sol.

No existían las secadoras automáticas solo las de rodillos, una vez ya secos los untabas por todos lados de crema transparente de las que se usaban para lustrar zapatos, se requerían varias latas para que quedaran totalmente engrasados, una vez más los sumergías en la misma Coca Cola del día anterior dejándolos otras 24 horas como mínimo, después los volvías a tender al sol para secarse y con un trapo mojado los planchabas por la parte interna del pantalón.

Después estaban listos para usarse y no los volvías a lavar, lo mejor de todo es que conservaban la apariencia de ser nuevos sin importar cuanto tiempo los usaras, el agua no penetraba en el tejido de la tela, el polvo y mugre se le quitaban con una simple cepillada, eran al clásico estilo norteamericano tal y como se veían en la película amor sin barreras que no era otra más que "West Side Story"

Nosotros los usábamos con un toque de distinción combinándolos con playeras tipo polo o camisas de vestir siendo obligado combinar el color de la playera con los calcetines que siendo del mismo color nos veíamos especiales según el gusto de esa época, así fue nuestra moda por varios años hasta que cambio la moda al pantalón acampanado, ya entrada la segunda mitad de la década de los 60's.

Los barrios competíamos deportivamente, musicalmente porque la música de rock estaba en la cúspide y cada barrio tenia uno o dos grupos musicales, los había buenos otros no tanto y los pésimos, pero ser miembro de uno de ellos te elevaba a un nivel de popularidad que no podías imaginar ni en sueños, los jóvenes nos dedicábamos a escuchar música de rock and roll, ver películas, jugar deportes y por supuesto tener noviazgos como pasatiempo. El deporte a nivel no profesional se convirtió en esperanza de muchos para convertirnos primero en jugadores de nivel nacional, luego de nivel internacional y más tarde como premio a la constancia y calidad convertirnos en jugadores profesionales.

DON TRISTE OTRA VEZ
HISTORIA TRISTE DE UN SUEÑO IMPOSIBLE

Dedicándonos también a lograr una carrera universitaria económicamente aspirando a una vida mejor que la que teníamos, debo decir que nuestra vida no era nada mala, pero lo normal era tener aspiraciones y metas para triunfar en la vida, económicamente.

Esa época nos brindó cosas divertidas, voy a decir una que llamo mi atención, la radio por lo regular terminaban sus transmisiones diarias alrededor de las 11:00 o 12:00 de la noche quedando los radios muertos sin transmisión alguna.

Era la época de los radios de bulbos, el descubrimiento del transistor con aquellos radios de baterías hechos todos ellos en Hong Kong y Alemania nos brindaron la portabilidad, así que después de las 12:00 de la noche buscaba estaciones de radio que transmitieran desde otros países, recuerdo bien que sintonizaba la BBC de Londres, lo divertido es que captaba la mejor radio difusora de rock del mundo que era conocida como Radio Rock que transmitía las 24 horas continuas desde un barco anclado en aguas internacionales cercanas a las costas del Reino Unido.

Aquella estación de radio era considerada ilegal al igual que otros 150 barcos que eran "Radio Piratas" ellos transmitían en idioma Ingles, pero el rock tenía un lenguaje propio que todos los jóvenes del planeta entendíamos sin pedir traducción alguna. se podían escuchar durante la madrugada disfrutando música de los Beatles, Kinks, Rolling Stones, Animals, Moody Blues, Caravan the Who, Herman Hermits, Zombies, Cream, Procul Harum, Turtles, Loving Spoonfull, en mi ciudad esos grupos y sus canciones se escuchaban con un retraso de 6 meses más o menos. Yo era pequeño de edad por eso nadie podía creer que estuviese al tanto de la música mejor que jóvenes mayores que yo. Por supuesto que mantuve mi secreto porque escuchaba durante las madrugadas cubriendo mi cabeza y al pequeño radio con la almohada para que mi madre no escuchara.

HISTORIA TRISTE DE UN SUEÑO IMPOSIBLE

Porque de enterarse me quitaría mi radio, porque en esa época los adultos no entendían la música de rock diciendo que era escandalosa, música del diablo etc. la iglesia se encargaba de satanizar el rock así que los sermones dominicales estaban llenos de prohibiciones de rock que nuestros padres seguían al pie de la letra porque no lo sé en esos tiempos los padres mandaban con o sin razón, su autoridad no se discutía respetando las reglas del hogar.

Por las madrugadas esas reglas no me importaban, escuchaba mi música de rock, brincando, danzando eufóricamente hasta quedarme dormido disfrutando lo que después descubrieron que no era satánico, eso si nadie se disculpó con la juventud y siguieron echándole la culpa al rock de todos los males que aquejaban a la sociedad encubriéndose unos a otros porque todos los males, guerras, corrupciones, depravaciones, exageraciones religiosas, asesinatos, cientos de errores políticos con consecuencias para los pueblos eran y siguen siendo errores cometidos por los adultos con toda la mala intención para enriquecerse o para tener más poder que otros adultos.

Los Beatles con su música, cabellos largos ropas ajustadas influyeron provocando el comienzo de la rebeldía juvenil, ya que solo buscábamos libertad de escoger lo que nos gustara, tener libertad religiosa, esto no implicaba dejar de estudiar e ir a la iglesia, seguíamos respetando a nuestros padres y a los adultos, solo pedíamos que ellos también mostraran respeto por nosotros.

Algunos adultos lo entendieron, fueron conscientes de darnos un poco de libertad aflojando el yugo en que nos tenían sometidos, otros no e inclusive les pusieron trabas a todas nuestras actividades modernas, el cabello largo en hombres era prohibido en escuelas, iglesias, trabajos, etc. Preferían que les mintiéramos para poder asistir a los tardeados musicales de los Domingos en las cuales bailábamos escuchando grupos musicales locales que interpretaban magistralmente.

DON TRISTE OTRA VEZ
HISTORIA TRISTE DE UN SUEÑO IMPOSIBLE

La música de rock. en las tardeadas por asistir menores de edad no se vendían bebidas alcohólicas, daban comienzo a las 3:00 pm finalizando a las 11:00 de la noche. los Lugares eran canchas de frontenis, pistas de patinaje, estacionamientos subterráneos.

Estacionamientos de varios pisos de altura, algunos salones de baile empezaban a participar haciendo ese tipo de tardeadas, pero resulta que eran clandestinas, lo curioso es que los organizadores obtenían permisos en las alcaldías del área a celebrarse las tardeadas.

Así que los policías vigilaban, pero no interrumpían el evento a excepción de que hubiese desorden por parte de la multitud participante o que los organizadores no tuviesen el permiso correspondiente.

En las tardeadas conocías músicos, chicas bonitas, gente con cabellos largos y ropa extravagante que te hablaban de poesía, de libertad que disfrutaban los jóvenes en los países desarrollados y más aún en los Estados Unidos y Canadá. Nos divertíamos a lo grande bailando y aprendiendo cosas que ocurrían en otras partes del mundo, lo que no cambiaba era el respeto a la unidad familiar. Por ser amiguero participaba en fiestas especiales, cenas y comidas familiares con una enorme cantidad de familias en el vecindario y fuera de él.

Veía con asombro aquellos matrimonios completos que bien o mal educaban a sus hijos, eso era normal la influencia y participación de ambos padres en la formación de sus hijos con la gran responsabilidad de mantener unida a la familia. Era respetable pertenecer a una de esas bellas familias en las cuales yo fui un invitado bien aceptado, pero no era miembro de la familia ser miembro implicaba responsabilidad, gusto, diversión, y mucho amor. Comprendí que yo carecía de muchas cosas porque yo no tenía padre o hermanos, mi madre y yo estábamos solos en esa gran ciudad.

Porque nuestros familiares radicaban en otras ciudades, otros en algunos países lejanos, así que yo era pobre por no tener una familia completa, eso no me amargo la existencia al contrario me hizo admirar y apreciar a las familias deseando tener algún día mi propia familia.

Recuerdo a una señora que acostumbraba lavar y planchar ropa de algunas personas del vecindario como manera para ganarse la vida, los chicos del barrio acostumbrábamos ir a su casa todas las tardes de verano porque mientras planchaba la ropa nos contaba historias antiguas de misterio, terror, etc. Dona Alta era excelente en sus narraciones, cuando terminaba de planchar era el final de sus narraciones alrededor de las 8:00 de la noche, le ayudábamos cargándole la ropa para todos ir con ella a entregarla porque de esa manera nos llevaba a cada uno de nosotros hasta las puertas de nuestras casas, porque nos daba miedo después de escuchar las historias que nos contaba, en fin todas las noches decía que no volvería a contarnos historias porque éramos más cobardes que un pollo, pero al día siguiente repetíamos la visita a su casa.

Los fines de semana teníamos actividades propias de nuestra edad, teníamos infinidad de travesuras y aventuras en que divertirnos, los días de la infancia Iván quedando atrás e íbamos cambiando, nuestro barrio tenía como alumbrado un foco colgado de un cable para alumbrarnos de noche, por supuesto que no era suficiente para toda la calle que de largo tendría unos 300 metros por lo tanto daba miedo caminar de noche ya que las construcciones en esa calle eran coloniales recordándonos las historias macabras de Dona Alta.

Después las obras publicas que realizo el gobierno entrando de lleno al modernismo contamos con 7 postes de alumbrado así que el barrio cambiaba igual que nosotros ya que dejábamos la infancia junto con aquel único foco que alumbro la calle. Entre semana cuando anochecía se escuchaban guitarras entonando canciones de moda.

DON TRISTE OTRA VEZ
HISTORIA TRISTE DE UN SUEÑO IMPOSIBLE

Que eran interpretadas desde la espectacularidad hasta horriblemente, era entretenido escuchar a esos intérpretes de barrio que te hacían transcurrir el tiempo. Que cuando te dabas cuenta eran ya las 10:00 de la noche así que padres y madres nos llamaban con gritos furiosos para que fuésemos a cenar para después dormirnos, dando fin a la diversión diaria del barrio.

Era también el fin de las historietas cómicas que empezábamos a guardar en libreros familiares o en un cajón porque no pudimos tirarlas ya que eran el recuerdo de nuestra infancia, aquel Sorprendente Hombre Araña que aun con sus súper poderes batallaba económicamente para pagar la renta de la casa, ocultando su identidad secreta a la tía May que lo adoraba como hijo propio. A mí me encantaba por ser pobre y honrado que no abusaba de sus poderes ni para pagar la renta, lo admire por el resto de mi vida identificándome con él por querer se justo y sencillo como él.

Claro había otras historietas que me gustaban como los Cuatro Fantásticos, Thor, Walt Disney, la entretenida Familia Burron, Rolando el Rabioso, los Súper Sabios, en fin, montones de historietas que le dieron diversión a nuestra infancia que se alejaba a toda prisa. sin darnos cuenta quedaron atrás las aventuras en bicicleta e ir por los alrededores de la ciudad con peligros y emociones memorables, los juegos de canicas, trompo, balero, diábolo, yoyo, carreras en patines, hoyo 16, y un sin fin de juegos.

La ciudad cambio los tranvías eléctricos desaparecieron junto con los viajes de mosca que era ir trepado atrás para no pagar, empezaron a construir el servicio de trenes subterráneos, edificios enormes aparecían de pronto, la radio y la televisión brindaban espectáculos sofisticados con variedad de canales, coberturas a red nacional con horarios de 24 horas continuas, todo cambiaba al igual que nosotros alcanzándonos la adolescencia.

AVENTURAS DE REFLEXION FILOSOFICA
HISTORIA TRISTE DE UN SUEÑO IMPOSIBLE

Con cambios físicos y también en nuestras mentes cambiando la manera de entender e interpretar la vida. Algo que perdimos, es que cuando jugábamos a policías y rateros peleábamos porque todos queríamos ser policías o ser los buenos, por lo menos en esa época así sucedía, decíamos que si llegásemos a ser doctores, abogados, etc. ayudaríamos a los humildes, aunque eso significara no ser ricos, sonábamos con hacer un mundo mejor, tristemente los que lograron ser agentes policiacos y ayudantes de agentes se dedicaban a robar.

Golpeando y asaltando hasta sexualmente a desconocidos inocentes ciudadanos, a los rateros los ponían a robar para ellos protegiéndolos para que no fuesen arrestados así que los mantenían libres y robando.

Otros lograron alcanzar puestos menores en el gobierno robando y estafando a mas no poder sin importarles que perjudicaban a los más humildes, los que se convirtieron en profesionistas jamás brindaron una consulta gratuita a los humildes cobrándoles lo mismo que a los ricos, engañándoles con tal de obtener más dinero. Así que aquella infancia dulce de blanco y negro se convirtió en cosa del pasado olvidando los sueños de mejorar el mundo, pero no para mí porque seguí sonando con mejorar el mundo sacrificando lo que otros no se atrevían ni siquiera a pensarlo.

Acudir a las tardeadas, escuchar la radio rock, y los guitarristas nocturnos del barrio, crearon en mí el deseo de aprender a tocar guitarra, pocos meses después aprendí ya que me agradaba más que cualquier otra cosa en la vida, cumplía con clases y tareas escolares pero el resto de la tarde y noche practicaba en mi casa con todo el deseo de unirme a un grupo de rock y ser músico profesional. Los Beatles dominaban el panorama mundial a mí me agradaban, pero no más que a mis amigos o conocidos, las mujeres pegaban alaridos al escucharlos a través de la radio.

DON TRISTE OTRA VEZ
HISTORIA TRISTE DE UN SUEÑO IMPOSIBLE

Eso era algo que no entendí, durante sus presentaciones había desmayadas, histeria colectiva, con gritos infinitos, todas las chicas lloraban de emoción, pero esto ocurría solo con los Beatles, era la famosa Beatles manía que no pudo ser entendida ni explicada por científicos o psicólogos. Escuche por primera vez el álbum de "El Sargento Pimienta" quede impresionado como lo hicieron millones de personas alrededor del mundo, no podía creer que eran los Beatles, escuche el álbum por ambos lados cerca de 7 veces en tan solo un día admirando la calidad del sonido, las composiciones, y la manera de interpretarlas, el álbum fue grabado con una orquesta sinfónica los Beatles escribieron las partituras de cada instrumento que eran cerca de 60 dándonos a saber que eran genios y que estábamos presenciando la historia musical con ese álbum como obra maestra del rock.

La primer transmisión global en vivo por satélite alrededor del mundo fue en Junio 25 de 1967 con la mayor audiencia de la época 350 millones de personas, se llamó "Nuestro Mundo" participando más de 25 países con el propósito de mostrar algo característico de cada nación, los Estados Unidos transmitieron el nacimiento de un bebe fue algo maravilloso porque habíamos personas que no habíamos presenciado nunca un nacimiento, otros países mostraron adelantos científicos, tradición y arte, contribuyeron 17 países en vivo nada grabado y ninguna participación política.

La nación que impacto al mundo fue el Reino Unido mostrando la grabación de la canción "Todo lo que necesitas es amor" de los Beatles por mandato de la Reyna Isabel, ahí vimos reunidos músicos como; Mike Jagger, Donovan, Eric Clapton, por decir algunos, nos dieron una experiencia deliciosa, imaginen la canción sonando simultáneamente en todo el planeta con un mensaje de paz y con el mejor grupo musical del mundo. He vuelto a ver y escuchar el video de esa transmisión y el mensaje sigue siendo válido porque lo único que necesitamos es amor.

Fui creciendo y participando en ensayos con grupos musicales en el barrio, pero no prometían éxito alguno, se comportaban como simples drogadictos ya que fumaban mariguana y tocaban una canción de 4 minutos a lo largo de 3 horas sin ton ni son, era absurdo porque no aprendías nada con ese tipo de prácticas.

Me fui a ensayar con otro grupo del barrio que no hacían drogas, pero en vez de ensayar para aprender más canciones y perfeccionarlas, lo único que les preocupaba era verse bonitos y creían que bastaba con solo tener instrumentos para tener éxito, pero no era el camino correcto.

Ensayar tratando de interpretar las canciones igualando el sonido original, requería esfuerzo y practica continua, un oído excelente para no confundir las notas que te ayudaban a que la interpretación sonara de acuerdo a la canción original.

Como yo no tenía hermanos solo tenía a mi Mami la cual trabajaba por largos turnos me daba tiempo para deleitarme con mi compañera la soledad, así que tenía tiempo de sobra para practicar con la guitarra, escuchar discos tratando de aprender las canciones escuchándolas miles de veces, era cansado pero no aburrido, descubriendo que aunque mejoraras tus habilidades musicales nunca terminabas de aprender, entre mejor tocaras las canciones tenías más necesidad de perfeccionar a tal grado que sonaras como profesional, así que mi mundo se convirtió en música de rock las 24 horas del día porque hasta durmiendo aprendía y practicaba.

Todos en el barrio decían que el mejor guitarrista indiscutiblemente era un tal Pancho, en cuanto alternamos musicalmente quedo demostrado que el mejor guitarrista era yo y la distancia entre uno y otro era enorme, porque él se dedicaba a tomar alcohol y fumar mariguana para según inspirarse.

DON TRISTE OTRA VEZ
HISTORIA TRISTE DE UN SUEÑO IMPOSIBLE

Qué pena porque tenía habilidad, cantaba bien, pero era más delincuente que músico, en cambio yo me dedicaba en cuerpo y alma al arduo trabajo de aprender practicando hasta el cansancio, me convertí en el mejor guitarrista del barrio, así que con tal de mejorar empecé a explorar y conocer otros grupos, dándome cuenta que los mejores músicos eran por lo menos una década más grande que yo por supuesto con mayor experiencia hasta de la vida misma.

Eran aquellos grandes grupos que se presentaban en las tardeadas y que sonaban igual a los discos de los músicos que interpretaban. Esos grupos ensayaban todos los días de la semana porque sábados y Domingos se presentaban en 4 o 5 diferentes lugares siendo los mejores por eso ganaban bastante dinero así que tenían buenos instrumentos y amplificadores comparables a los de los grupos internacionales que escuchaba en la radio rock.

Por fin logre colocarme en un grupo que proponía ensayar toda la semana de las 4:00 de la tarde a 8:00 de la noche en un cuarto localizado en la casa del baterista, ellos me contactaron por ser un músico desconocido pero que demostraba cualidades musicales, ellos fueron un grupo de regular a bueno pero se desintegraron a raíz de que el guitarrista líder renuncio, diciendo que los demás miembros del grupo carecían de calidad musical fundando otro grupo con el mismo nombre de ellos "Las Flores" porque según el merecía conservar el nombre del grupo por ser el único con calidad musical y ser el líder. El grupo con nuevo nombre "La Expedición" conformado por Chava que era el baterista y líder del grupo, el Orejas que era el bajista, Ramiro que era el cantante, y yo el nuevo guitarrista. empecé el arduo trabajo de aprender las canciones que ellos tocaban anteriormente, para lo más pronto posible presentarnos en las tardeadas de los sábados donde acostumbraban presentarse, decían que yo no tenía la habilidad del guitarrista anterior.

Eso no me molestaba al contrario me motivaba a superarme y ser mejor guitarrista, incremente los ensayos en mi casa practicaba de 9:00 de la noche hasta la 1:00 de la madrugada, despertaba alrededor de las 7:00 de la mañana a desayunar e irme a la escuela, salía a las 2:00 de la tarde regresaba a casa comía, me cambiaba de ropa y me trasladaba a la casa de Chava para ensayar de Lunes a Sábado, los Domingos asistíamos a las tardeadas de los grupos famosos con la idea de aprender y disfrutar escuchando a esos grupos que eran los mejores de la ciudad y del ambiente musical del momento.

Transcurrieron 3 semanas y en Sábado hicimos la primer presentación en un barrio lejano, participamos 3 grupos de los cuales uno era mejor que nosotros, el otro no muy bueno siendo nosotros solo un grupo regular, Fili un joven universitario metido en política, propuso ser nuestro representante musical ofreciéndonos la garantía de presentarnos en mítines políticos cobrando poco pero todos los Sábados y Domingos por la mañana proporcionándonos el transporte más los Sábados por la tarde presentarnos en aquel lejano barrio. pidió que repartiésemos las ganancias a 5 partes iguales como miembros iguales del grupo, nos pareció bien y de inmediato nos presentamos por las mañanas los sábados en mítines políticos y por la tarde en 2 diferentes tardeadas de barrios lejanos del centro de la ciudad donde ensayábamos.

El público nos aceptaba comenzando a ser populares en aquellos lejanos barrios, presentábamos una o dos nuevas canciones cada semana, el cantante propuso cobrar el doble porque según él, era la atracción del grupo y sin él no éramos nada, por decisión unánime prescindimos de sus servicios comenzando Chava a como primera voz, yo la segunda voz y el Orejas ayudaba un poco con voces así que de golpe incorporamos tres voces al grupo que sonaba mejor que cuando teníamos a Ramiro, todas las canciones las manejábamos con voces no practicadas antes.

DON TRISTE OTRA VEZ
HISTORIA TRISTE DE UN SUEÑO IMPOSIBLE

Él usar al mismo tiempo los instrumentos requerían de más horas de ensayo porque anteriormente solo contábamos con una voz, así que nos convertimos en un grupo musical como los Beatles con voces sonando mejor, de inmediato aquel grupo que sonó mejor que nosotros en la primera presentación se quedó sorprendido porque sonábamos mejor que ellos por la incorporación de las voces.

Tuvimos cuidado de seleccionar bien las canciones integrando música y voces de grupos como Beatles, Wallace Collection, Box Tops, Classic 4, Turtles, Marmalade, America, Kinks, Eric Burdon y los Animales, Three Dog Night, Guess Who, etc. fuimos explorando rock más agresivo como Ratless, Led Zeppelin, Crow, Deep Purple, Grand Funk Railroad, Jimi Hendrix, Black Sabath, etc. esos grupos estaban de moda pero escogíamos las canciones de los álbumes que otros grupos no interpretaban porque nos habría hecho parecer un grupo más, habría comparaciones y quizás no serían buenas para nosotros o quizás sí, pero para que arriesgar.

El grupo subió de nivel presentándonos en mejores lugares, alternando con grupos grandes ya en Domingo en los 4 puntos cardinales de la ciudad, teniendo seguidores que acudían a nuestras presentaciones creando para nosotros una popularidad desconocida por lo menos hasta ese momento. Algunos grupos con los que alternábamos eran espectaculares.

Eran los mismos que anteriormente íbamos a escuchar durante las tardeadas de los Domingos como Love Army, Last Soul Division, Factory, Peace and Love, La Sociedad Anónima, Los Leo, La Tropa Loca, el Cactus, así como muchos otros grupos más que no eran de los grandes, pero eran populares como el Three Souls in my Mind que hasta la fecha sigue activo pero conocido como el Tri, de Alejandro Lora que era amigo y vecino mío.

Caminábamos por rumbos distintos, pero éramos rocanroleros de corazón, había otros grandes grupos como los Cousins, las Naciones Unidas, Javier Batiz que fue el maestro de Carlos Santana, la Tinta Blanca, la Tribu y muchos más que les pido disculpas por no mencionarlos solo porque tengo mala memoria y últimamente practico mi Alzheimer.

Imaginen la emoción que sentí al alternar con aquellos grandes grupos que eran mis ídolos, aun no alcanzábamos su nivel pero estuvimos a 5 niveles debajo de ellos y en eses momento a solo 3 niveles y seria solo 2 si tuviésemos mejor equipo de sonido como ellos, así que habíamos progresado en tan solo 6 meses, cuando empecé con ellos tenía una guitarra marca patito japonesa, y en ese momento tenía una Fender americana modelo Dúo Sonic, la compramos usada pero estaba en perfectas condiciones pero la mandamos pintar quedando como de fábrica además sonaba de lo mejor, teniendo guitarra para competir con los mejores guitarristas dependiendo todo de mi practicando más tiempo y con más esfuerzo que nunca.

Algunas veces el mundo es chiquito y que bueno porque comencé a conocer músicos buenos de los grupos grandes. mi Mami tenía una amiga que se convirtió en su comadre por bautizarle a su hija, esa señora tenía un hermano que le decían Satanás porque vestía de rojo casi a diario, él era miembro de un grupo llamado la Yerba que ensayaban en un barrio no muy lejano, donde ensayaba también La Sociedad Anónima que tenían un guitarrista Alejandro que le decían Don Gato, que era el maestro musical de Satanás y que lo ayudo a colocarse con el grupo la Yerba.

Después de conocer a Satanás me invito a presenciar sus ensayos agradándome la invitación fui a escucharlos, a manera de ser originales interpretaban casi todas las canciones de los Credence Clear Water Revival grupo internacional de gran popularidad ellos las interpretaban bien alrededor del 80%

DON TRISTE OTRA VEZ
HISTORIA TRISTE DE UN SUEÑO IMPOSIBLE

Al 85% tenían un buen equipo de sonido casi de grupo grande, ensayaban en un establo donde criaban borregos, puercos y vacas que ordeñaban y vendían leche, el hijo de los dueños que era la segunda guitarra el proporcionaba los instrumentos y los amplificadores ya que el negocio familiar les proporcionaba buenas ganancias teniendo bastante dinero.

Al término de su ensayo nos fuimos Satanás y yo a 4 calles de distancia a un taller mecánico, al fondo había un pequeño cuarto donde ensayaba La Sociedad Anónima mejor conocida como la "S.A." entramos al cuarto sin hacer ruido porque estaban practicando la canción "vivo por el sol" de "Vanity Fair" el sonido de los instrumentos y las voces sonaban 100% igual que el disco. Whow como llegue ahí? el Satanás era amigo de Alejandro, además eran vecinos separados a tan solo una calle uno del otro, así que íbamos por Alejandro para juntos irnos de regreso a casa, yo habitaba a 8 calles de distancia de ellos siendo vecino también.

Fue un placer conocer cara a cara a los elementos del grupo Dayton el baterista, Panchillo el bajista, Carlos el tecladista, líder del grupo y Alejandro Don Gato el guitarrista, fue como un sueño estar en su ensayo, ellos decidieron darle un repaso a la canción "Let it be" de "los Beatles"

Para estrenarla en su siguiente presentación, el sábado, cuando la interpretaron sonaban exactamente al disco original, cada instrumento, cada voz, el piano en fin todo era igual en cada detalle de la canción. Fui presentado con ellos diciéndoles que yo era músico guitarrista de "La Expedición" dijeron de seguro por amabilidad haber escuchado el nombre de nuestro grupo que empezábamos a tener fama, Carlos tenía un sentido del humor bellísimo, conto varios chistes, me hizo algunas bromas sin usar malas palabras, el me pareció un tipo fantástico, que siendo bromista no dejaba de ser bien educado y de buenos modales.

Para mi buena suerte se presentó don Nino dueño del taller y representante de ellos invitándonos a cenar a todos sin excepción en su casa que estaba al lado del cuarto de ensayo, ya en su casa nos acomodamos alrededor de una mesa grande para deleitarnos con platillos preparados por la señora de la casa, observe unas miradas de complicidad entre Patricia la hija de Don Nino y Alejandro, se me hizo curioso porque ella tendría 15 abriles de edad mientras Alejandro tendría 25 abriles así que se me figuro divertida la situación.

Patricia tenía un cuerpazo de mujer, de cara bonita tentación para cualquier hombre, pero respetuoso como debería de ser me dedique solo a observar, más tarde nos despedimos de todas las personas, pero Alejandro Don Gato, Satanás y yo nos fuimos caminando hasta la parada del camión que abordaríamos de regreso al barrio, ellos cargaban sus estuches donde Iván sus guitarras.

Yo no traía mi guitarra, ese día no ensaye porque Chava tuvo cita con el doctor así que aprovechando me fui con Satanás y que bueno que así lo hizo porque fue el principio del ascenso de mi incipiente carrera musical.

Durante el trayecto de regreso charlamos Alejandro me hizo saber que vivía con su Mami igual que yo con la diferencia que él tenía 3 hermanitos tal y como él se refería a ellos. Fue divertido conocerle ya que me invito a sus ensayos o verlos en "El Cortijo" una plaza de toros localizada en frente del taller donde ensayaban, al siguiente Domingo se presentarían por cierto ahí era como su casa por ser el grupo local, después caminé hacia mi casa demasiado contento sonreía y agradecía la buena suerte que tuve de conocer a los jóvenes de aquel grupo que tanto admiraba.

Al día siguiente fui al ensayo con mi grupo, pero mis compañeros no creían que había estado con "La S.A." en su cuarto de ensayo, pero eso no me preocupo.

DON TRISTE OTRA VEZ
HISTORIA TRISTE DE UN SUEÑO IMPOSIBLE

Llego el sábado y fuimos a presentarnos a 2 diferentes lugares, como ganábamos más dinero adquirimos en pagos un amplificador Fender súper rever así que solo rentábamos un amplificador para las presentaciones para ser más competitivos, para ensayar era suficiente con el nuevo Fender y otro amplificador no muy bueno que usábamos para el bajo.

Ese Domingo temprano fuimos presentándonos en los mítines políticos de Fili y en la tarde les pregunte si querían ir "Al Cortijo" pero prefirieron ir al "Centro Deportivo Nader" un lugar cercano donde también se presentaban grupos musicales de los denominados grandes y famosos.

Ya estando en "El Cortijo" pagué mi entrada y fui a saludar a mis amigos de "La S.A." Carlos y Alejandro fueron amables y corteses mostrando alegría de verme, también se presentaban "las Naciones Unidas" con canciones de "Electric Flag" interpretándolas entre 90% y 95% comparado a las originales.

Mientras tantos La S.A. mis amigos terminaron de montar el equipo de sonido comenzando su presentación, Carlos saludo al público y pregunto si habíamos escuchado el álbum de "Los Beatles" "Abbey Road" todas las personas contestaron que si mencionando algunos títulos de canciones del álbum.

Carlos dijo que dedicado para todo el público interpretarían el lado 1 del álbum, de inmediato comenzaron y claro sonaban al 100% igual que el disco, tocaron una tras otra todas las canciones y en el mismo orden del lado 1 del disco cuando finalizaron Carlos imitando el sonido de un tocadiscos y haciendo la mímica de voltear un disco, dijo ahora el lado 2 y continuaron tocando todas y cada una de las canciones del lado 2 hasta finalizar el álbum, el público aplaudía con locura como si fuesen los reales "Beatles" y no "La S.A." quedamos impresionados luego interpretaron "Let it be" al 100% igual despidiéndose tocando el Reprise del sargento pimienta y Un día en la vida.

HISTORIA TRISTE DE UN SUEÑO IMPOSIBLE

Al término de la presentación el público no dejaba de aplaudir elogiándolos como el mejor grupo del mundo en lo que se refería interpretar a "los Beatles" me sume al clamor del público y corrí a felicitarlos mostrándoles musicalmente mi respeto, Don Gato Alejandro me pregunto si vivía cerca del Deportivo Nader? conteste que si además a solo 2 calles de donde ensaya con mi grupo, amablemente dijo que se dirigían a presentarse en ese lugar así que si quería ir con ellos era bien aceptado y me pidió ayudarlos a trasladar el equipo al camión que nos llevaría, o solo cuidar su guitarra, por cobardía y para seguir vivo escogí ayudar con los amplificadores.

Ya en el camino me pregunto porque escogí lo más difícil y pesado que cuidar su guitarra sonriendo conteste que una guitarra Gibson estéreo negra igual que la de "BB King" era enorme responsabilidad y no dudo que alguien me asesinara para robarla. Don Gato y Carlos que había escuchado se rieron y continuamos el camino hacia el Centro Deportivo Nader, una vez ahí entramos por un portón de servicio que nos condujo hasta un elevador de carga donde amigos y músicos nos dimos a la tarea de introducir el equipo al elevador y luego subir hasta el tercer piso donde estaba el salón de recepciones más grande.

De inmediato escuchamos la música del grupo "Factory" que en ese momento interpretaban casi al 100% las canciones de grupos como "Chicago" mientras tanto en un balcón enfrente de ellos nos dimos a la tarea de montar el modesto equipo, no tan grande para ser un grupo de primer nivel, calidad y prestigio.

Don Gato estuvo contento de que le ayude a cuidar y cargar su guitarra dijo que si yo sabía el modelo y quien de fama internacional tenía otra igual que por cierto eran las únicas dos guitarras construidas en el mundo en ese tiempo, de seguro yo no permitiría que nada malo le ocurriera a Lola Patricia nombre dado a su guitarra.

DON TRISTE OTRA VEZ
HISTORIA TRISTE DE UN SUEÑO IMPOSIBLE

Como de costumbre Carlos saludo al público dedicándoles la presentación y comenzaron con "Let it be" deleitando a los presentes por lo perfecto de su interpretación, mis compañeros de grupo que veían desde el segundo nivel mezclados entre el público y sorprendidos que yo estaba en el balcón con "La Sociedad Anónima" los salude con gusto y a partir de ese momento no dudaron que eran mis amigos en especial Don Gato y Carlos que eran mis vecinos porque Carlos vivía a solo tres calles de Don Gato, aunque yo no tenía la calidad musical de ellos, me sentí grande como nunca antes.

Tenía poco tiempo de conocer a Alejandro cuando su mami murió, el Satanás me lo hizo saber le dije a mi Mami la triste noticia y ella menciono que le dijera a Alejandro que si necesitaba ayuda para atender a sus hermanitos podría contar con nosotros solo bastaría que nos dijera.

Más tarde el Satanás y yo fuimos a la funeraria para estar con Alejandro, cuando entramos la gente estaba triste llorando en fin eran momentos terribles, Alejandro estaba triste pero no lloraba sus hermanitos lloraban desconsolados, para mi sorpresa la hermana tenía 22 años, el hermano 18 y la más chica 16 años como yo, pero entendí que para el siempre serían sus hermanitos.

Alguien le dijo a Alejandro que llorara para desahogar su dolor y que no tenía por qué ocultarlo, el respondió que si sus hermanitos lo vean llorar estarían más tristes, él debía mostrar fortaleza como hombre de la casa dándoles confort, dijo que para que llorar en ese momento si la lloraría toda su vida. Me dio gusto saber que se expresaba tan bonito de su Mami y hermanitos, supe que fue buen hijo, buen hermano y por supuesto un buen hombre, sentí orgullo de conocer a alguien con tan buen corazón uniéndome a él en su dolor. más tarde después de abrazar a Alejandro y hermanitos salimos de ahí el Satanás y yo rumbo a nuestras casas, callados por la tristeza que tenía nuestro mutuo amigo.

La S.A. descansaban los viernes en ese primer descanso pidieron visitarnos a nuestro lugar de ensayo, cuando Carlos y Don Gato nos escucharon dijeron que éramos mejor grupo de lo que decía Satanás, dijeron que teníamos estilo propio, la selección de nuestro repertorio era excelente, el contraste de ser solo 3 elementos, pero cubriendo bien los vacíos musicales, las voces teníamos que mejorarlas, pero sonaban bien, como si su visita fuese un examen nos aprobaron.

Él satanás nos visitó solo una sola vez para vendernos discos de música porque necesitaba dinero para ir con su novia esposa, pero meses después dejo de ser músico, se buscó un empleo cotidiano trabajando para tener una vida matrimonial olvidándose del rock, confieso que no lo busque ni supe nada más de él. la situación de nuestro grupo cambio porque empezamos a usar las técnicas de ensayo de "La S.A." por consejo de ellos descansábamos los lunes así que esos días me iba a casa de Don Gato, o al lugar donde ensayaban.

Él amablemente se convirtió en mi maestro a manera de que perfeccionara mi estilo musical para ser un guitarrista completo. el amor parecía ser enemigo del rock como epidemia también contagio al Orejas se consiguió novia empezando a hacer planes para casarse renunciando al grupo de manera amigable. la vida teje enredadas telarañas que cruzan caminos a veces complicándolos otras veces facilitándolos como sucedió en el caso de encontrar el reemplazo adecuado del Orejas.

Tan solo una semana antes habíamos alternado con "The Flowers" el grupo de Chava el gordo como le decían al guitarrista que yo había reemplazado, antes de alternar dijo que musicalmente éramos un grupo malo y que nos darían una paliza, pidió que la tardeada fuese un mano a mano así que el ganador cobraría dos sueldos, y el grupo perdedor nada. aceptamos porque mis compañeros se sintieron ofendidos, estuve de acuerdo.

DON TRISTE OTRA VEZ
HISTORIA TRISTE DE UN SUEÑO IMPOSIBLE

Porque quise quedaría claro quién era mejor guitarrista. después ganamos el mano a mano así que el humillado fue chava el gordo y su grupo porque nosotros cobramos doble.

Dos días después llegaron a nuestro ensayo Chava el gordo y Guti con la idea de incorporarse a nosotros musicalmente, pensando en el beneficio del grupo decidimos que yo tocaría teclados, chava el gordo seria el guitarrista principal y Guti la guitarra de armonía, trayendo 2 amplificadores no teniendo que rentar equipo durante las presentaciones siguientes.

Conseguí prestado un teclado box jaguar que sonaba de maravilla, chava el gordo no pudo con el paquete renunciando ese mismo día así que volví a la guitarra principal.

Más tarde el Orejas renuncio sabiendo que Guti seria su reemplazo, musicalmente fue un cambio positivo Guti era mejor bajista e incorporo una tercera voz de calidad, así que después de aprenderse nuestras canciones nos presentamos sonando mejor ya que trajo su amplificador para el bajo. nuestra superación musical nos trajo la necesidad de un equipo para voces, pero sería más adelante cuando tuviésemos más trabajo y dinero para invertir.

La S.A. decían que el problema de equipo era solucionable proponiéndonos algo que no podíamos rechazar, que nos abría un camino exitoso en nuestra corta carrera musical.

Tenían demasiado trabajo y varios salones para presentarse, pero carecían de un gran equipo, nosotros no teníamos tanto trabajo como ellos y no un gran equipo, así que, si nos presentábamos juntos, ellos nos conseguirían contratos en sus presentaciones así que juntaríamos los equipos, de esa manera ambos tendríamos buen equipo para las presentaciones, y competiríamos con los grandes grupos sin tener que rentar o pedir prestado equipo.

De ahí en adelante nos presentábamos juntos en 2, 3, o 4 lugares sábados y domingos. nuestros lugares de ensayo eran pequeños para poder los dos grupos ensayar, pero musicalmente convivíamos tanto que fuimos los beneficiados por estar con ellos ensenándonos tanto que subimos a solo un nivel de distancia de los mejores grupos del momento no importando que solo éramos 3 elementos.

Como mencione al juntar el equipo la batería se convirtió en una doble que solo los grandes bateristas la podían usar y créanme cuando chava la usaba lo hacía tan bien que subieron sus bonos musicalmente, él era también todo un rompe corazones con las chicas en nuestras presentaciones.

Por lo regular nuestras presentaciones eran antes que las de La S.A. después de ellos salíamos prácticamente volando a la siguiente presentación, así que juntamos los ayudantes que transportaban el equipo, el encargado en jefe de la logística de la transportación, instalación, verificación de sonido le llamaban "secretario" porque no lo sé, el de nosotros era buen amigo, inteligente, gran colaborador se llamaba Lalo.

Créanme Lalo fue parte importante del grupo tanto que el manejaba un presupuesto dedicado a pagar el transporte, cargadores, mantenimiento del equipo como todo lo eléctrico, cuerdas para guitarras, cueros de batería, cables de micrófonos, realizando un sin número de reparaciones menores, lo mejor es que se mezclaba entre la multitud para escucharnos dando la correcta modulación y volumen a cada instrumento y voces del grupo.

Su cariño y lealtad hacia nosotros lo hizo elaborar un plan para la condición especial que teníamos en el grupo, chava estaba enfermo tenía una amiba estolitica en el cerebro provocándole ataques con convulsiones con duración de entre 3 a 4 minutos durante los cuales quedaba inconsciente Los ataques no eran frecuentes.

DON TRISTE OTRA VEZ
HISTORIA TRISTE DE UN SUEÑO IMPOSIBLE

Pero impredecible saber cuándo seria el siguiente. Lalo después de instalar el equipo se encargaba de la modulación y volúmenes, lo hacía durante la primera canción de nuestra presentación, después se sentaba al lado de chava muy cercano al control central eléctrico donde el conectaba todos los amplificadores, cuando chava tenía un ataque Lalo cortaba la electricidad así que el equipo se apagaba e inmediatamente colocaba a Chava en el piso con una almohada debajo del cuello.

Lo cubría con una cobija preparada para el momento, todo lo hacía al lado de la batería por el lado interior donde el público no podía observarlos, también le colocaba un lápiz en la boca para que no se mordiese la lengua sin dejar de frotarle su frente diciéndole palabras que lo mantuviesen en calma, mientras tanto nosotros actuábamos sorprendidos porque la electricidad se había interrumpido haciendo que la atención del público estuviese conmigo y no con chava.

Poco después Chava se sentaba en su banco y mientras se recuperaba totalmente Lalo reintegraba la electricidad, yo ofreciendo disculpas decía que fue algo fuera de nuestro control pero que nuestro técnico de sonido tenía ya todo bajo control, momentos después Chava daba el clásico conteo musical de un dos, un dos tres cuatro y recomenzábamos la misma canción que habíamos interrumpido. eso nos ocurría en promedio de 10% de las presentaciones.

Lalo eran tan eficiente y buen amigo que hasta esa situación especial siempre la tenía bajo control. Lalo fue el precursor de lo que después les llamaron ingenieros de sonido, al tiempo gente sin calidad musical ni conocimiento alguno se auto nombraban ingenieros de sonido, pero no sabían modular, ni tenían oído musical, cualidades que Lalo tenia naturales y enormes que aplicaba de manera modesta tal y como él siempre fue.

AVENTURAS DE REFLEXION FILOSOFICA
HISTORIA TRISTE DE UN SUEÑO IMPOSIBLE

Él universo conspiro a mi favor porque al no tener hermanos siempre estaba solo, pero me regalo amigos especiales que he recordado a lo largo de la vida, han sido demasiados quizás sin merecerlo, Benito, Gutierritos, Gerardo el guapo, Lalo el patotas, Lalo y Chava compañeros del grupo musical, Villicana, Alex, Alejandro Don Gato, Carlos el director de La S.A. el Campana, María la dedotes.

Luis y su hermano Beticus, Gerardo el borrego, Arturo el chivo, Daniel el zurdo, Mario, Nacho el perico, Juan el concho, Conchita, Juanis, Jorge el pinocho, Lupita, Arturo mi compadre, Andy, Carito, Marcos, Tono avandaro, Irma, Marisela, Laura, Trini, y muchísimos más, de todos ellos lo característico que recuerdo con cariño y respeto es que fueron excelentes hijos e hijas, aprendí que amar a tu padre o madre o a ambos si eras afortunado de tenerlos es la base que guiara tu vida por el resto de tu existencia, les agradezco lo que me dieron, lo mucho que me ensenaron, lo que compartimos durante nuestra infancia y adolescencia.

Nuestro grupo musical y a partir del segundo año durante el cual alcanzamos el reconocimiento de ser grupo de segundo nivel y cercanos al primer nivel, disfrutaba sin darme cuenta de estar toda la semana con mis compañeros, en los ensayos, en las presentaciones, vestíamos igual, en las giras musicales comíamos lo mismo y dormíamos juntos, como si fuésemos hermanos, así que con ellos aprendí a vivir con la relación diaria de hermanos, inclusive nos enojábamos, nos peleábamos pero nunca nos ofendimos, nos protegíamos uno al otro.

Chava me protegió como si fuese mi hermano mayor por lo tanto se ganó mi cariño, así que no volví a estar solo. la vida cuando va bien se altera de manera que no eternamente va bien, o así me pareció en ese momento.

DON TRISTE OTRA VEZ
HISTORIA TRISTE DE UN SUEÑO IMPOSIBLE

Mi mami como la mayoría de las personas adultas de esa época se oponían a la música de rock, a los hombres de cabello largo, a los grupos musicales de rock, las vacaciones escolares estaban por terminar teniendo que regresar a clases, mi mami tenía planes de que yo abandonara por completo a mi grupo para concentrarme en el colegio, yo me opuse a dejar la música, pero ella dijo que tenía dos opciones, una era vivir en su casa e ir al colegio y no mas grupo de rock, o irme de la casa como segunda opción.

Yo amaba la música, al grupo que era mi universo así que opte por irme de la casa, por el momento Chava y su familia me dieron alojamiento, tenían una recamara disponible porque una hermana de chava se había fugado con el novio dejando a su familia sumida en la tristeza, demostrando que la epidemia de amor podía contagiarte en cualquier momento, la familia me trato bien, gozaba de la compañía de Chava compartiendo como hermanos, me agradaba pero también me preocupaba porque me convertí en una carga económica para la familia.

Así que me dedique a buscar un alojamiento económico, que me diese independencia para dedicarme al grupo musical, además dejarme crecer el cabello al estilo de los rocanroleros de moda. Alejandro y sus hermanitos habitaban en cuartos de azotea de un edificio donde su mami fue la encargada de la limpieza, uno de los cuartos lo acondicionaron como cocina tenían otros tres cuartos que eran las recamaras, había dos baños con regaderas que se compartían entre un total de doce cuartos que eran el total de cuartos en la azotea.

Para mi buena suerte un cuarto estaba vacante, así que don gato hablo por mí con la persona que rentaba el cuarto y por un accesible precio, Dona Trastupijes me lo rento incluyendo la electricidad y mobiliario. ella no se llamaba así, pero Alejandro la había nombrado y yo también sin que ella se enterase. que alegría fue el tener a Don gato de vecino.

Así que de la noche a la mañana me convertí en músico profesional de tiempo completo ya que mis ingresos provenían tan solo de las presentaciones del grupo. Una vez instalado en mi cuarto, mi vida cambio positivamente tanto musicalmente como en mi comportamiento, a las 11:30 de la mañana despertaba, me banaba y desayunaba con mi vecino Alejandro, su hermana mayor cocinaba de manera más que exquisita, estudiábamos las canciones a ensayar cada uno con su grupo hasta alrededor de las 2:30 de la tarde hora en que deteníamos la práctica.

Preparándonos para ir a ensayar con nuestros grupos. los ensayos eran de 4:00 a 7:00 si yo terminaba primero iba en busca de Alejandro hasta su lugar de ensayo cosa que disfrutaba en grande por escucharlos, aprender y con gusto saludar a Carlos, otras veces Alejandro terminaba primero y me buscaba en casa de Chava donde estaba nuestro cuarto de ensayo.

Alrededor de las 9:00 de la noche cenábamos por lo regular en un modesto café de chinos donde la comida era barata y casera, otras veces cenábamos en su casa así que a las 10:30 de la noche ensayábamos y platicábamos hasta las dos o tres de la madrugada para después irme a mi cuarto a dormir. al día siguiente se repetía el mismo ciclo.

Los sábados y domingos era cuando trabajábamos en las presentaciones de nuestros grupos, a veces juntos, otras veces cada quien cubriendo por separado las presentaciones por tener contratos en lugares diferentes, al final del día ya en la noche alrededor de la 1:30 de la madrugada volvíamos a reunirnos en el café de chinos cenábamos y corríamos a casa a dormir. las practicas musicales con o sin grupo eran de 14 a 16 horas diarias, además contaba con la tutela y enseñanzas de Alejandro. mi progreso se aceleraba a pasos gigantes así que cada día me convertía en mejor y más completo guitarrista.

DON TRISTE OTRA VEZ
HISTORIA TRISTE DE UN SUEÑO IMPOSIBLE

En lo referente a voces y arreglos musicales le preguntaba a Carlos y como siempre me ensenaba amablemente. cierto día le pregunte a Alejandro que porque el sobre nombre de "Don Gato" sonriendo me pregunto que si vi las caricaturas de "don gato y su pandilla" en la televisión? claro que si le respondí además todavía me seguían gustando eran divertidas, menciono que cuando comenzó a tocar en su primer grupo, algunos amigos que querían ser guitarristas lo seguían a sus ensayos, le cargaban la guitarra a manera de ser sus ayudantes y lo seguían a todas partes, sus compañeros de grupo y también de otros grupos cuando lo veían seguido de sus ayudantes decían ahí viene don "Gato y su pandilla"

luego Alejandro se integró a otros grupos cada vez más profesionales los cuales no permitían gente extraña en los ensayos así que tuvieron que dejar de seguirlo no sin ocultar su tristeza, pero el sobre nombre de "Don Gato" se le quedo para siempre, sus amigos lo llamábamos Alejandro, yo era su mejor amigo y el mío. El imitaba a la perfección a "Cantinflas" y me hacía reír cuando decía cosas a la manera especial de Cantinflas, pero era curioso que solo lo hizo conmigo para hacerme reír porque todos los que lo conocían no sabían que, hacia esa imitación tan perfecta, pero a mí me divertía y si estaba un poco triste lo hacía para hacerme reír y olvidar la tristeza. Al comienzo del tercer año con el grupo teníamos contratos por toda la ciudad, nuestros ingresos eran grandes y el grupo sonaba bien, el público nos comparaba con los grandes grupos del momento. La S.A. compraron en pagos 4 amplificadores marca "Kustom" que eran buenísimos y sonaban de maravilla las columnas de bocinas eran acolchonadas de manera muy especial que los hacia ver elegantes porque eran de color negro, eran 2 de 200 watts para la guitarra y el teclado, otro de 400 watts para el bajo todos con 2 columnas cada uno, el de las voces era de 600 watts y con cuatro columnas utilizando 2 de ellas atrás de ellos junto a las de los instrumentos y las otras 2 al frente para el público.

Con ese equipo La S.A. sonaban mejor que los grupos originales que interpretaban, cuando nos presentábamos juntos nos permitían usar su equipo y sonábamos como cualquier grupo grande de primer nivel, eran los mejores tiempos de ambos grupos. visitaba a mi mami cada 5 semanas, a veces 8 semanas porque viajábamos para presentarnos en lugares lejanos, pero la llamaba por teléfono. seguí con mi carrera musical dejando por completo de ir a la escuela porque era músico profesional de tiempo completo. La S.A. llego a un nivel donde ganaban tanto dinero que el baterista y el representante hicieron manejos ilícitos del dinero para ellos dos ganar más dinero que el resto del grupo.

Así que decidieron prescindir de los servicios de Dayton, reemplazándolo con Jessé un veterano baterista que venía de Tijuana, musicalmente era mejor que Dayton así que la s.a. sonaba de lo mejor. sus problemas económicos por la deuda contraída por la compra del súper equipo y otras cosas más los llevaron al límite de su capacidad, el representante los robaba ya de forma descarada teniendo que prescindir de él.

Él les quito el equipo porque lo compraron a su nombre así que regreso parte del equipo, renegocio la deuda y se quedó con tres amplificadores uno de 400 watts y otro de 200 watts también con el de 600 watts de voces, pero solo con dos columnas, total que de 4 amplificadores y 10 columnas de bocinas solo conservo 3 amplificadores y 6 columnas de bocinas y con la deuda que seguía siendo grande. no teniendo grupo que representar necesitando uno para usar el equipo, seguir haciendo pagos y ganar algo de dinero para él, pero su mala reputación lo hacía ver como alguien no confiable, no sé qué fue de él ni del equipo.

La S.A. se quedó sin equipo, el que tenían lo dieron como pago inicial para comprar el gigantesco equipo así que ensayábamos y compartíamos nuestro equipo cuando nos presentábamos juntos.

DON TRISTE OTRA VEZ
HISTORIA TRISTE DE UN SUEÑO IMPOSIBLE

En ocasiones teníamos presentaciones por separado así que tenían que rentar el equipo, otros grupos también les ayudaban prestándoles equipo durante presentaciones en el mismo lugar, ya decepcionados de la situación, optaron por separarse siendo un golpe duro no solo para ellos también para mí porque eran mis ídolos.

Nosotros conseguimos un tecladista el cual compro en pagos un teclado Box modelo Jaguar que sonaba de lo mejor, pero nos duró poco el gusto ya que su padre y el hermano mayor de Gerardo lo obligaron a salirse del grupo por motivos religiosos y que no tocase jamás rock and roll en toda su vida y que tristeza que así fue. Carlos me ayudo y aprendí lo básico para poder usar aquel teclado, mientras tanto Alejandro no se quiso integrar a ningún grupo amaba ser independiente así que se dedicó a echar palomazos como se decía en el ambiente musical que no era otra cosa más que lo que se conoció como freelance.

Participaba con algunos grupos pero no de manera permanente, algunas veces se presentaba con nosotros claro que como guitarrista principal, yo como segunda guitarra y tecladista, con Alejandro el grupo sonaba como la misma s.a. así que nos colocamos en el gusto de la gente como grupo de primer nivel, cuando Alejandro iba con nosotros rentábamos un amplificador twin Fender para la guitarra y voces usando el amplificador súper reverb Fender para el teclado o para la segunda guitarra y voces, Guti seguía usando su amplificador Golden Gate copia de baseman Fender que sonaba hermoso así que por fin éramos el grupo que soñamos ser.

Cuando Alejandro tenía otro compromiso, entonces Carlos iba con nosotros como tecladista y voz principal así que rentábamos el amplificador twin Fender, pero para mí como guitarrista principal y sonábamos igual que La S.A. en sus mejores tiempos. así pasaron varios meses, yo iba a casa de Carlos su mami y el eran originarios del norte del país.

AVENTURAS DE REFLEXION FILOSOFICA
HISTORIA TRISTE DE UN SUEÑO IMPOSIBLE

Él aprendió inglés a temprana edad y queriendo ser maestro de escuela, se trasladaron a la ciudad capital para ingresar a la escuela normal de maestros en la cual se graduó, pero no ejerció porque su pasión era la música de rock, su mami lo apoyo así que cuando Carlos no tenía grupo o contrato para presentarse la que sostenía el hogar era su mami cociendo, lavando y planchando ropa que los clientes le llevaban a su casa.

Cuando Carlos ganaba dinero el pagaba los gastos, llevaba a si mami a pasear, se compraban ropa, zapatos, etc. ellos vivían humildemente en cuartos de azotea al igual que Alejandro y yo, a mí me acechaba la tristeza por estar distanciado de mi mami, a mi ella no me apoyaba ni siquiera sabía que había progresado musicalmente porque el equipo que teníamos, los instrumentos y nuestros salarios eran obtenidos gracias a las presentaciones musicales donde el público pagaban por escucharnos y vernos, pero repito mi mami no tenía idea de los logros alcanzados con mi propio esfuerzo.

Al comenzar el tercer año como grupo teníamos tanto trabajo que corríamos de un salón a otro por los cuatro puntos cardinales de la ciudad, las presentaciones eran exitosas con Carlos o Alejandro.

Desgraciadamente por conflictos con nuestro representante y luego con Chava optamos por desintegrar el grupo cuando estábamos en nuestro mejor momento. vendimos parte del equipo así que quede como propietario de mi guitarra dúo Sonic Fender, un wha wah Box, mi distorsionador Boston, y mi micrófono Shure de volumen.

Me dedique a seguir mi propio camino musical convirtiéndome en "freelance" como Carlos y Alejandro, con ellos viaje a otras ciudades en giras artísticas, otras veces en palomazos con grupos por toda la ciudad, yo me acomodaba a tocar guitarra, teclado o el bajo.

DON TRISTE OTRA VEZ
HISTORIA TRISTE DE UN SUEÑO IMPOSIBLE

Alejandro me presentaba como su primo porque de esa manera los músicos de otros grupos confiaban y me daban más trabajo y no deje mal a nadie porque en realidad fui buen músico con gran capacidad sobre todo a la hora de improvisar que era nuestra mejor característica.

Después Carlos fundo La S.A. con elementos nuevos, poco tiempo después también yo fui reclutado eso equivalía a una graduación profesional, ellos fueron el grupo que admiraba al convertirme en el guitarrista principal ocupando el honorable lugar de Don Gato, así que por un tiempo no lo pude creer, viví un sueño maravilloso. teníamos carencia de equipo gastando parte de las ganancias en rentar amplificadores, así que la economía nos asfixio de manera que tuvimos que desintegrar el grupo. Carlos era propietario del nombre "La Sociedad Anónima" ante "discos Capítol" de la ciudad de México en agradecimiento de que yo los admiré tanto y fui tan leal con ellos me llevo a la disquera Capítol para nombrándome el nuevo propietario del nombre, por respeto a ellos no utilice el nombre con ningún grupo en México.

Presentándome con varios grupos por mi cuenta, en ocasiones con Carlos, otras con Alejandro y pocas veces los tres juntos con algún baterista para completarnos como grupo. fueron tiempos inolvidables donde aprendí el arte de la improvisación con los mejores músicos del género musical rocanrolero por lo tanto hacíamos presentaciones magistrales la mayor de las veces sin ni siquiera haber practicado o conocer los tonos originales de las canciones pero ellos eran maravillosos, Alejandro era el mejor guitarrista de México superando a músicos como Javier Batís que fue el maestro de Carlos Santana, pero él no tenía la fama internacional ni gano el dinero que ellos porque? porque Alejandro fue muy sencillo y modesto que le bastaba con disfrutar su guitarra lo demás carecía de importancia. Me enseño el arte de mantener tu guitarra en condiciones óptimas, como octavarla, cambiarle los viejos trastes por nuevos de plata alemana.

Rebobinar las pastillas de sonido para aumentar su capacidad acústica, la primera enseñanza que recibí por parte de él fue la limpieza del instrumento como base para así poder ser buen músico. Nos involucramos en las giras con "Caravanas Artísticas" de las principales compañías cerveceras del país como "Moctezuma", "Corona" acompañando a cantantes famosos, por urgencias de calendarios en las presentaciones no había tiempo para ensayar, pero salíamos bien y el público disfrutaba al grado de no darse cuenta que no habíamos tocado o practicado juntos esas canciones, otras veces teníamos minutos de conocer a los otros miembros del grupo.

Él rock en sus inicios los 50's se interpretaban canciones extranjeras con letras en español por lo tanto los artistas se convirtieron en pioneros e ídolos del rock en México, yo ni siquiera había nacido. a principio de los 70's cuando sucedió mi historia.

Aquellos músicos famosos hacían sus grandes retornos sin importarles que los grandes éxitos y los grandes intérpretes cantábamos en inglés, pero ellos tenían su público fiel que no los habían olvidado presentándose exitosamente como en sus mejores tiempos, pero recurrían a músicos como nosotros sin tener que rehacer sus propios grupos. también hacíamos presentaciones de nuestro grupo interpretando el rock en ingles que nuestro público gustaba, además así eran nuestros contratos en esas caravanas artísticas.

Acompañamos musicalmente a artistas como; Enrique Guzmán, Cesar Costa, Alberto Vázquez, Manolo Muñoz que fue la mejor voz del país, en las presentaciones de ellos yo tenía que hacer segundas y terceras voces según como se necesitase inclusive en enfermedades de ellos yo cantaba por ellos en fin me convertí en parte importante del grupo por la facilidad de cantar en ambos idiomas, presentándonos en palenques, ferias nacionales, salones de baile y casinos, y en el recién inaugurado Casino Terrazas.

DON TRISTE OTRA VEZ
HISTORIA TRISTE DE UN SUEÑO IMPOSIBLE

Acompañando a "Romano" que era un cuarto lugar del internacional festival "OTI" por cierto contare aquella presentación magistral. El cantante Romano contrato a Alejandro y a mí un día miércoles, nos dio discos con las canciones que interpretaríamos, entre ellas estaba el famoso tema de "El Padrino" claro el la cantaba en español. nos dimos a la tarea de estudiar y aprender las canciones ese día miércoles y la madrugada del jueves, ese día temprano viajamos hacia Cuernavaca en el estado de Guerrero, México donde nos reuniríamos en la tarde con un tecladista y un baterista y completar el sencillo grupo musical, en esa ocasión yo tocaría el bajo.

Eran las 6:00 de la tarde cuando nos reunimos en el salón de las presentaciones para ensayar el baterista llego no apareciendo ningún tecladista, de emergencia buscamos un tecladista o un bajista, pero no conseguimos a nadie. esa noche aprendí y practiqué las armonías y figuras de todas las canciones en un teclado "Hamond" de doble teclado (maravilloso instrumento).

Estaba en el salón a nuestra disposición, tenía más de 200 registros de sonido que al mezclarse hacia miles de sonidos, tenía pedales a manera de bajo. durante la noche del jueves y la madrugada del viernes ensayamos Alejandro en la guitarra, yo en el teclado y el baterista la totalidad de las canciones de la presentación.

Viernes a mediodía nos reunimos con el baterista y con romano a ensayar hasta la noche quedando ajustadas todas las canciones con figuras y armonías, aun teníamos el problema de no tener bajista, los pedales del teclado sonaban perfectamente como un bajo pero la sincronización para usarlos era complicada ya que todos los grupos de esa época usábamos teclados portátiles sin pedales y el bajo era interpretado por un bajista, en este caso teníamos que hacer el bajo con los pedales más el doble teclado.

HISTORIA TRISTE DE UN SUEÑO IMPOSIBLE

Use mi pie izquierdo para alcanzar y poder tocar la mitad de los pedales del lado derecho, Alejandro con su pie derecho tocaba la otra mitad de los pedales sonando el bajo de manera excelente, créanme en la mañana del sábado ensayamos el bajo con nuestros pies, en ocasiones Alejandro me pisaba, en otras ocasiones yo lo pisaba. Ese sábado por la noche y la noche del domingo que fueron los días de las presentaciones ante el público, nadie noto la ausencia del bajista, por fortuna no me equivoque con tantas armonías y figuras con los dos teclados, no me confundí con tantos registros de sonido, Alejandro toco la guitarra maravillosamente como era de esperarse, eso si al final de las presentaciones terminamos con pies y espinillas golpeados como si hubiésemos jugado la final de un campeonato de futbol.

Estuvimos tan adoloridos que al caminar cojeábamos, Romano quedo contento y sorprendido de la calidad y habilidad música por eso nos compenso el esfuerzo pagándonos a los dos el salario que hubiese sido para el bajista y otro dinero extra felicitándonos por la magia de nuestra improvisación para salir con bien del compromiso tan grande.

Dos días después fui a visitar a Carlos que se preparaba para una presentación en un hotel donde sería el tecladista acompañando a una cantante de música romántica, sus zapatos se veían bien lustrados, pero Carlos les colocaba un pedazo de cartón en el interior para cubrir los agujeros en la suela, eso era porque estaban desgastados de tanto uso, pero por arriba no se notaba nada, su mami le plancho un bonito saco al cual se le colgaba un poquito la manga izquierda por estar roto el forro interior que no tenía remedio ni remendándolo, ya que el saco tenía más de diez años de uso.

Carlos se veía bien, súper listo para la entrevista sin importarle el hoyo en los zapatos o lo viejo del saco, él y su mami se mostraban contentos por tener una oportunidad de obtener un buen contrato musical. al observarlos créanme que pensé que si hubiese un dios me gustaría estar como ellos.

DON TRISTE OTRA VEZ
HISTORIA TRISTE DE UN SUEÑO IMPOSIBLE

Feliz y optimista en los momentos difíciles. ambos nos despedimos de su Mami dirigiéndonos al hotel que estaba cerca de su casa, por el camino Carlos dijo que la cantante era bonita y que le gustaría salir con ella.

Por fin llegamos al bar del hotel donde rápidamente Carlos integrado al grupo comenzaron a ensayar, mientras tanto yo dejaba volar mi imaginación deseando estar como Carlos y su Mami porque ellos tenían una relación bonita de mutua comprensión que cualquiera envidiaría, me prometí en silencio que, si pudiese vivir de esa manera con mi Mami, sería la felicidad más grande para mí.

Al tiempo tocando en Tijuana con Alejandro, algo así como 6 meses con diferentes grupos rocanroleros mexicanos y norte americanos por la cercanía de San Diego, California empecé a sentir que estaba lejos de lo que deseaba en la vida porque amaba la música, a diferencia de Carlos y Alejandro yo no disfrutaba mi carrera musical si estar al lado de mi madre, se lo dije a Alejandro y me entendió, porque esa madrugada después de tocar me dijo que si él fuese yo partiría hacia la capital buscaría a Mami y empezaría la universidad, en realidad dijo estar sorprendido de que teniendo al alcance ser profesionista graduado de universidad estuviese alejado de los estudios y me dijo que sería lo mejor que haría si regresase a estudiar.

Muy temprano Alejandro después de comprarme un boleto para viajar de regreso a casa, me invito a desayunar y me encamino a la estación para empezar el regreso a casa con mi Mami, Alejandro dijo que me extrañaría pero que él deseaba lo mejor para mí y que, aunque estuviese triste solo con los recuerdos sería suficiente para estar contento por mí y por él, por guiarme en el camino correcto. Ya a bordo del camión a través de la ventanilla nos despedimos y le vi limpiarse las lágrimas de su rostro.

Ese fue un gran honor para mí porque cuando su madre murió no derramo lágrimas, pero en mi despedida lo hizo, se lo agradecí eternamente. De regreso a la capital abandone mi cuarto y regrese a casa con mi Mami, vendí mi guitarra y mi equipo para ese dinero usarlo en comprar libros y ropa para ingresar a los últimos dos semestres de colegio para ingresar a la universidad. no volví a casa de Alejandro o Carlos porque existía la tentación de volver a la música así que me alejé de ellos sin ningún problema entre nosotros solo que fue lo mejor para dedicarme a estudiar.

Coincidencia o lo que sea Carlos y Alejandro eran buenos hijos y eran buenas personas seguí su ejemplo y quise ser buen hijo, ellos y yo no tuvimos padres a nuestro lado, pero tuvimos mucha Mami que nos sacaron adelante en nuestras carreras y fueron motivo de alegría y orgullo. Me ensenaron infinidad de habilidades musicales, pero me ensenaron a ser buen hijo lo cual hasta mi vejez lo disfrute y se los agradezco, fueron como hermanos mayores que no tuve.

No tengo palabras con que agradecerles, pero seguro saben que los extrañe como personas más que como músicos porque la enseñanza había llegado a su fin la música solo era práctica diaria ser buen hijo es práctica de por vida.

Me dedique a estudiar y recobrar el amor a los estudios tal como lo hice con la música, fue bonito convertirme de nuevo en estudiante, me gustaba estar en la escuela con compañeros y muchachas bonitas en fin me involucre con alegría y vocación estudiantil.

Entre a estudiar al vocacional número 4 de ciencias físico matemáticas, así que los estudios requerían gran concentración, conociendo un mundo diferente ya que la escuela estaba en la carretera que te llevaba al Ajusco, atrás de la escuela había una serie de cuevas habitadas por gente que, como los pica piedra de las caricaturas.

DON TRISTE OTRA VEZ
HISTORIA TRISTE DE UN SUEÑO IMPOSIBLE

Tenían luz eléctrica, refrigeradores, televisores, pero dentro de cuevas que ellos escarbaban y hacían más cuartos, era como cuento de fantasía, pero eran reales. Teníamos clases de taller durante 3 semanas cada semestre participando en actividades todo el día de 8 de la mañana a 8 de la noche con un descanso de 2 a 4 de la tarde para comer, así que nos trasladábamos a las cuevas porque se dedicaban a preparar comida casera por cierto a la casa que íbamos le decíamos el "Dennis" como restaurante de cadena internacional, eran comedores económicos, limpios y sobre todo a un paso de la escuela esa fue una experiencia única en mi vida.

Permanecí estudiando por 6 meses consecutivos hasta terminar el semestre para descansar dos semanas para comenzar el siguiente y final semestre, los sábados y en especial los domingos caminaba por las calles de la ciudad que no tenían el bullicio y tráfico de los días de la semana, así que era delicioso caminar por todo el centro de la ciudad. me sentía inactivo porque los domingos eran los días más activos durante la época del grupo así que estrenaba la actividad musical, pero me dedicaba a continuar con mi carrera y sobre todo recobrar la relación con mi madre.

Caminando un domingo me encontré con un amigo que estuvimos en la misma secundaria, él era más joven así que estaba en un grado escolar menor que yo, me caía bien porque era conflictivo, problemático, etc. durante esa época escolar se metió en broncas con un miembro de la banda de Iza zaga que eran el terror de los alrededores pero amigos míos por lo tanto lo saque de apuros porque de no ser así la hubiese pasado muy mal así que hicimos un poco de amistad gracias a mi intervención para salvar su pellejo. Por esos tiempos el me recordaba con aprecio, pero lo que el en realidad admiraba y apreciaba fue mi participación en el grupo musical, él nos escuchó en varias ocasiones, le fascinaba la idea de hacer un día su propio grupo.

HISTORIA TRISTE DE UN SUEÑO IMPOSIBLE

Así que nos detuvimos a platicar por cerca de 30 minutos o más invitándome a escuchar el coro musical de la iglesia ya que tocaban canciones católicas, pero en realidad eran baladas modernas cantadas por chicas bonitas, los jóvenes entre ellos el las acompañaban con guitarras así que era todo un show musical.

Después de insistir acepte que iría a escuchar la presentación del coro musical en la iglesia el próximo domingo. ya se imaginaran que por no tener actividad musical al domingo siguiente me hice presente en la iglesia escuchando a las chicas bonitas y los guitarristas improvisados que no lo hacían del todo mal, cantaban regular pero no se ponían de acuerdo en las primeras, segundas voces y sobre todo que no había el esquema donde utilizaran voces que pitaran a manera de altas y bajas para realizar las presentaciones magistralmente, el material humano lo tenían lo reconocí al instante pero tenían que educar las voces.

Al finalizar la misa y presentación musical nos reunimos en el salón de la iglesia donde fui presentado por Gilberto a su novia y hermana que eran integrantes del coro musical, también me presentaron a su hermana mayor sencilla y linda persona no cantaba solo iba a misa y acompañaba a sus hermanas para que pudieran participar y verse con Gilberto porque como eran hijas de familia a la antigua salían siempre acompañadas o no las dejaban salir.

Ellas eran jovencitas de 17 y 18 años de edad igual que Gilberto, yo tenía 20 abriles la hermana mayor contaba con 30 abriles, trabajaba en un banco siendo una persona trabajadora que ayudaba en los gastos del hogar siendo soltera hasta ese momento. las pláticas donde mis conocimientos musicales fueron realzados por Gilberto nos condujeron al ofrecimiento para que me convirtiese en el director del coro, acepte solo por tres semanas con ensayos de 3 días por semana para ubicar sus voces y acoplar guitarras.

DON TRISTE OTRA VEZ
HISTORIA TRISTE DE UN SUEÑO IMPOSIBLE

Con voces así que no se necesitaba mucho tiempo solo esfuerzo por parte de ellas y ellos lo cual aceptaron sabiendo que no me quedaría más del plazo acordado. Esa semana ensayamos por tres días a razón de dos horas por día ubicando el sitio de cada voz esperando al siguiente domingo una presentación con ajustes de calidad en las voces e incorpore el uso de bajo acústico para realzar las voces bajas que antes no utilizaban porque no tenían idea de lo que era cantar cada quien con su tesitura de voz. ese domingo se escucharon fantásticamente la gente noto la mejoría, así como ellos mismos esperando mejorar más durante las próximas dos semanas.

Ese domingo me presentaron a otra bonita hermana que era de mi misma edad y que fue a la iglesia solo para conocerme, a los ensayos no acudió porque trabajaba en unos almacenes comerciales al lado de tres hermanas mayores que ayudaban al sostén del hogar como hijas de familia bien educadas.

Ese día durante las cuatro horas que estuvimos juntos no nos separamos y platicamos de mil tonterías con la idea de conocernos, ella me escogió como alguien especial o así lo sentí y me invito a que fuese por ella al salir de su trabajo para juntos caminar hacia su casa que estaba a la vuelta de la iglesia.

Era tan bonita que dije que quería ir por ella a su trabajo pero no podría porque mis clases eran por la tarde y salía alrededor de las 7 de la noche más el regreso a casa que sería alrededor de la 8 de la noche, pero quedamos de vernos al siguiente domingo, por supuesto que antes de ir a la escuela me presente a su trabajo en el departamento de libros e intercambiamos comentarios de autores que disfrutábamos de sus obras como Edgar Allan Poe, Julio Verne, Oscar Wilde entre otros, luego me despedí y salí camino a la escuela.

Así pasaron semanas en las que compartimos tiempo juntos, cumplí mi trato con el coro de la iglesia no aceptando quedarme como su director en forma definitiva porque eso incurriría en sacarme del retiro de la música que yo mismo escogí como mi nueva vida donde solo existía la escuela como meta y el romance que se convertiría en una historia triste.

Nuestra relación fue algo más que especial porque nos conocimos recién saliendo de la adolescencia entrando en la edad adulta donde debíamos madurar juntos. Vivimos un amor tormentoso que duro toda una década y nunca maduramos, cuando novios salíamos en grupo con sus hermanas, los amigos y novios de ellas porque era la única manera permitida para salir porque eran hijas de familia educada a la antigua, por lo que salían juntas o no salía ninguna.

Lo divertido era salir a platicar, lo hacíamos por horas ya que en realidad nos sentíamos felices estando juntos. Virginia era una joven sumamente bella, con un toque de distinción que la hacía única, caminaba de una forma especial que solo de verla venir hacia ti podías enamorarte perdidamente como me sucedió a mí, me hacía sentir feliz y afortunado de que fuese mi novia.

Los Domingos nos reuníamos en la iglesia, y después de la misa íbamos a un café cantante, a una nevería, o tan solo a caminar, pero siempre platicando y con las manos entrelazadas, o abrazados, en fin, era hermoso pasar ese día juntos. Ella trabajaba en el mismo lugar con sus hermanas mayores y menores, yo iba por ella al salir, y caminábamos hasta su casa, claro lo hacíamos con las manos entrelazadas, platicando de miles de cosas con o sin interés, solo para disfrutar de la mutua compañía. En ocasiones, yo salía tarde de la escuela o me atoraba en el trafico así que corría como si quisiera ganar un maratón, corriendo como loco por calles y calles hasta llegar con ella, a decir verdad, me salve de ser atropellado en un sin número de ocasiones.

DON TRISTE OTRA VEZ
HISTORIA TRISTE DE UN SUEÑO IMPOSIBLE

Eso no importaba ya que corría con desesperación para llegar junto a ella, de verdad que nos queríamos, porque ella me esperaba con el deseo de que llegara para realizar nuestra diaria caminata abrazados. Al tiempo, le hicimos respetuosamente saber a su Padre que éramos novios y con su consentimiento permanecíamos en la puerta de su casa platicando hasta cerca de las nueve o nueve y media de la noche, tiempo en que yo partía hacia el barrio para platicar con mis amigos, o simplemente ir a casa para realizar mis tareas escolares que eran bastantes.

Debo hacer un paréntesis para decirles que ocurrió con Gilberto que fue el causante de haber conocido a Virginia. Como les mencione era joven pero no veía más allá de sus ojos, era irresponsable, se gastaba el dinero de la colegiatura en drogas y locuras que no lo condujeron a ningún camino positivo. Él trabajaba los fines de semana al lado de su padre que tenía un negocio de abarrotes al mayoreo ganando dinero a manos llenas. Gilberto le robaba al padre cada que iba a trabajar convirtiéndose en el tonto que invitaba todo a todos para ser popular en el barrio y sobre todo con Teresa su novia.

Le hice saber lo equivocado que estaba, que podría ser popular, pero por sus acciones positivas, además si quería robar estaba bien pero que ahorrase porque nunca sabes que puede pasar, por supuesto que no me entendió continuando su vida con drogas defraudando a sus padres. Poco tiempo después su padre murió dejándole su negocio al hijo mayor de su primer matrimonio dejando a la familia de Gilberto con escases económica donde su Mami tuvo que mantenerlos y educarlos tanto a él como a su hermano y hermana menores que él. Sin dinero dejo de ser popular en el barrio, descubriendo que Teresa no lo quería ya que termino su relación con el cuándo no tenía dinero, se volvió loco de tristeza e intento suicidarse por ella, el único que acudió a consolarlo fui yo.

Porque sabía que todo era consecuencia de sus irresponsables actos, trate de confortarlo diciéndole que hay ilusiones por alcanzar y tratar de lograrlas es lo hermoso de la vida. Con la cabeza baja menciono que su ilusión más grande era pertenecer a un grupo musical de rock, pero, cuando me lo hizo saber en varias ocasiones le conteste que yo estaba retirado así que no podía hacer nada por él y que no contara conmigo. Llorando dijo que yo estaba retirado después de haber logrado el sueño más grande de un rocanrolero, pero el no y que sería feliz de nuevo si yo lo ayudaba a lograr ese sueño. Después de pensarlo detenidamente sentí que me necesitaba como amigo y como músico así que le dije que de guitarrista se moriría de hambre, pero podría ser un buen bajista.

Que tendría que seguir mis instrucciones y ensayar con dedicación absoluta para lo más pronto posible estar listo para comenzar una nueva etapa de su vida y convertirse en músico como su sueño. Prometió seguir mis enseñanzas para iniciar al instante si así lo decidía yo.

Como él era un guitarrero se conocía los tonos así que no hablaba yo con un ignorante musicalmente, además adoraba la música de Los Beatles, comenzamos a ensayar con dos guitarras acústicas pero el usaba la del cómo bajo, aprendiendo las canciones del repertorio de La Expedición para que tuviese una base de cómo se ensayaba cada quien su parte y que pronto tocaríamos con un baterista probándose como miembro de un grupo.

Mientras yo estaba en la escuela y con Virginia el practicaba con los discos, pero de manera formidable con una dedicación no conocida, en solo ocho semanas estaba listo en cada una de las canciones del repertorio del desaparecido grupo La Expedición. Así que empezó la enseñanza de la improvisación que era una técnica con habilidad exquisita, créanme tenia tantas ganas de ser músico.

DON TRISTE OTRA VEZ
HISTORIA TRISTE DE UN SUEÑO IMPOSIBLE

Que lo logro y en base a sus propios esfuerzos recordándome a mí mismo cuando inicie aquel camino musical, créanme me agradaba el sonido logrado por ambos y como él hacia voces lo acomode a hacer la segunda y sonábamos de manera muy aceptable recibiendo felicitaciones de quienes nos escuchaban en el barrio.

Pensé que Gilberto estaba listo para presentarse en público y ver como se comportaba, tendría que dominar al monstruo que te aplaude o te chifla según sea tu presentación. Llame a uno de los salones donde nos presentamos antes con La Expedición dejándoles saber que estábamos de regreso, pero queríamos probar al nuevo bajista sin tener que llevar equipo solo usar el equipo del grupo que estuviese tocando solo llevaríamos guitarra y bajo.

Los organizadores mostraron su alegría por el retorno del grupo diciendo que nos proporcionarían todo el equipo incluyendo bajo y guitarra, solo tendríamos que presentarnos alrededor de las 8 de la noche así que estábamos en horario pico así que era un horario de lujo. Hable por teléfono con Chava el cual dijo que con mucho gusto se presentaría para revivir aquellas presentaciones inolvidables, por supuesto que me pregunto si el bajista podría con el paquete, le dije que estaba listo para tocar todo el repertorio anterior del grupo.

Ese Domingo llevamos a Virginia, Teresa y hermanas, así como amigos del barrio que estaban emocionados de escuchar al grupo de Nuevo, por supuesto que Lalo fue también para ayudarnos a modular en pocos minutos durante la primera canción como acostumbraba hacerlo.

Cuando subimos al escenario la gente aplaudió porque gratamente nos recordaban así que comenzamos a tocar, Gilberto estaba tan bien acoplado que no se notaba que era nuevo con el grupo. Llegamos a una parte de la canción donde teníamos que cantar sin música.

Para posteriormente continuar con la música y voces al mismo tiempo, confieso que estaba temeroso de que Gilberto no cantara o que se saliese del tono, pero para sorpresa de todas las voces sonaron magistralmente así que a partir de ese momento el público se nos entregó y cada canción que interpretamos las aplaudieron como en los mejores tiempos del grupo. Hicimos cerca de 10 presentaciones y una en una fiesta de los XV de uno de los amigos del barrio, mencione que solo era cuestión de tiempo para que yo continuara mi retiro así que deberían conseguirse un guitarrista para continuar con las presentaciones musicales sin mí.

Chava mostro disgusto diciendo que si yo me salía él también lo haría, porque el regreso solo por mí. Me fue a buscar un súper cantante conocido mío diciendo que supo de mi retorno musical y que junto a otros músicos tenían un grupo bastante bueno llamado La Odisea, que me querían como guitarrista ofreciendo instrumentos y amplificadores les hice saber que aceptaba con la condición de llevarme a mi bajista y gustosos aceptaron.

Esa semana nos presentamos a ensayar, aprendiendo del repertorio de ellos y ellos aprendiendo de nuestro repertorio así que después de dos semanas armamos un grupo sumamente competitivo presentándonos con éxito mi amigo el Campana cantaba súper bien así que en el aspecto de voces estábamos bien organizados, la música era formidable porque Mario era buenísimo en los teclado, su hermano Jorge era polifacético ya que estuvo a punto de ser el bajista pero por llevarme a Gilberto se convirtió en el baterista tocando de manera más que aceptable, en pocas palabras éramos un grupo de Segundo nivel pero a un pasito del primer nivel.

Permanecí con ellos cerca de 6 semanas diciendo que por la escuela tendrían que buscar un guitarrista para retirarme nuevamente, dos semanas más y consiguieron mi reemplazo, Gilberto quiso salirse conmigo.

DON TRISTE OTRA VEZ
HISTORIA TRISTE DE UN SUEÑO IMPOSIBLE

Le asegure que todo lo hice por él, para que tuviera un grupo, instrumentos, además el poder hacer su soñada carrera musical.

Obedeciéndome por su bien acepto quedarse y fue el inicio de su carrera que fue exitosa por cerca de 40 años hasta el día de su muerte porque nunca se cuidó y siguió siendo activo fumador de marihuana, cigarrillos y alcohol, pero murió siendo feliz haciendo lo que le gustaba porque estaba orgulloso de ser rocanrolero.

Volviendo a la historia de amor que fue tormentosa, porque deseábamos estar juntos más tiempo, pero no solucionábamos el problema, porque la única manera era casarnos, pero ella no acepto mis proposiciones por estar jóvenes y no preparados para algo tan serio como el matrimonio, así que seguimos juntos, pero sufriendo por solo vernos como novios a la antigua. Deberás que no importaba lo de a la antigua porque el poco tiempo que estábamos juntos lo aprovechábamos al máximo, descubriendo tantas cosas de nosotros mismos y enamorándonos cada vez más.

Estando en la Universidad, después de ver a Virginia regresaba a casa por las noches convivía en el barrio con los amigos disfrutando de fumar marihuana y platicar hasta la una de la madrugada para irnos a descansar y estar listos para el siguiente día de actividades, durante esa veladas los vecinos pensaron que al crecer nos habíamos convertido en los sucesores de los jóvenes malos que abusaban de los vecinos y hasta de los negocios del barrio porque la generación anterior así lo hicieron pero para su grata sorpresa nosotros solo nos divertíamos y hacíamos ruido porque cantábamos canciones de rocanrol pero respetábamos a todos los vecinos y transeúntes del barrio, así como los negocios, así que hasta nos escondían en sus casas cuando llegaban los policías y querían arrestarnos aunque no éramos delincuentes.

En esas reuniones nocturnas nos involucramos con todo tipo de amistades razón por la cual me vi involucrado en un choque de auto cuando íbamos de regreso al distribuidor de autos donde Jaime trabajaba y habíamos tomado prestado el auto según él y el Grillo íbamos a cobrar un dinero que les debían, así que Jaime me pagaría el préstamo que le hice el cual yo necesitaba para pagar unos gastos escolares.

Para mi sorpresa querían asaltar una zapatería, pensando que yo por ser inteligente podría desconectar la alarma, pero ya enojado les quite las llaves del auto para ir de regreso a la distribuidora de autos e irme a casa, por supuesto que iba enfadado porque me dijeron que en la cajuela había dos kilogramos de marihuana para entregarla y que me pagaría su adeudo, no los escuche y seguí de camino a la distribuidora.

Un auto que se pasó la señal de alto nos impactó y después del susto tratamos de huir por un paso a desnivel, pero el auto se detuvo, inmediatamente Jaime y el Grillo salieron huyendo sin esperarme así que corrí en dirección opuesta y tras una persecución de 12 o 15 calles no recuerdo exactamente logre escapar de la policía, huyendo al negocio de mi madre y su socio un restaurant bar.

Jaime y el Grillo para según ellos salvarse dijeron que yo era jefe de la banda obligándolos a robar y distribuir drogas razón por la cual me convertí en fugitivo.

Abandonando la ciudad refugiándome en una lejana pequeña ciudad portuaria dedicándome a trabajar y jugar football como acostumbraba. Virginia y yo quedamos sumergidos en la tristeza, ella creía en mi inocencia, pero debíamos estar lejos uno del otro, nuestro amor se incrementó continuando el romance durante 12 meses así que nos escribíamos casi a diario, algunas veces le llamaba por teléfono diciéndonos que estaríamos juntos lo más pronto posible.

DON TRISTE OTRA VEZ
HISTORIA TRISTE DE UN SUEÑO IMPOSIBLE

Se comprobó que el chofer del auto con que nos impactamos estaba ebrio y drogado, un video mostro que el no respeto la señal de alto provocando el accidente, se demostró que el auto que yo manejaba no fue robado solo que lo usamos sin permiso de la distribuidora, Jaime y el Grillo confesaron que yo no tenía nada que ver con la droga encontrada en el auto. Quede absuelto de los cargos pudiendo regresar y continuar con mis estudios y el romance. Fue muy triste saber que según amándome rechazo el casarnos para regresar al lugar donde yo tenía un buen empleo y un futuro económico asegurado.

Ya de regreso en la gran ciudad continuamos el romance llegando a la etapa sexual que nos apasionaba tanto que quedó embarazada y al hacérmelo saber que era bonita noticia porque podríamos casarnos y estar juntos para siempre, ella solo dijo que quería abortar razón por la cual decidí respetar su decisión porque era su cuerpo, la tristeza me embargo porque era la segunda ocasión en que rechazaba ser mi esposa.

Fuimos a una clínica de abortos convirtiéndonos en una pareja más de la estadística de abortos en el país, como la quería demasiado me hice responsable de los gastos y estuve con ella en todo momento sin soltar su mano, después de dormir y descansar unas horas fui a dejarla en su casa con su familia que solo se enteraron que estaba enferma y que yo la acompañé al doctor. Me fui a casa y lloré porque hubiese sido feliz de convertirme en padre.

Descubrí que cuando una pareja lleva a cabo un aborto para cubrir apariencias sociales el daño emocional se siente de por vida, algo se muere dentro de la pareja, yo no me recupere de haber matado a una inocente criatura.

Así que me convertí en un criminal pagando para que realizaran el crimen, oculte esa maldad por cuatro décadas hasta el día de hoy.

Sus hermanas Teresa y Georgina buscaban libertad y se fueron cambiando de trabajo para trabajar en varias sucursales bancarias, así que empezaron a disfrutar el conocer amistades nuevas y a reunirse con amigos de una sucursal y de otra. Haciendo una relación, de libertad exagerada donde empezaron a fumar y a tomar bebidas, alcohólicas algo que no hicieron antes, por supuesto que, a escondidas de su familia, pero cada vez más frecuente. Afectando nuestra relación ya que Virginia, también se fue a trabajar a una sucursal de banco para seguir a sus hermanas y amigos, comportándose como ellas, reduciendo el tiempo para estar juntos al mínimo.

Participaba en todas sus actividades fuera del trabajo, tratándome como si yo fuera poca cosa, como si los del banco fueran superiores a mí, nunca supe en que aspecto. Aprovechando el tiempo extra que me daba, acabe mis estudios y trabajando en el Consejo Nacional de Turismo dedicado al Diseño y Relaciones Publicas.

Empezó a manejar mi propio dinero que resulto fácil de ganar, porque tenía tiempo y habilidad para realizar infinidad de eventos turísticos dentro y fuera del país, comenzando a viajar al extranjero necesitando aprender idiomas, primero francés, luego Ingles, por cierto, a Virginia la invite a estudiar inglés conmigo y pague el curso para ambos en el Anglo Mexicano de Cultura un Colegio bastante reconocido en la enseñanza del idioma Ingles.

Fuimos el primer y segundo curso, pero no más porque Virginia prefirió ir con Teresa, Georgina y amigos del banco para divertirse. Mientras tanto, yo seguí superándome intelectualmente y económicamente, Virginia en vez de estar orgullosa de mi, se sintió ofendida, porque para graduados e inteligentes nadie se podía comparar a sus hermanos, nunca supe cuál fue el problema porque yo no competía con ellos ni con nadie.

DON TRISTE OTRA VEZ
HISTORIA TRISTE DE UN SUEÑO IMPOSIBLE

Me dediqué a tratar de subir posiciones en el Consejo Nacional de Turismo y como consecuencia obtuve relaciones de primer nivel, útiles en todo trabajo.

Por fin nuestra relación rebaso los siete años siendo cada vez más tormentoso para ambos, su Padre le dijo que era tiempo de formalizar nuestra relación, y como Virginia siempre obedecía a su Padre decidió casarse conmigo aunque no fue de su agrado ni en el momento justo para ella, ya que no quería casarse conmigo pero acepto porque creyó estar embarazada y no quiso pasar por la pena de otro aborto, lo malo para ella es ya casados volvió a la normalidad no habiendo estado embarazada pero ya estaba casada no gustándole el sacrificio vano de unirse a mí de por vida.

Antes de la boda, por medio de un arreglo económico, le pague a su familia por el traspaso del destruido apartamento que fue de la familia y que sería nuestro hogar. Me llevo cerca de dos meses el remodelarlo y repararlo, porque los techos se tuvieron que instalar nuevos, así como el piso, incluyendo puertas y ventanas, hasta dejarlo en condiciones de ser habitado. Luego la pintura, el amueblamiento y la decoración que incluyo cuarenta y siete cuadros de arte, todos ellos enmarcados en aluminio y con cristal anti reflejante para una inversión total de $60,000 dólares aproximadamente.

De los cuarenta y siete cuadros solo dos fueron obra mía y mande a hacer un Follón al estilo Huichol realizado por un artista originario de la sierra de Nayarit que lo hizo con estambre y cera como una obra genial, después me hizo otros 5 cuadros más también de Follón que los regale a distintas personalidades entre ellas al conductor del primer programa noticiero matutino el señor Guillermo Ochoa y Lourdes Guerrero presentando al ingenioso artista en red nacional siendo una promoción turísticas y cultural para el estado de Nayarit. También tuve un segmento semanal de 15 minutos para presentar aspectos turísticos de México durante 12 meses.

Quedaban 43 cuadros de artistas como Follón, Vasarelli, Stewart Moskowits, todos ellos representantes del arte moderno contemporáneo con fama internacional, mi meta era ir reemplazando cada copia por originales como regalo a Virginia y herencia para nuestros hijos.

Era un sueño difícil de alcanzar, pero no imposible porque el precio de los cuadros era accesible ya que ahorrando podría comprar uno o dos por los primeros dos años, después teniendo más contratos y experiencia quizás 5 por año. Parecía locura, pero no tenía yo cuadros de Picasso o de Miguel Ángel así que sería una aventura Hermosa, lograrla seria demostrar el amor hacia Virginia por todo el tiempo que hubiésemos estado juntos. En el apartamento, fui a vivir y a trabajar, porque instalé un estudio de diseño con el cual obtenía ingresos económicos, ya que comenzó a tener más y más contratos con el Consejo Nacional de Turismo encargándome de eventos internacionales viajando al extranjero frecuentemente.

Cuando nos casamos, Virginia mando hacer copias de las llaves de la casa y les entrego un juego de llaves a cada miembro de su familia, algo así como dieciséis juegos de llaves. La luna de miel en California fue un rápido viaje, ya que pidió solo tres días en el banco, porque para ella era importante volver al trabajo lo más pronto posible. En San Francisco y sus alrededores, nos dedicamos por tres días a comprar regalos para cada uno de los miembros de su familia, convirtiendo nuestra luna de miel en un vil viaje de compras.

Sin visitar un lugar romántico, cenar o bailar, solo compras por el día y noches para dormir por el agotamiento de elegir compras y regalos. Una vez ya instalados en el apartamento, yo feliz me dedicaba de lunes a viernes muy temprano a prepararle la ducha para que cuando ella se levantara tuviera lista el agua caliente para bañarse, le cocinaba el desayuno y la despedía cuando se marchaba a su diario trabajo.

DON TRISTE OTRA VEZ
HISTORIA TRISTE DE UN SUEÑO IMPOSIBLE

Virginia decidió seguir trabajando, ya que fue muy clara cuando me dijo que ella jamás dependería de mí, como si fuera una ofensa el depender de mí. En fin, así fue en un principio nuestro matrimonio. Por las tardes, si yo quería comer con Virginia, era posible si me trasladaba hacia el restaurante que sus compañeros de trabajo hubiesen elegido para después marcharme y continuar cada quien con su trabajo. Por las noches el apartamento se llenaba con la presencia de sus hermanas menores, novios y amigos que se entretenían fumando y tomando hasta la hora en que pasaba Irma con su carro para llevárselas a casa.

Los fines de semana, nos trasladábamos desde el Viernes a casa de sus Padres permaneciendo hasta la noche del Domingo, sin tener salidas al cine o a cenar, excepto si Teresa y Georgina querían salir al cine, a bailar o a cenar, entonces Virginia si quería salir conmigo o sin mí, para ella era lo mismo, así que opte por dejarla ir con su familia desde el Viernes en la noche, quedándome en casa con Kicho y Kimba mis dos gatos siameses, yendo a comer a casa de mi Madre que habitaba a tan solo dos calles del apartamento.

Cuando viajaba y regresaba tarde, encontraba el apartamento convertido en fiesta privada, por supuesto estaban Teresa, Georgina, amigos y novios del banco, sin susto ni remordimiento se despedían, saliendo del apartamento quedando solos Virginia y yo, nunca dije nada porque no sabía que pensar, o que podía decir si estaba claro lo que pasaba en mi ausencia.

El apartamento siempre estuvo totalmente a mi cargo, pagando todos los gastos, incluyendo los servicios de limpieza, lavado y planchado de ropa que se llevaban un día y la entregaban al siguiente día, hacia las compras de la despensa porque seguía cocinando para ella el desayuno y cocinando para mí porque comía y cenaba solo, ya que Virginia comía y cenaba como siempre con sus hermanas y amigos del banco.

Así fue mi vida matrimonial por los doce primeros meses. De las cosas buenas, recuerdo que ya casados prepare un evento con la línea Aeroméxico en el lujoso hotel Ciudad de México, donde prepare su "Informe Anual de Actividades y Cena Gala", participando el gobierno, la industria privada y contando con las personalidades del medio turístico del país. Invitaron a la Srta. Aeroméxico, la Srta. Ciudad de México, la Srta. Latinoamérica, y un sin fin de bellas mujeres.

Dando aspecto de certamen de belleza. Virginia acepto ir y llevaba un atuendo elegante como era su costumbre, se veía con tanta clase y tan bonita, recuerdo con orgullo como todos y todas la miraban opacando en cierto grado a varias de las bellezas presentes. Todos me felicitaban, porque tenía por esposa una mujer bellísima fue algo maravilloso, pero regresamos temprano a casa, porque al siguiente día, ella tenía que ir al banco a trabajar.

Después, hice amistad con el esposo de una amiga de Virginia que trabajaban en la misma sucursal del banco, con ellos disfrutábamos un poco de la vida en pareja porque nos invitaban a salir, así que se hizo muy agradable el conocer a esa pareja de amigos maravillosos. Él y yo, jugábamos football los Domingos en el equipo de uno de mis cuñados, así que salíamos los fines de semana a pasear, comer, cenar, etc. y el Domingo por la mañana íbamos los cuatro al juego de football, y solo al termino del juego íbamos a casa de los Padres de Virginia, así que permanecíamos juntos los fines de semana.

La amistad creció entre nosotros, nuestras esposas entraron al equipo femenil de voleibol del banco, así que, apoyándolas, íbamos con ellas a los entrenamientos y por supuesto a los juegos donde participaban. A Virginia, en casa le ayudaba a entrenar, jugaban tan bien y cada vez mejor que se coronaron campeonas del torneo, lo cual fue hermoso y un logro casi increíble porque empezaron muy mal.

DON TRISTE OTRA VEZ
HISTORIA TRISTE DE UN SUEÑO IMPOSIBLE

Nadie creía en ellas, excepto nosotros y al final fueron las campeonas, whow que bonito recuerdo. Por supuesto que fuimos a celebrar los cuatro, así que nuestra vida matrimonial se veía mejor que en el principio.

Un jugador del equipo de football, me hizo saber que Virginia iba a tener un bebe, ya se imaginaran, que al felicitarme le agradecí actuando como si yo supiera la noticia. Al termino del juego, fui a casa de sus padres, enterándome que todos sabían de su embarazo excepto yo, cuando le pregunté porque no me lo dijo y porque no fui el primero en saberlo, respondió con enfado que eso era asunto de ella y no asunto mío.

Más tarde, supe que se embarazo porque su Padre le dijo que cuando le daría un nieto, así que ella obedeció como buena hija que era y se embarazo. Cada mes o antes, la acompañaba al doctor para ver que todo estuviera bien, por supuesto iban sus hermanas lo cual era normal y bueno para ella, por causa del embarazo, Virginia pasaba más tiempo en casa de su familia.

Así que iba a visitarla como cuando visitas a una amiga enferma pero no era mi amiga ni estaba enferma, era mi esposa Yo seguí trabajando y viajando, por lo mismo el distanciamiento creció a tal grado, que perdí la noción de la realidad o no enfrente la realidad que vivía, fui malo y grosero con Virginia, cierto día en que caminábamos los dos cerca de una pastelería, menciono que, si podía tener un pastel para su cumpleaños, conteste que sí. Inmediatamente lo compramos, nos trasladamos a casa de su familia con el pastel y celebramos su cumpleaños.

Hubo un tiempo en que hubiese dado mi vida por ella y, sin embargo, esa vez no recordé que era su cumpleaños, fue triste, porque era la señal de que comenzaba el final.

Tiempo antes de nacer él bebe, Virginia me dijo que él bebe no podría estar en el apartamento a menos que no estuviesen los gatos, ya se imaginaran queriendo al bebe en casa, fui a visitar un amigo que rogaba y suplicaba que quería a mis gatos, así que para su grata sorpresa se los regale con sus juguetes y cama, así que kicho y kimba fueron a dar a la casa de un extraño, ya se imaginaran que llore como niño pequeño, sintiéndome de una manera que no sabía si era bueno o malo por lo que hice, de ahí en adelante comía y cenaba solo, porque para colmo no estaban conmigo kicho y kimba.

Por fin, fuimos al hospital donde nacería él bebe, toda la familia estaba presente, así como mi madre, tras largas horas de espera, fuimos informados que él bebe había nacido y era hombre, todos corrieron a ver al bebe al piso superior, yo me quede preguntando como estaba ella, porque me preocupaba, porque seguía queriéndola ese día lo supe, ya que me sentí feliz cuando dijeron que estaba bien, que solo dormía a causa de la anestesia.

Corriendo fui a verla, estaba dormida, pero se veía tan bonita que tomando una de sus manos y besándola, le agradecí que quizás sin merecerlo me había dado un hijo, después alcance a los demás viendo al bebe a través de un cristal, quedando maravillado por lo bonito que era.

Al siguiente día, me traslade muy contento al hospital para recoger al bebe y a Virginia, pero los planes, eran de que permanecieran en casa de su familia porque los cuidarían y atenderían mejor que yo. Fui a pagar la cuenta del hospital, casi tuve que pelear con uno de sus hermanos mayores porque insistía pagar la cuenta, explique que tenía ahorrado el dinero tiempo atrás, sabía que era mi responsabilidad y que no veía bien porque tenían que pagar ellos, así que, sin escuchar protestas, pague la totalidad de los gastos.

DON TRISTE OTRA VEZ
HISTORIA TRISTE DE UN SUEÑO IMPOSIBLE

Se llevaron a Virginia y al bebe, así como los arreglos florales, abandonando en el hospital los arreglos florales obsequiados por mi madre y el mío. Fui a visitarlos a casa de sus padres, ofrecieron el poder quedarme con ellos todo el tiempo que quisiera, pero no acepte, porque tenía que estar en el apartamento teniendo trabajo por hacer en mi estudio de diseño.

Las familias en general eran de lo mejor, las hermanas mayores Cristina y Yolanda, firmaron por mí y me prestaron dinero para comprar equipo de fotomecánica, para crecer mi negocio de diseño.

Por supuesto que les pague agradeciendo la ayuda, el problema real eran las hermanas menores que por falta de libertad en su casa y por el exceso de libertinaje al que se acostumbraron, aprovechaban la excusa de que salían con Virginia y que estaban en el apartamento, pero no decían que era su refugio amoroso involucrando la tomadera y fumadera, por eso al regreso de mis viajes, encontraba la casa convertida en fiesta privada del banco.

Al poco tiempo, Virginia regreso a trabajar al banco, pero seguía viviendo en casa de sus padres, así que yo visitaba al bebe mientras Virginia trabajaba, una vez estuve con él bebe en el apartamento, porque ella fue al doctor, así que por fin estábamos él y yo juntos, tuve que ir al Consejo de Turismo así que, tomando pañales, biberones y al bebe me fui a trabajar. En las oficinas del Consejo todos estuvieron contentos con la visita del bebe, regresamos a casa y más tarde paso ella a recogerlo para ir a casa de sus Padres.

Por segunda ocasión sucedió lo mismo Virginia fue al doctor y me dejo al bebe, yo teniendo que ir al Consejo de Turismo lleve al bebe con mi Mama, ya se imaginaran mi Madre se volvió loca de felicidad con él bebe y me fui a trabajar, mientras tanto Virginia fue enojada a recoger al bebe.

Le pregunte, que cuando presentaríamos al bebe ante el registro civil, porque como yo viajaba quería saber cuándo lo haríamos, le expresé mi deseo de hacerlo juntos, contesto que no había prisa y que me haría saber cuándo, pocos días después, viaje al extranjero y a mi regreso, me entere de que lo registro, así que, en su acta de nacimiento, no estuvo mi firma como debería de ser, por supuesto que le reclame, pero obtuve por respuesta, que era su hijo y que con su firma bastaba.

Perdí el interés de seguir involucrado en un matrimonio falso, así que le dije que teníamos que arreglar la situación o divorciarnos, ella escogió el divorcio. Le mencione que, para casarnos, hablamos con sus padres, así que para el divorcio deberíamos de hablar con ellos. Nos reunimos en casa de sus padres, su Padre, Virginia y yo, actuando el sr. como modulador. Le dije a él, todo lo que ocurría en el apartamento en mi ausencia, por supuesto que se molestó y no le agrado saber algo tan desagradable de sus hijas menores, aunque él ya tenía indicios de su comportamiento.

Virginia dijo que yo tenía el apartamento lleno de amigos, conteste que no era cierto ya que tenía empleados, que de nueve a cinco de la tarde trabajaban en mi estudio y claro que eran amigos míos, uno de ellos, fue novio de Teresa una de sus hermanitas y por él nos conocimos, el otro era el mejor amigo de Alejandro uno de sus hermanos mayores, por eso le di trabajo, además él era amigo de su familia, y al tiempo se convirtió en amigo mío y solo trabajaban.

Virginia dijo que yo era un inútil y que "yo no le servía ni como hombre" en ese momento no conteste, porque lo único que podía responder hubiese sido "comparado con quien" así que opte por entender lo que quiso decir y le dije al sr. que quería el divorcio.

DON TRISTE OTRA VEZ
HISTORIA TRISTE DE UN SUEÑO IMPOSIBLE

Su Padre dijo que ambos fallamos, porque no respetamos el apartamento que representaba nuestro hogar, que debiéramos pensar las cosas antes de divorciarnos, pero que si no había otra solución, el me garantizaba el divorcio y mi libertad porque le exprese que solo quería ser libre y no estar atado en una unión sin sentido, Virginia siguió ofendiéndome amenazando que nunca me dejaría ver al bebe ni a mi Madre tampoco, que el divorcio me lo daría con la condición que desapareciera para siempre, respondí que así seria.

Algo sucio, fue que tuvo el descaro de perderme, que dejara el apartamento porque Jorge uno de sus hermanos que se robó a la novia, y vivían de arrimados con sus padres, necesitaban el apartamento, así que tendría que largarme, sin importar lo que había gastado en remodelarlo, amueblarlo, decorarlo etc. por un valor aproximado de $60,000 dólares, así que yo tendría que ser el padrino involuntario de casa para su hermano, lo cual nunca me lo agradecieron, ni me regresaron el dinero que invertí.

Antes del nacimiento del bebe, Virginia se fue con sus padres y como magia se suspendieron las fiestas en mi casa, así que estaba claro, lo planearon de antemano y lo único que les hacía falta era que yo me largara. Recogí mis cosas de trabajo, ropa, y discos, dejando mi anillo de matrimonio, en el cajón donde guardábamos cosas personales. Fui al negocio de su Padre, y entregándole las llaves del apartamento, le hice saber que no volvería jamás.

Me fui a vivir a casa de mi Madre, mientras tanto Jorge el hermano de ella y su galana, se fueron a vivir en lo que fue mi casa, preparaba mi partida definitiva del país, ya que vivir en el mismo lugar no sería conveniente, fui el perdedor en esa historia romántica, quede solo, sin esposa, sin bebe, sin casa, sin lugar de trabajo, y hasta sin mis queridos kicho y kimba.

Seguí viajando, preparando mi salida del país, pero a mi regreso, visitaba al bebe llevándole regalos, ropa, y dinero, Cristina la hermana mayor me veía y trataba bien, porque sabía que era bonito que viera al bebe y que fuera responsable. Otras veces fui al banco, a dejarle a Virginia el dinero para él bebe, porque el banco estaba cerca del Consejo Nacional de Turismo, ella aceptaba el dinero a fuerzas mencionando que no necesitaba nada de mí, en fin, mostraba un odio nunca visto en su rostro, o al menos así lo sentí. Semanas antes de mi partida definitiva, aquel matrimonio de amigos nuestros, buscando la manera de reconciliarnos, fueron un fin de semana, por Virginia y él bebe.

Luego pasaron por mí para que juntos paseáramos, fuimos de compras, a comer, compramos la cena para ir a su casa a pasar la noche. Todo el tiempo me la pase con él bebe y compre cosas para él, no fui grosero en ningún momento, pero evitaba hablar con Virginia porque no sabía que decirle. Esa noche nos acostamos, pero al bebe lo acostamos en medio de los dos, de común acuerdo y hablamos de cosas que ya no tenían remedio, porque éramos dos extraños, habíamos dejado de ser pareja.

Le mencione, que estaba a punto de irme con el deseo de permanecer en los Estados Unidos y no volver más que de visita. Virginia dijo que, si yo quería, se iría conmigo, pero no le creí, le respondí que ella no podría estar lejos de su familia. Pensé de seguro el Padre le había dicho que debía de estar conmigo y como ella obedecía me lo dijo, pero no sentía hacerlo, así que de seguro me abandonaría en la primera oportunidad que tuviera, sin hablar más nos dormimos como enemigos. Si deberás quisiera estar conmigo, porque no dijo no te vayas, vámonos a nuestro apartamento a seguir con nuestro matrimonio. Claro que no porque ahí vivían Jorge su hermano y cuñada, seguirme a mí, era para asegurarse de que saliera del país y luego abandonarme. Al amanecer, nuestros amigos se sorprendieron.

DON TRISTE OTRA VEZ
HISTORIA TRISTE DE UN SUEÑO IMPOSIBLE

Esperaban que hubiésemos arreglado nuestras diferencias, pero no fue así y les pedimos que nos llevaran a nuestras respectivas casas. En silencio fuimos primero a casa de mi Madre, despidiéndome de ellos, así como del bebe sabiendo que era el adiós definitivo.

Días después, quise despedirme de Virginia y del bebe porque mi partida estaba programada para el siguiente día, hable por teléfono acordando vernos en casa de sus Padres, cuando me presente, le pedí que saliera y habláramos afuera de la casa.

Porque la última vez que estuve dentro se comportó de forma grosera humillándome, pero ella mando decir con uno de sus cuñados, que ella no hablaría conmigo afuera de la casa, respondí que esperaría afuera y que de no salir entendería y partiría sin molestarlos.

No sé cuánto tiempo espere, quizás 30 minutos, no recuerdo exactamente el tiempo, convencido de que no saldría opte por marcharme, de eso hace muchos años, durante los cuales no los volví a ver, ni siquiera en las pocas ocasiones que volví al país para visitar a mi Madre, ni tampoco los busque cuando fui a recoger a mi Madre para traerla a vivir conmigo.

No los visite, porque vi en Virginia un odio tan grande que lastimaba mis sentimientos, no podía creer, que era la misma persona dulce y bella, solo veía una persona con odio destructivo. Yo seguro estaba, que se había casado y que al bebe lo había engañado con que yo no existía.

Y que el esposo de ella era su verdadero padre, pensé para que destruirle la vida al bebe, tenía Padre y Madre, así como familia, era preferible cumplir el deseo de ella desapareciendo de sus vidas, además, su Padre cumplió, porque a casa de mi Madre, llego el acta de divorcio al poco tiempo de que partí al extranjero.

HISTORIA TRISTE DE UN SUEÑO IMPOSIBLE

Los recordé a ambos en sus cumpleaños, mentalmente les mandaba abrazos y besos, deseando y creyendo que estuviesen bien, sabía que no les hacía falta, así me hizo sentir ella, fue mi error el aceptar su condición de desaparecer de sus vidas, fui tonto e inexperto en todo lo que sucedió entre nosotros.

No todo fue malo en nuestra relación, creo que debimos casarnos tres años antes cuando se lo pedí, o no casarnos y olvidarnos el uno del otro para siempre.

Por supuesto que me porté mal, ya que fumaba mariguana, en la casa durante el tiempo que Virginia estaba afuera trabajando, en casa de su familia, o con los del banco, en fin, creí tener la excusa perfecta, pero no fue así simplemente me hundía en ese vicio y en la tristeza que no era justificación, pero para mí en ese momento de torpeza lo fue.

Lo bueno que, en mi trabajo y contratos, me comporte como un profesional, no presentándome con el vicio, no en los eventos ni exposiciones, dentro y fuera del país. En fin, ella con sus hermanas Teresa, Georgina y amigos del banco, y yo con el vicio, fuimos caminando cada vez más lejos el uno del otro hasta nuestra separación final.

Ya en el extranjero, con poco dinero, sin trabajo, no contando con la residencia permanente solo con una visa de turista, tuve un comienzo difícil, además la tristeza de haberla perdido, así como al bebe y para colmo lejos de mi Madre. Fue doloroso, porque después de convivir con Virginia por diez largos años, no sabía cómo estar sin ella y sin poder hablarle, aprendí a caminar en la lluvia, porque nadie nota que estas llorando. No culpe a nadie, no me queje con nadie, solo espere a que las cosas cambiaran.

Atrapado en el tiempo en que viví con ella, películas, música, todo lo de esa época me rodeo, al grado de que tuve un cuarto de Los Beatles.

DON TRISTE OTRA VEZ
HISTORIA TRISTE DE UN SUEÑO IMPOSIBLE

Donde tenía libros que ella me regalo porque son parte de aquella maravillosa vida que viví con ella, recuerdo como corría desesperadamente para llegar a tiempo y verla salir de su trabajo con sus hermanas mayores, recuerdo aquellos Domingos donde platicábamos como enamorados, aquellas caminatas con manos entrelazadas, quede atrapado en el tiempo, pero fue mi decisión.

Aquí viene lo triste de esta historia, fui enlazando cada detalle de nuestra relación descubriendo la verdad que oculte hasta llegar al día de hoy donde diré la verdad que me atormento durante toda mi existencia.

Cuándo nos casamos ella lloraba mientras yo era feliz por qué Porque no quería casarse conmigo, pero el miedo de abortar nuevamente el motivo a continuar con la mentira y casarse conmigo. No dejar de trabajar era que no quería implicarse conmigo de manera económica porque todas sus hermanas dejaron de trabajar al casarse, pero ella no. La luna de miel fue solo de tres días porque ella necesitaba regresar al banco para demostrarle a su enamorado que se casaba conmigo solo para cubrir las apariencias.

Registrar en el registro civil al bebe en mi ausencia era que no quería mi firma por no ser el padre del bebe. Hacia solo 12 meses que nació un sobrino de ella y lo llamaron Jorge Alberto sin embargo al bebe lo llamo Sergio Alberto, porque otro Alberto Porque en el banco había un Alberto que esperaba mi desaparición para decir que era el padre.

En el hospital escogió cesárea porque de esa manera yo no entraría al quirófano porque no era yo el indicado a estar en el nacimiento de su hijo no el mío. Sus familias sabían la verdad porque eso de que querían pagar la cuenta del hospital los delataba como que algo estaba mal. Llevársela a ella y al bebe a su casa casi a escondidas delataba que tenían temor que al enterarme la agrediera o algo por el estilo.

AVENTURAS DE REFLEXION FILOSOFICA
HISTORIA TRISTE DE UN SUEÑO IMPOSIBLE

En realidad fueron tantas señales que lo supe de inmediato, quise ser caballero y no dije nada pero en cuanto ella se recuperó corrió al banco a seguir su romántica historia en la cual yo quedaba fuera, más tarde me pidió el apartamento porque querían eliminarme del panorama pero hipócritamente y para cubrirse ante la sociedad, yo quede como que fui el que abandono el hogar, deje al bebe sin padre, claro que así no fue pero es lo que la familia se encargó de manifestar para cubrir su sucia manera de proceder.

Ella la única vez que invirtió dinero en el apartamento fue cuando compro un librero de toda una pared para los libros de sus hermanos como preparando el momento en que ya no estaría en esa casa.

Podría enumerar más situaciones que comprobaban esa sucia maniobra de ella y su familia contra mí, imaginen quede traicionado en lo que pudiese ser motivo para que me suicidara, me robaron mi apartamento donde yo vivía dejándome en la calle, ahí mismo tenía mi estudio donde trabajaba así que me quede sin lugar para trabajar arruinando mi economía.

Fue una conspiración familiar haciéndome saber que eran muy unidos hasta en lo malo y miserable porque fueron sucios y no les valió ser una familia respetable, yo no hice nada para desenmascararlos porque ante todo yo era un caballero y valía más que todos ellos que se prestaron a tan sucia acción.

Tuve una vida difícil porque estaba destrozado por la separación y por la traición tan elaborada contra mí y creando el cuento de que yo era el malo y el que abandoné a mi hijo. Me dedique a viajar por el Mediterráneo dedicándome a interpretar música de Los Beatles, Joan Manuel Serrat, Julio Iglesias, Mocedades, etc. en ferris y cruceros que fueron mi refugio porque tenía hogar, alimentos, trabajo viajando por África, Europa descubriendo lugares y personas sumamente.

DON TRISTE OTRA VEZ
HISTORIA TRISTE DE UN SUEÑO IMPOSIBLE

Interesantes así que fue mi distracción vivir así durante mis primeros 10 años. Más tarde regrese al Consejo Nacional de Turismo como representante turístico y comercial de México en el extranjero con misiones diplomáticas alrededor del mundo por 25 años hasta llegar al retiro temprano en Houston, TX y regresar a mi actividad musical para disfrutar los últimos anos de mi vida haciendo lo que más me gusta brindando satisfacción a mi vida. Durante todo ese tiempo sufrí porque extrañé a Virginia deseando que fuese feliz y que mi sacrificio hubiese sido de lo mejor para ella y su bebe. ¿Hay una canción de Los Beatles que se llama "¿Cuando tenga 64" se me hizo fantástico el llegar a esa edad, pero pensé porque el numero 64? Pues bien 6 y 4 son 10 uno y cero son 1 así que pensé que si llegaba a esa edad seria el momento de descubrir mi dolorosa pena que cargué a mis espaldas por casi 40 años.

Descubrí que el número 1 era donde debería descubrir aquella triste historia para abandonarla para siempre y ser feliz por el resto de mis días, por eso es que la estoy narrando para que sea escrita y compartida como el sacrificio de un simple ser humano con bondad, digna de respeto porque la gente me conoció como una persona honorable aunque mi mirada siempre fue triste pero brinde alegría a todas las personas y más al interpretar la música con toda la calidad obtenida con anterioridad con tantos músicos que llenaron mi vida musical con alegría y anécdotas divertidas.

En ese momento hice una pausa mientras el hombre del espejo se limpiaba las lágrimas de su rostro que reflejaba una tristeza profunda pero que por fin se había despojado de aquella verdad que lo martirizaba por tantas décadas. Se disculpó por haberse mostrado débil, pero sonrió y dijo que la verdad dejo de lastimarlo porque en realidad Virginia y su familia podían avergonzarse, pero no el, el honor y respeto mostrado durante su existencia era más valioso que todo lo que le hubieron robado.

AVENTURAS DE REFLEXION FILOSOFICA
HISTORIA TRISTE DE UN SUEÑO IMPOSIBLE

Comento que, si me gusto la historia, tenía su permiso para escribirla, pero sin mencionar su nombre, eso desde el principio supe que así debería de ser para no provocar una imagen de hombre sufrido, porque él era todo menos sufrido, el ante mis ojos era una víctima que no realizo venganza, ni rencores contra nadie así que era respetable como persona y todo un hombre de bien.

Fueron semanas hermosas durante su relato interesante, me deslumbro con su elegancia sus gabardinas, abrigos, sacos, y sus sombreros tipo boinas italianas que le daban un toque de distinción, en fin, nos despedimos a sabiendas que era el final de aquellas reuniones y que no lo volvería a ver como todos los personajes de mis historias, así que después de un abrazo caminamos por rumbos opuestos.

Ya en casa con la nueva historia terminada la agregue a mi libro como el ultimo capitulo teniendo como meta publicarlo de una vez por todas. Estando frente al espejo me quité el elegante abrigo, la boina italiana que vestía ese día y mirando mi figura que aun mostraba elegancia lejana por la edad me despedí para seguir mi vida siendo feliz con mis recuerdos.

Es bello no guardarle rencor a nadie sin importar todo lo malo que te hagan con o sin razón, cuando amas a alguien eres capaz de hacerte a un lado pensando que será feliz, por cierto, aquel amigo que me presento a Virginia me hizo saber que ella nunca se casó y su romance no prospero quedando tan sola como yo, así que de nada le valió su perversa acción porque no mereció ser feliz.

La felicidad se gana a base de sacrificios y voluntad que nunca tuvo, a mí eso me sobro porque se convirtió en mi manera de vivir día a día.

FIN DEL VOLUMEN I

La gente les vio sonreír, besarse e ir amorosamente abrazados por los rincones de calles, senderos, pueblos y ciudades compartiendo sus vidas solos al ritmo del amor que los encadeno para vivir felizmente condenados al romance esplendoroso que nunca los abandono.

Se dedicaron a criar amorosamente a sus hijos que eran pajaritos con alas rotas temerosos de volar como todos los hijos, pero ellos los cobijaron con su amor convirtiéndose en el viento que los empujo a ser pájaros voladores de altura que enfrentaron todos sus temores recordando el amoroso ejemplo de sus padres.

Aun en la soledad del ocaso de sus vidas continuaron despertando con los amaneceres dorados bañados con intensas tonalidades amarillas recordándoles que estaban juntos para empezar otro día de felicidad y lucha compartida para esperar los atardeceres donde el cielo se convertía en un espectáculo lleno de colores de miel con azules que anunciaban el arribo de las noches en las cuales daban rienda suelta al amor que los unió hasta el final de sus días.

Este no fue el real final de esta historia, al contrario, fue el principio de mi eterna soledad esperándola con la misma emoción que cuando jugábamos a que nos amábamos.

Recordare su hermosa sonrisa, sus ojos con aquel brillo que me transportaban al mundo de las emociones más sublimes que un ser humano puede sentir, sé que la ame como no se puede amar a nadie más.

Ella peligrosamente bella vivirá en mi hasta el último latido de mi corazón, su bello recuerdo mantendrá el brillo en mis ojos, seguiré siendo Don triste otra vez para narrar historias y aventuras.

Amor es un alma en dos cuerpos que se buscan locamente para amarse sin condiciones, uniéndose como un solo cuerpo, un solo espíritu condenándose mutuamente a vivir y sufrir por su amor, siguiendo el ritmo de sus corazones porque el universo conjura y se inclina con respeto a favor de los que se aman.

Fin del volumen I
Volumen II en verano del 2017